VALLEY OF OPPORTUNITY

VALLEY OF OPPORTUNITY

Economic Culture along the
Upper Susquehanna, 1700–1800

Peter C. Mancall

CORNELL UNIVERSITY PRESS

ITHACA AND LONDON

First published 1991 by Cornell University Press.

International Standard Book Number 0-8014-2503-4
Library of Congress Catalog Card Number 90-55719

Printed in the United States of America

Librarians: Library of Congress cataloging information
appears on the last page of the book.

⊗ The paper in this book meets the minimum requirements
of the American National Standard for Information Sciences—Permanence
of Paper for Printed Library Materials, ANSI Z39.48–1984.

FOR LIS AND SOPH

Contents

Maps

Preface

This book analyzes the economic culture of the upper Susquehanna Valley in the eighteenth century. Its aim is straightforward: to explain how different peoples perceived the natural resources of the area and how they created economies based on the production and allocation of these resources. The book considers three different groups of people: Indians, colonists, and post–revolutionary war settlers. But in spite of the differences between, and at times within, these groups, all of the peoples who inhabited the upper valley in the eighteenth century came to define their lives in relation to the market economy of eastern North America. They did so, in large measure, because of the efforts of traders and landholders. These developers encouraged valley residents to look at the natural world—the region's forests, fields, and streams—and see commodities. Those who directed this development of the hinterland sought to transform the environment and make nature yield what they believed was its bounty and their due. By 1800, they had succeeded; in the process, they had initiated the industrial revolution in the hinterland.

Although historians have written some splendid studies focusing on eastern Indians, colonists, or post-Revolution settlers, analyses of regions inhabited over time by all of these peoples are lacking. This

book seeks to move beyond provincial boundaries to find the underlying attitudes and behavior that transformed a region where Indians, colonists, and post-Revolution settlers all actively shaped the
economic culture. Yet this is not a traditional economic history. The
text contains few statistics, although tables in the Appendix provide
quantitative evidence for parts of the argument. In focusing on the
disparate cultures that created the valley economy, this book treats
issues such as the relationship between law and economic development and the impact of religious sensibilities on economic behavior.
In addition, it reconstructs the relationships between valley residents
and their physical world, an approach derived from the work of Fernand Braudel and developed by historians who have studied the
process of settlement in the American West.

To illustrate economic development in the upper Susquehanna
Valley I have chosen a chronological organization. The book begins
with a description of the regional environment (the best starting
point for the study of any economic system) and how people thought
about it in the eighteenth century. The environment does not recede
into the background in this history as in many others; it remains at
the center, both the stage on which the historical actors played out
their parts and also, in its own way, a major determinant of valley
residents' economic behavior. Later chapters deal with the establishment of the Indian population in the area, the development of
intercultural trade between Indians and colonists, the emergence of
the colonial economy, the destruction of the existing valley communities during the revolutionary war, and the creation of the postwar
economy.

One of my goals is to describe what seems, to twentieth-century
minds, utterly illogical economic behavior: Why would Indians overhunt furbearing animals for quickly depleted fungible goods, with
the result that they became even poorer than when they began procuring pelts for traders? Why would settlers become tenants of
wealthy landlords instead of purchasing land for themselves? Why,
if they did own land, did settlers have any economic dealings with
these landholders?

The answers to these questions are vital for understanding what
some historians have termed the "capitalist transformation" of the
countryside. At the beginning of the eighteenth century economic
ideals reflected a strong sense of community. Indians and colonists
alike, in their own ways, worked to enhance the "common wealth";

religious sensibilities and ideals such as the "moral economy" shaped commercial and ritual exchanges between disparate peoples. Most of them did not define their lives in response to the larger Atlantic market. By the end of the century the situation was far different. A demographic revolution had reshaped eastern North America; peoples of European descent controlled most of the territory from the Atlantic to the Appalachians. The economic world inhabited by these peoples was decidedly market-oriented, and working for the "common wealth" had an entirely new meaning. Only in times of distress, which were infrequent, did traditional economic sensibilities reemerge. Rather than restricting economic development, which might bring a mix of benefits as well as troubles for a community, Americans after the Revolution oriented their lives to the larger market and sought government assistance to help them in their private ventures. This new economic climate nourished the developers and encouraged them and those who followed them to seek profit through industrialization.

Yet these developments, so clear in retrospect, did not happen spontaneously, nor did those involved always understand the changes they had initiated. The market spread into the backcountry not in a single moment but over time and in a myriad of often subtle and ambiguous ways. Indians did not become individualistic market-oriented capitalists even though they participated in a market-oriented economic system. When settlers engaged in long-distance trade and exchanged their wares in local trade centers, they did so not because they had read Adam Smith but because such behavior proved, for these often cash-poor farmers, the surest way of providing for themselves and their families. And even when the countryside appeared to have become transformed by the expansion of the Atlantic market into the backcountry, traditional impulses, at times religious or ethical, reminded those directing the economic development of the upper valley that residents of the hinterland were not strict economic determinists whose desires could be calculated like the prices of commodities. Instead, most valley inhabitants expressed their economic desires in already existing, culturally defined ways of looking at the world around them.

The upper Susquehanna Valley is an ideal setting for a study of the economic development of the backcountry. For the peoples who lived there, the move toward modernity was hardly inexorable or predictable. These hinterland residents did more than adopt mar-

ket-oriented strategies; they reshaped their physical world in response to the transatlantic commercial system. As witnesses to a his-
toric shift in economic sensibilities, these peoples of the backcountry
have much to teach us. They migrated to the upper valley seeking
opportunity, but many of them never prospered. By reconstructing
their economic world, we gain new insight into the economic forces
that continue to shape the world we inhabit.

During the years that I gathered materials for this book I received
much assistance from many historical societies and libraries. I am
grateful to the staffs of the manuscript divisions of the Historical
Society of Pennsylvania (particularly Linda Stanley), the New-York
Historical Society, the New York State Library, the New York State
Historical Association, the Public Record Office (Kew), and the Brit-
ish Library. In addition, the map librarians at the Public Record Office, the Map Library of the British Library, and the Map Library of
Harvard University provided great help. Further, the staffs of the
Wyoming Historical and Geological Society, the Broome County
Historical Society, the Lycoming County Historical Society, and the
Office of the County Historian of Montgomery County (N.Y.) also
provided much assistance. I especially thank Frederick Reed, the
register and recorder of Northumberland County, and the staffs of
his office and the Prothonotary's Office of Northumberland County,
both located in the Northumberland County Court House in Sunbury, Pennsylvania.

Financial support for the project came from the Charles Warren
Center at Harvard University, an Artemas Ward Dissertation Fellow-
ship at Harvard, and a Michael Kraus Research Grant from the
American Historical Association. The Small Grants Fund of the University of Kansas provided funds for the maps, which were drawn by
David Brower under the supervision of Barbara Shortridge at the
university's cartography lab.

Part of Chapter 6 appeared as "The Revolutionary War and the
Indians of the Upper Susquehanna Valley," in *American Indian Cul-
ture and Research Journal* 12 (1988). Part of Chapter 7 appeared as
"Independence and Interdependence in the Upper Susquehanna
Valley after the American Revolution," in *Locus* 2 (1989).

I accrued even more important debts by having my work read by
an insightful group of historians. Neal Salisbury read two chapters
dealing with Indian-colonist relations; Alan Taylor allowed me to see

one of his essays before its publication and discussed the book with me; and Colin Calloway, in commenting on a paper I gave at the Southern Historical Association meeting in 1987, helped me realize the larger significance of the Susquehanna Valley Indians' wartime experiences. In addition, several friends and colleagues read parts of the manuscript or commented on parts of the argument. I thank them for their insights, especially Kathleen Kete, Beth LaDow, Josh Rosenbloom, Tom Siegel, Russell Snapp, Cindy Taft, and Eric Hinderaker, who provided me with information about a crucial eighteenth-century manuscript. I owe an even greater debt to friends who read the entire book manuscript, especially Helena Wall and Don Worster, each of whom made important comments during the last stages of its preparation. Christopher Clark provided me with a superb analysis of the book which proved of great use during my final revisions. Peter Agree, my editor at Cornell University Press, has proved supportive throughout.

Two individuals, both associated with my graduate training, went well beyond what anyone could have expected of them. One is Bernard Bailyn. Like those of many of his other students, my insights about early America have been shaped by his always probing inquiries, and I could not have asked for a more astute and challenging adviser. The other is Patty Limerick, who read the manuscript several times; each of her critiques was more helpful than the one before. Her remarks did much more than polish my prose; they also showed me how to sharpen my argument and thus give it much more explanatory power than it would have possessed.

Finally, Lisa Bitel's keen historical insights, sharp-eyed stylistic criticisms, and understanding of how to describe a world long since past enriched the book more than I can describe. To her, and to the other woman in my life, I dedicate this book.

PETER C. MANCALL

Lawrence, Kansas

Notes on the Text

Punctuation and spelling have been silently corrected in places to make quotations more readily understandable. Whenever it was possible I have left quotations in their original form. When modernized, quotations follow the guidelines presented in Frank Friedel, ed., *Harvard Guide to American History*, rev. ed. (Cambridge, Mass., 1974), 1:27–36.

The following abbreviations are used for sources frequently cited:

ABV: John B. Linn, *The Annals of Buffalo Valley, Pennsylvania, 1755–1855.* Harrisburg, 1877.

Add. Mss.: Additional Manuscripts, British Library.

AHR: *American Historical Review.*

CO: Colonial Office, Public Record Office (Kew).

DAB: *Dictionary of American Biography.*

Doc. Hist. NY: E. B. O'Callaghan, ed., *The Documentary History of the State of New York*, 4 vols. Albany, 1849–1851.

HSP: Historical Society of Pennsylvania, Philadelphia.

JAH: *Journal of American History.*

Johnson Papers: James Sullivan et al., eds., *The Papers of Sir William Johnson*, 14 vols. Albany, 1921–1965.

LCHS: Lycoming County Historical Society, Williamsport, Pennsylvania.

NCCH: Northumberland County Court House, Sunbury, Pennsylvania.

NY Col. Docs.: E. B. O'Callaghan, ed., *Documents Relative to the Colonial History of the State of New York*, 15 vols. Albany, 1856–1887.

NY Hist.: *New York History.*

NYHS: New-York Historical Society, New York City.

NYSHA: New York State Historical Association, Cooperstown, New York.

NYSL: New York State Library, Albany.

PaCR: *Pennsylvania Colonial Records*, 16 vols. Harrisburg, 1838–1853.

Pa. Hist.: *Pennsylvania History.*

P. Arch.: *Pennsylvania Archives*, 138 vols. Harrisburg, 1852–1935.

PHMC: Pennsylvania Historical and Museum Commission, Harrisburg.

PMHB: *Pennsylvania Magazine of History and Biography.*

SCP: Julian Boyd and Robert Taylor, eds., *The Susquehannah Company Papers*, 11 vols. Wilkes-Barre, Pa., and Ithaca, N.Y., 1930–1971.

WHGS: Wyoming Historical and Geological Society, Wilkes-Barre, Pennsylvania.

WMQ: *William and Mary Quarterly.*

Introduction

William Penn (1644–1718) and William Cooper (1754–1809) lived in different worlds. Penn initiated the settlement of Pennsylvania and devised its famous policies of religious toleration. He recruited thousands of German-speaking Protestants to make the arduous transatlantic passage and establish themselves in his province. While some in the late seventeenth century scrambled to make a profit, Penn cherished more traditional views of economic behavior and believed that economic development should serve a moral purpose. The philosophes, who cherished the human faculty for reason and praised tolerance in a world of intolerance, celebrated Penn's ideals and policies and saw in his endeavors a model for the Western world. William Cooper never received such praise. The founder of Cooperstown and father of novelist James Fenimore Cooper, William Cooper was, first and foremost, a land speculator and landlord. He cared most about making a profit from his investments. Like Penn, he lured settlers to a largely unpopulated region and offered them land and economic opportunity. Cooper attracted a fond following during his life and in the years after his death, helped along no doubt by the parallels between his life and that of Judge Temple in his son's novel *The Pioneers*, yet he was an archetype of an age vastly different from Penn's. In Cooper's world economic development, not reason, was the cherished ideal.

For all their differences, however, Penn and Cooper shared the belief that economic success could be found along the banks of the Susquehanna River and its tributaries, the most extensive waterway in eastern North America. This book analyzes the economic culture of that region and how it changed from the age of Penn to the age of Cooper.

To understand the upper Susquehanna Valley we need first to understand how its residents' economic patterns compared to those of peoples in other parts of British America. With this larger picture in mind, we can then analyze the economy of the upper Susquehanna Valley and comprehend its peculiar features and how the region fit into the larger economic history of eighteenth-century North America.

Over the past generation historians have demonstrated the diversity of the economy of British America.[1] The inhabitants of New England, the middle colonies, the Chesapeake region, the Deep South, and the West Indies created distinctive commercial systems based on local resources and the demands of the Atlantic market. The development of these discrete but related economies influenced vital aspects of North American society and culture in the early modern period: race relations, marketing systems, land and resource use, political affiliations. Everyone in these disparate subcultures throughout British America felt the pull of the distant European market. Some were able to capitalize on the opportunities while others, among them slaves and servants, found the market and its entrepreneurs to be cruel taskmasters.

Colonists in New England, a first home to many migrants to the upper Susquehanna Valley, typically inhabited tightly organized villages where small-scale agriculture dominated economic activity. Adult males, usually the heads of households, retained control over their holdings for the duration of their long lives and organized their family farms; adult women directed the household economy, at times producing goods for sale. In port towns, especially Boston and Salem, merchants maintained connections to both the farming hin-

1. A recent overview of the field is presented in John J. McCusker and Russell R. Menard, *The Economy of British America, 1607–1789* (Chapel Hill, N.C., 1985). See also Ronald Hoffman et al., eds., *The Economy of Early America: The Revolutionary Period, 1763–1790* (Charlottesville, Va., 1988).

terland and the larger Atlantic commercial world. Embracing the
European market, they capitalized not on the production of goods
but on vital services, especially the shipping and merchandising of
commodities. Although at times this economic orientation caused
conflicts with their rural neighbors, as at Salem in the late seventeenth century, few New Englanders wished to sever their ties with
the market.[2]

Far from the shores of the Atlantic, at least by colonial standards,
a market-oriented economy also thrived in the backcountry. Unlike
that of coastal settlements, however, this economy was peopled
mostly with Indians and, in places, with colonists seeking the furs the
Indians brought to trade. Both the gentry and yeomanry of western
Europe wanted furs, particularly beaver pelts, and they created a
virtually insatiable demand for North American peltry. The force of
these market pressures emerged in Indian villages where residents
adopted, and soon came to rely on, various European-produced
commodities: metal kettles and needles, axes, guns and gunpowder,
glass beads, mirrors, and blankets. Indeed, soon after the beginning
of the seventeenth century, and certainly by the mid-eighteenth century, most New England Indians had come to rely on European
goods.[3]

To the south, around the banks of the Chesapeake Bay, a different economy emerged. There the first settlers, who sought profitable exports from the start, established themselves along waterways so
they could maintain contact with other communities and have access
to the tidewater commercial system. They oriented their economy
around the production of goods valued in Europe. While a few settlers experimented with a variety of crops for export, but many by
the mid-seventeenth century concentrated on tobacco. But tobacco
production proved highly labor-intensive, and when planters could
no longer obtain necessary laborers from Europe they began to import human chattel to produce the crop. Although English cultural

2. Philip Greven, Jr., *Four Generations: Population, Land, and Family in Colonial An-
dover, Massachusetts* (Ithaca, N.Y., 1970); Bernard Bailyn, *The New England Merchants in
the Seventeenth Century* (Cambridge, Mass., 1955); Paul Boyer and Stephen Nissen-
baum, *Salem Possessed: The Social Origins of Witchcraft* (Cambridge, Mass., 1974).

3. Neal Salisbury, *Manitou and Providence: Indians, Europeans, and the Making of New
England, 1500–1643* (New York, 1982); Stephen Innes, *Labor in a New Land: Economy
and Society in Seventeenth-Century Springfield* (Princeton, N.J., 1983); Eric Wolf, *Europe
and the People without History* (Berkeley, Calif., 1982), chap. 6.

attitudes contributed to the development of slavery, the emerging
tobacco economy and later the development of rice and indigo production encouraged slaveholding and shifted the demographics of
the colonies south of Pennsylvania: by 1720 forty percent of Virginia's labor force and two-thirds of South Carolina's were of West
African descent, many of them living under the worst forms of op-
pression. The West Indies, where sugar production predominated,
experienced a similar economic evolution.[4]

The slavers and their human chattel reshaped the economy of the
Chesapeake and the South. Those able to afford slaves found themselves in a better position than their neighbors and soon began to
force less wealthy planters onto marginal uplands. Slavery's impact
was also evident in transitional areas, where people abandoned tobacco and produced grain but continued to keep slaves, even though
the demands of cereal agriculture had inhibited farmers farther
north from keeping laborers bound for life. Since planters owned
not only slaves but their slaves' progeny, much of the regional economy centered around growing slave populations guided by strict social hierarchies and export-oriented economies.[5]

Although we can identify these major components of the economies of New England and the southern colonies, our knowledge of
the middle colonies is less complete. The connections there between
urban and rural peoples, between colonists and Indians, between the
free and the unfree, and even, in many areas, between settlers in the
same environs, have yet to receive the scholarly attention devoted to
New England and the Chesapeake.

Certainly we know much about specific aspects of the regional
economy. Philadelphia became the primary shipping center for the
region's thriving grain trade, and Albany and Oswego served similar
functions for the fur trade. We know, too, about commercial relations in the agricultural communities of southeastern Pennsylvania

4. Winthrop Jordan, *White over Black: American Attitudes toward the Negro, 1550–
1812* (Chapel Hill, N.C., 1968), chaps. 1–2; Edmund Morgan, *American Slavery, Ameri-
can Freedom: The Ordeal of Colonial Virginia* (New York, 1975); Peter H. Wood, *Black
Majority: Negroes in Colonial South Carolina from 1670 through the Stono Rebellion* (New
York, 1974); Richard S. Dunn, *Sugar and Slaves: The Rise of the Planter Class in the
English West Indies, 1624–1713* (Chapel Hill, N.C., 1972).

5. Paul G. E. Clemens, *The Atlantic Economy and Colonial Maryland's Eastern Shore:
From Tobacco to Grain* (Ithaca, N.Y., 1980); Ira Berlin, "Time, Space, and the Evolution of Afro-American Society on British Mainland North America," *AHR* 85 (1980),
44–78.

and about settlements, such as Germantown, which grew up on the periphery of the urban core. But these areas were only partly representative of the middle colonies. Only major urban centers like Philadelphia could support nonagricultural communities in their periphery; without its service-oriented establishments, Germantown with its poor soils never would have attracted such a large population. Southeastern Pennsylvania, which had productive soils, softly rolling hills, and access to the Philadelphia market, has been the most thoroughly studied area in the middle colonies, and recent interpretations have challenged the eighteenth-century notion that this region was the "best poor man's country." Yet southeastern Pennsylvania was geographically and economically distinct from settlements in more rugged terrain far from the Atlantic.[6]

In regions well away from the major ports, and especially in river valleys along the banks of the Hudson, Mohawk, and Susquehanna rivers, many groups established communities with successful, profit-oriented local economies. Along these avenues of commerce, early Americans learned vital lessons about the Atlantic economy. They discovered, in very tangible ways, how the larger market functioned. They found out which goods could be sold, how to transport commodities to coastal markets and up inland riverways, and how to establish stable communities in the backcountry. These lessons were of vital importance to a quickly growing population always seeking western lands and commodities for the larger market.[7]

In some ways, the development of the economy of the upper Susquehanna Valley resembled that of the Chesapeake and the South. Those with control of valuable commodities shaped the regional

6. Thomas M. Doerflinger, *A Vigorous Spirit of Enterprise: Merchants and Economic Development in Revolutionary Philadelphia* (Chapel Hill, N.C., 1986); Thomas E. Norton, *The Fur Trade in Colonial New York, 1686–1776* (Madison, Wis., 1974); James T. Lemon, *The Best Poor Man's Country: A Geographical Study of Early Southeastern Pennsylvania* (1972; rpt. New York, 1976); Stephanie Grauman Wolf, *Urban Village: Population, Community, and Family Structure in Germantown, Pennsylvania, 1683–1800* (Princeton, N.J., 1976). Among the most important recent studies of the economy of southeastern Pennsylvania are Lucy Simler, "Tenancy in Colonial Pennsylvania: The Case of Chester County," *WMQ* 3d ser., 43 (1986), 542–569, and Paul G. E. Clemens and Lucy Simler, "Rural Labor and the Farm Household in Chester County, Pennsylvania, 1750–1820," in Stephen Innes, ed., *Work and Labor in Early America* (Chapel Hill, N.C., 1988), 106–143.

7. The best study of economic development along any of these channels during the colonial period is Sung Bok Kim, *Landlord and Tenant in Colonial New York: Manorial Society, 1664–1775* (Chapel Hill, N.C., 1978).

commercial system, with long-lasting implications for the resident population. Trade involved different commodities over time. Peltry initially brought profits, at least to traders; later valley residents bought and sold maple sugar, potash, fish, grains, lumber, coal, and real estate. Some involved with marketing these goods made a fortune, and they promptly enlisted laborers to extract and sell existing resources. Thus Indian hunters became involved in commercial relationships with fur traders, an economic relationship benefiting colonial traders far more than the Indians. Similarly, landlords attracted people to work their lands and produce marketable goods. Those who profited most in this hinterland economy were often those who were already wealthy. Many had connections to influential political figures who helped them gain possession of prime parcels of real estate; they also organized trade networks, connecting their back-country entrepôts to external markets. Finally, those who succeeded often had the capital with which to finance varied commercial enterprises.

Some profited more than others, and these landholders and traders needed few indentured servants and fewer slaves than their southern neighbors. They succeeded because the emerging economy of the valley also proved attractive to thousands of less wealthy people. No one forced the Indians to reorient their traditional economies to obtain peltry for traders. The Indians chose to do so. Similarly, people who became tenants, either farming grains or operating mills for wealthy landlords, did so for their own profit; no heritable ties bound them to the land of the emerging gentry. Tenants chose to migrate to the area for reasons sensible to people of limited means.[8]

But if these groups willingly participated in the emerging market-oriented economy, they did so because their choices were limited. Larger demographic, epidemiological, and political phenomena influenced the economic choices available to valley residents. The available opportunities prompted some to adopt economic strategies that promised short-term gain but often had high long-term social, economic, and environmental costs. Thus, though the fur and lumber trades initially proved profitable, each eventually declined when stocks of animals and trees dwindled from overzealous hunting and cutting.

8. See Innes, *Labor in a New Land*, epilogue.

The economy of the valley fluctuated constantly, and not every resident succeeded. Some, indeed, failed miserably; a few wealthy speculators, who had the greatest chance for success because of their access to land and markets, ended their lives in relative poverty or debtors' prison. Failure lay not in ignorance or even deception, although many traders and wealthy colonists acted duplicitously at times. Economic instability resulted instead from the dynamic and shifting nature of the Atlantic commercial world, which reached into every household and processing center in the region. Few sought to escape this market. In establishing themselves and their economy in this frontier, valley residents—Indians, colonists, and post-Revolution settlers—forged an economic relationship between the rural backcountry and the Atlantic commercial world.

This book seeks to reconstruct the economic world of valley residents, including rich and poor, Indian and colonist. Its aim is to understand the economic choices available to these people. Many forces influenced valley residents' lives. The Indians received more than European commodities; Old World pathogens and alcohol devastated their communities. Indians and colonists alike suffered and inflicted the destruction of the revolutionary war and the animosities that conflict engendered and sustained. And perhaps most important and yet least readily understood, valley inhabitants responded to the series of demographic upheavals reshaping eastern North America. In addition to the spread of epidemics among the Indians, the flood of immigrants into the middle colonies and a high rate of natural increase among colonists influenced valley residents in profound and at times unsettling ways.

Yet though such phenomena often reoriented the lives of valley residents, so did events that seem, on the surface, far less remarkable. Individual exchanges—between colonial fur traders and Indian hunters, between landlords and tenants—could have as great an impact as an epidemic or a rise in the price of wheat. To decipher the economic culture of the upper valley, we need to be aware of the lessons such localized interactions reveal. Thus, to cite but one example, when a valley trader drowned in an overflowing creek, his death did not threaten the fur trade in the region. But the tragedy swept beyond the trader's family if his demise meant that Indians counting on his visit to purchase needed goods had to forgo this planned exchange or had to spend a great deal of time finding other traders to supply them with the desired commodities. The importance of individual episodes could have a long-term impact as well; for example, one valley resident attempted to use his will to control the future construction of a mill on his lands with proceeds to go to his heirs. Thus individual acts, such as the decision to travel by water during the time of the spring runoff or to write certain provisions into a will, constituted components of the valley's preindustrial economy. Taken together, these often idiosyncratic episodes created and shaped the attitudes governing economic behavior in the backcountry.[9]

Social, political, and demographic changes are central to the argument of the book, but certain parts of the region's history need not be analyzed here at great length. Some readers may be disappointed to find that the dispute between Pennsylvania and Connecticut over the northern tier of Pennsylvania is a minor part of this story. That conflict has already been chronicled by numerous historians, and though it raised profound legal and political questions, its impact on economic development is less clear. Many people in the Wyoming Valley had their origins in Connecticut but were living under Pennsylvania's jurisdiction; some from elsewhere in Pennsylvania also inhabited the region, eventually trading and living with former New Englanders. The ongoing battle between Connecticut and Pennsylvania did not greatly influence the economic culture of the region. Indeed, even though disputes over titles impeded settlement, at some times enterprising would-be landlords purchased both Pennsylvania and Connecticut deeds, expecting that the greater costs involved would eventually pay handsome returns.[10]

The valley economy is best understood through the eyes of its

9. Will of Benjamin Harvey, probated December 16, 1795, Luzerne County Will Book A, 1787–1836 (typescript in WHGS), 15. The story of the trader is described in chapter 3, below. Daniel Usner has drawn attention to the importance of "small-scale, face-to-face marketing" in his important essay "The Frontier Exchange Economy of the Lower Mississippi Valley in the Eighteenth Century," *WMQ* 3d ser., 44 (1987), 165–192.

10. The most important source collection relating to the dispute is *SCP*. In addition to the invaluable introductions provided in each of these volumes, see also Julian Boyd, "Connecticut's Experiment in Expansion: The Susquehannah Company, 1753–1803," *Journal of Economic and Business History* 4 (1931), 38–69; Edith A. Bailey, "Influences toward Radicalism in Connecticut, 1754–1775," *Smith College Studies in History* 5 (1920), 179–252; Robert J. Taylor, "Trial at Trenton," *WMQ* 3d ser., 26 (1969), 521–547; and Richard T. Warfle, "Connecticut's Western Colony: The Susquehannah Affair," *Connecticut Bicentennial Series* 32 (1979). For one landlord's response to the situation see Robert D. Arbuckle, *Pennsylvania Speculator and Patriot: The Entrepreneurial John Nicholson, 1757–1800* (University Park, Pa., 1975), 107.

residents. When the Susquehannocks, who inhabited the region during the initial period of North American colonization, suffered a demographic catastrophe because of contact with Europeans and struggles with other Indians, the region became a home for displaced Indians; Nanticokes, Mahicans, Conoys, Delawares, and Tutelos thought they found in its fertile vales the promise of security but eventually had to confront land-seeking colonists who again displaced them. English, Scottish, Irish, and German migrants also hoped to find homes in the valley, although many of them ultimately found that reality did not measure up to the promises of land promoters. French men and women fleeing their country's revolution thought they would find a refuge along the Susquehanna's banks. So did the scientist Joseph Priestley, who hoped to lure both French and English refugees to lands he owned in the upper valley. Priestley and his associates, the scientist's son later recalled, "thought that by the union of industry and capital, the wilderness would soon become cultivated and equal to any other part of the country in everything necessary to the enjoyment of life." Over the course of the eighteenth century, thousands of valley residents came to share this vision.[11]

All valley residents realized that their local economy was part of a larger commercial system. People in the upper Susquehanna Valley were witnesses to, and participants in, a vital chapter of Western civilization: the development of the Atlantic economy. This development forever altered the people and resources of the entire world. At its core lay complex relationships between those who sought to develop economic opportunity and who had the political power to act on their acquisitive impulses and others who actually spread the European market across the ocean. And in the eighteenth century, when the shackles of the *ancien régime* loosened everywhere, those enterprising groups inhabited a commercial world that nourished the notion that economic development was always best for the common good; available resources, most believed, should be channeled toward any developing commercial opportunities, regardless of the potential social, ethical, and even economic costs of such pursuits.

11. Elsie Murray, "French Refugees of 1793 in Pennsylvania," *Proceedings of the American Philosophical Society* 87 (1944), 387–393; Durand Echeverria, *Mirage in the West: A History of the French Image of American Society to 1815* (Princeton, N.J., 1957), 209; John T. Boyer, ed., *The Memoirs of Dr. Joseph Priestley* (Washington, D.C., 1964), 103, 130–132.

The peoples of the upper Susquehanna Valley, from the age of William Penn to the age of William Cooper, shared this economic mentality and its power to shape social relations. In the process, they helped establish patterns of economic behavior central to the modern world and the coming of the industrial era.

1 The Physical World

The upper Susquehanna Valley, stretching almost from the Finger Lakes region to the Susquehanna's confluence with the Juniata River and from western Pennsylvania to the edge of the Delaware Valley, encompasses twenty thousand square miles. In 1700, after the decline of the Susquehannocks, almost no one lived in this vast tract of Pennsylvania and New York. Within the next one hundred years Indians, colonists, and postrevolutionary settlers peopled the region and created a new economic order there.

In the eighteenth century, the Susquehanna River dominated the lives of those who inhabited the upper valley. All wanted to live near it, seeing in its waters the promise of economic opportunity. Many wanted the rich stocks of fish; others sought to impound the water for milldams; still others believed the river and its tributaries to be wondrous natural highways, the most extensive in eastern North America south of the St. Lawrence, which residents could use to transport valuable commodities hundreds of miles through the rugged terrain of the rural interior. Proximity to the river or one of its major tributaries allowed residents to take advantage of many opportunities. When the opportunities arose, few resisted.

The economic history of any people must take into account the physical world they inhabited. The local geography, climate, fuel

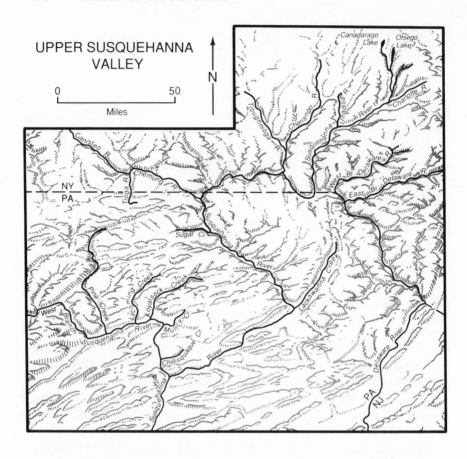

sources, and flora and fauna all influenced the valley economy. The contours of the valley inhabitants' world—their mountains and rivers and vales—defined settlement patterns and trade routes; local animal populations and supplies of lumber and coal became the staples of the valley economy. (The tables in the Appendix present a statistical account of some of the changes in the valley.)

Geography and Climate

Two great forces of nature, plate tectonics and erosion, shaped the physical contours of the upper valley. Shifting plates lifted the region known today as the original Appalachia; in the Paleozoic Era this land mass rose high above an inland sea to its west. But the land masses, in constant movement, then reversed their positions; the deep trough that had held the sea filled with layers of sediment and came to tower over Appalachia. Dense swamps formed along the banks of the trough and soon began to fill with sediment. Layers of peat gathered in many areas but were soon covered by sand and mud. Then, in a length of time unimaginable to the historian, the peat hardened into coal and the other sediment into limestone, shale, and sandstone. The various upward and downward movements of different parts of the region led to the layering of these substances, likened in a report by the Pennsylvania Topographic and Geologic Survey to a massive closed book "with every twentieth page made of black paper to represent the coal seams."[1] With subsequent shifting of the regional landmass some of these coal seams appeared at the surface while others remained deep underground.

Coal formed only in parts of the valley. Anthracite, hard coal, developed around the confluence of the Susquehanna and the Lackawanna and between the Lehigh and the Susquehanna. Bituminous or soft coal formed along the Tioga and in rich sections along the upper West Branch and some of its tributaries. The location of these coal seams, laid thousands of years before people ever walked through the region or fished in its waters, would eventually determine much about the human geography of the valley. In the eighteenth century, valley residents discovered exposed coal seams and soon realized their utility. The Susquehannocks apparently knew coal could burn; so did the colonists whom Hector St. John de Crèvecoeur observed at Wyoming in the 1770s. And in the nineteenth century, when an industrializing nation needed fuel, the mining of valley coal supplies reoriented local settlement and commercial patterns.[2]

Erosion also shaped the upper valley's topography. Water cut into rock from the formation of the original Appalachia, and the power

1. This discussion of the shaping of the regional environment is based largely on William Voight, Jr., *The Susquehanna Compact: Guardian of the River's Future* (New Brunswick, N.J., 1972), chaps. 1–2; the quotation is on page 17.

2. On Susquehannocks, see ibid., 15; on Crèvecoeur see H. L. Bourdin and S. T. Williams, eds., "Crèvecoeur on the Susquehanna, 1774–1776," *Yale Review* 14 (1925), 570–571; on the later importance of coal see Anthony F. C. Wallace, *St. Clair: A Nineteenth-Century Coal Town's Experience with a Disaster-prone Industry* (New York, 1987); and Edward J. Davies II, *The Anthracite Aristocracy: Leadership and Social Change in the Hard Coal Regions of Northeastern Pennsylvania, 1800–1930* (DeKalb, Ill., 1985).

of erosion later increased. In particular, the upthrusting of the western part of the regional landmass in the Mesozoic Era caused streams to flow to the southeast and gave them the force to cut more effectively through softer rock surfaces. The ageless battle between the rock and the water is evident throughout the region today. Where the landmass was less resistant, the Susquehanna and its tributaries have cut deep valleys; the gorge cut by Pine Creek, one of the major tributaries of the West Branch, is so steep that today it is known as the "Grand Canyon" of Pennsylvania. Where the rock was stronger, the waters formed wider and shallower valleys, especially evident south of the confluence of the Susquehanna's two branches and becoming more pronounced as the river moves closer to the Atlantic. When the Pleistocene glaciers retreated, the river incorporated water from the melting ice, increasing the force of erosion. The melting of the icecaps also created numerous ponds and lakes in the region.

The movement of water, in both its liquid and solid states, defined the region's topography. The watercourse that became the Susquehanna River was particularly active, capturing other major channels, including the Unadilla, Chemung, and Chenango. The Susquehanna did not, however, maintain all the streams that flowed into it. Over time, further tectonic activity and continued erosion altered the course of some streams, which eventually drained into the Mohawk and thence to the Hudson. The east and west branches of the Delaware may also once have been part of the Susquehanna, but they too changed course. Still, the Susquehanna's drainage system remained largely intact, its drainage basin constituting, as a result of these changes, a vast network stretching through the area that became the middle colonies.

Today, the initial source of the river is Lake Otsego, fourteen miles south of the Mohawk in central New York. Several miles below the southern end of Lake Otsego the Susquehanna acquires water from Canadarago Lake. The river's major tributaries in New York, including the Chemung, the Tioughnioga, and the Unadilla, stretch into the Finger Lakes region and the heart of Iroquoia. In southern New York the river flows close to the Delaware; in Pennsylvania it runs near the Schuylkill and the Lehigh, both of which flow into the Delaware. By any of these routes travelers on the Susquehanna could make overland passages to rivers that run directly to Philadelphia. The West Branch of the Susquehanna, rising in western

Pennsylvania and swelling as it gathers the waters of important tributaries such as Pine Creek and Lycoming Creek, joins the main branch of the Susquehanna in north-central Pennsylvania. The West Branch itself can be followed to two points where portages once connected eighteenth-century travelers with the Ohio River.[3] After the confluence of its two main branches, the Susquehanna flows almost directly southward, much straighter than at any point farther upstream; the Juniata joins the Susquehanna roughly sixty miles south of this point. Eventually the river drains into Chesapeake Bay, providing much of the aquatic life in that body.

The vast territory drained by the river invited Indians and colonists to take advantage of possible trade and travel along regional waterways. Such travel was always quicker and less expensive than overland movement by foot, horse, or wagon through the forests and over or around the mountains. But as early travelers soon realized, water levels in the Susquehanna drainage basin change dramatically over the course of the year in direct response to seasonal conditions. During the winter, when one hundred inches of snow usually fall in the region, the Susquehanna and many streams and lakes in the region ice over, some into more or less solid blocks, others with a thin ice coating or floating ice blocks. Travelers who failed to take account of these conditions risked exposure or drowning if they tried to navigate the waters amid the ice flows. At times the ice was so thick that it blocked the river and prevented boat travel, isolating and endangering groups that needed supplies. During the winter of 1756–1757 Pennsylvania soldiers at Fort Augusta, at the confluence of the Susquehanna's two branches, often had great difficulty performing their duties; rain, hail, snow, wind, cold, and ice constantly interrupted their work and at times threatened their lives.[4]

The winter freeze often lasted from December to April; certain areas, such as Canadarago Lake, were generally free of frost only between May and October. When the ice broke and the snow on the

3. The portages from the Susquehanna can best be seen in the map in Francis Jennings, "Susquehannock," in William Sturtevant, ed., *Handbook of North American Indians*, vol. 15, *Northeast*, ed. Bruce Trigger (Washington, D.C., 1978), 362.

4. Thomas E. Harr et al., "Limnology of Canadarago Lake," in Jay Bloomfield, ed., *Lakes of New York State*, 3 vols. (New York, 1978–1980), vol. 3, *Ecology of the Lakes of East-Central New York*, 155; "Journal of Col. James Burd While Building Fort Augusta at Shamokin, 1756–7" *P. Arch.* 2d ser., 2:743–820, esp. 754–766.

surrounding hills drained into the Susquehanna and its tributary streams, flooding destroyed settlements in the low-lying areas, which generally had the most fertile soil. Deforestation usually followed in the wake of human settlement, and the cleared land was less able to hold water, increasing the forces of erosion and flooding.[5]

In summer, water levels in the drainage basin ran very low. Some streams, navigable during other parts of the year, were completely dry in July and August. Even the main branch of the Susquehanna at the confluence with the West Branch became so shallow that travelers could easily walk across the river; one surveyor found that the depth of the water in this area was only two feet during August. The thickly wooded environment, with numerous shallows of slow-moving or even stagnant water, provided ideal breeding grounds for disease-carrying mosquitoes. These pests, thriving in the summer heat and ubiquitous humidity of the area, plagued eighteenth-century residents of the upper valley; if they carried certain pathogens, these insects could transmit illness and, at times, death. Autumn brought respite from many of the problems of the summer, but the river often did not rise to a navigable depth until heavy rains or the first snows fell.[6]

Weather conditions varied with dominant wind patterns. Dry polar air from Canada buffeted the region from late autumn through early spring. When the winds blew strongly and crossed Lake Ontario, heavy snow squalls buried much of the valley, thoroughly disrupting movement along paths and roads. From May through October the dominant weather patterns generally originated in the Gulf of Mexico; winds from the south brought warm and humid weather, often plaguing travelers and settlers who constantly complained about the conditions. The third major source of weather was the Atlantic Ocean. When winds blew directly from the east the weather became cool, damp, and cloudy.[7]

5. Harr et al., "Limnology of Canadarago Lake," 155.

6. Robert Albion and Leonidas Dodson, eds., *Philip Vickers Fithian: Journal, 1775–1776, Written on the Virginia-Pennsylvania Frontier and in the Army around New York* (Princeton, N.J., 1934), 86; "Journal of General James Whitelaw, Surveyor-General of Vermont," *Proceedings of the Vermont Historical Society* (1905–1906), 135. On water conditions in general see the writings of the Moravian missionaries in William Beauchamp, ed., *Moravian Journals Relating to Central New York, 1745–1766* (Syracuse, N.Y., 1916), passim.

7. Willard N. Harman and Leonard P. Sohacki, "The Limnology of Otsego Lake (Glimmerglass)," in Bloomfield, ed., *Lakes of New York State*, 3:16.

Valley residents were acutely aware of local weather patterns. Snow and cold threatened travelers with exposure. Heat and humidity made summer movement almost intolerable. Rain at any time of the year could turn paths into pools of mud that made horse, foot, and wagon travel treacherous.

Given the importance of meteorological patterns, it was not surprising that some in the valley attempted to predict the weather. In August 1743 the naturalist John Bartram, the cartographer Lewis Evans, and Conrad Weiser, who was sometimes a trader and sometimes a political envoy for colonial governments negotiating with eastern tribes, were walking through part of the upper valley with several Nanticokes. On the tenth of the month Bartram angered his Indian traveling companions by rolling a stone down a hill near the West Branch of the Susquehanna. They believed that his action would bring rain the next day. Bartram wrote in his journal: "I told them I had sufficient experience it signified nothing, for it was my common practice to roll down stones from the top of every steep hill, and could not recall that it ever rained the next day." The following day was dry, but it rained two days later, and, much to Bartram's surprise, the Nanticokes attributed the wet weather to his stone-rolling. When Bartram pointed out that if their reasoning was sound it would have rained the day before, one of the Nanticokes "cunningly replyed that our *Almanacks* often prognosticated on a day, and yet the rain did not come within two days."[8] Although neither Indians nor colonists could successfully predict the weather, each group tried to determine weather patterns because these meteorological events greatly influenced their lives.

The survival of place names provides some clues to valley residents' perceptions of the natural world. Valley Indians, like other Indians in North America, often used place names to describe specific elements of the environment. This is clear in the varied meanings for the name of the river. The precise meaning of the Algonquin word *Susquehanna* remains obscure, but it apparently referred to the river's length and the terrain it traversed. The Delawares once called the West Branch the Quenischachagekhanne, shortened to

8. John Bartram, *Observations on the Inhabitants, Climate, Soil, Rivers, Productions, Animals and Other Matters Worthy of Notice. Made by Mr. John Bartram, in His Travels from Pensilvania to Onondaga, Oswego and the Lake Ontario, in Canada* (1751; rpt. Barre, Mass., 1973), 82–84.

Quenischachki, meaning *the river which has the long reaches or straight courses in it*, and they referred to the North Branch by the name M'chewamisipu or Mchwewarmink meaning *the river on which are extensive clear flats.*[9]

Other parts of the valley bore names indicating prominent geographic features. Owego, probably a corruption of Ah-wa-ga or A-o-we-gwa, referred to the place where the valley widens. To the Oneidas, Unadilla, and its variant De-u-na-dil'-lo, referred to the "place of meeting," indicating the confluence of two rivers. When Conrad Weiser traveled through the valley in 1737, he ventured up Lycoming Creek, one of the tributaries of the West Branch. "The stream we are now on," he wrote, "the Indians call *Dia-dachlu* (the lost or bewildered,) which in fact deserves such a name. We proceeded along this stream between two terrible mountains; the valley was however now about a half mile in width, and the stream flowed now against this and then against the other mountain, among the rocks." Weiser also discovered the apt name of a stream known as Oscohu, "the fierce." This watercourse, a tributary of the North Branch, "is a rapid impetuous stream," he wrote, "because it flows among mountains, and because the wind has melted the snow in the high forests."[10]

Colonial observers similarly used descriptive terms to identify important geographical features. They adopted Indian names for the river and many of the towns along it but substituted their own terminology for other environmental features. T. C. Lotter's map of the middle colonies, printed possibly as early as 1720, showed that mountains dominated the upper valley. Lotter filled the region between the two main branches of the river with mountains and labeled it "Montes inaccessi." The area north of Wyoming was similarly dominated by imposing peaks and labeled "Montium juga continua." Other maps bore similarly menacing translations: "The End-

9. George P. Donehoo, *A History of the Indian Villages and Place Names in Pennsylvania, with Numerous Historical Notes and References* (Harrisburg, Pa., 1928), 215–219; William Beauchamp, *Aboriginal Placenames of New York*, New York State Museum Bulletin 108 (Albany, N.Y., 1907), 27–30, 173.

10. Donehoo, *Indian Villages and Place Names*, 143; Beauchamp, *Aboriginal Placenames*, 172, 175, 43; "Narrative of a Journey, made in the year 1737, by Conrad Weiser, Indian Agent and Provincial Interpreter, from Tulpehocken in the Province of Pennsylvania to Onondaga, the head quarters of the allied Six Nations, in the Province of New York," trans. H. H. Muhlenberg, *Pennsylvania Historical Society Collections* 1 (1853), 9–11.

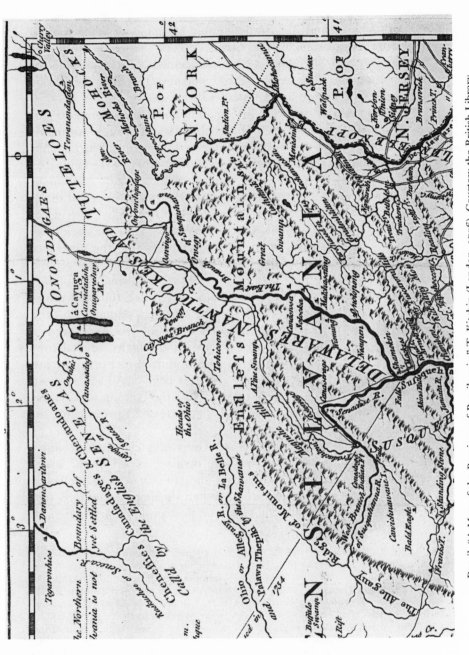

Detail, "A Map of the Province of Pensilvania," T. Kitchin (London, 1756). Courtesy the Briitish Library

less Mountains," and the "Impenetrable Mountains." Some warned
of specific hazards such as a "Steep Descent" between "Anthony's
Wilderness" and Shamokin or routes deemed "Scarce passible for
Steep Mountains." Travelers feared journeys through one thickly
wooded region known as the "Shades of Death."[11]

Place names also provided information about the mountains surrounding the Susquehanna and its tributaries. Although not nearly
as tall as the White or Green mountains, they were still formidable.
Many were too steep to support agriculture; others were cultivable,
but their distance from reliable sources of water made continuous
use problematic. All of the mountains in the region impeded direct
travel. Travelers frequently referred to the "Ant Hills," a string of
small but distinct mountains which covered much of the region between the two branches of the river, demonstrating the itinerants'
frustration when confronting these impediments; traveling around
or over these large hills proved troublesome and time-consuming.
Paths along the edges of the mountains were often thin and unstable, capable of giving way and sending travelers plunging to their
death. Livestock, as some Continental army soldiers discovered in
the late 1770s, could not traverse some of the paths; several cows
they were herding along the top of a two-hundred-foot precipice lost
their footing and dropped to the river far below. "All was not lost,
however," one of the soldiers recalled. "At the bottom, luckily, was
the river; the boats coming up had them dressed," presumably for
that night's dinner.[12]

But if the hills and mountains were imposing, eighteenth-century
residents knew about areas far more inviting, especially the many
fertile vales along the floodplain of the river and its major tributaries. *Wyoming,* in all of its variant Indian spellings, meant *large flats*
or *great meadows*; Indians, colonists, and postrevolutionary settlers all

11. [T. C. Lotter], "Pensylvania Nova Jersey et Nova York cum Regionibus ad Flu-
vium Delaware in America Sitis, Nova Delitione ob oculos posita per Tobr. Conr.
Lotter" [1720?]; Lewis Evans, "A Map of Pensilvania, New-Jersey, New-York, and the
Three Delaware Counties" [1749], and Evans, "A General Map of the Middle British
Colonies in America" [1755], in Lawrence H. Gipson, *Lewis Evans* (Philadelphia,
1939). Lotter's map is undated, but a copy in the Map Library of the British Library
indicates it was apparently engraved in 1720; see #7400.(3); a later version of this
same map is by Matthias Seutterum (Augsburg, ca. 1740). On the "shades of death"
see Frederick Cook, ed., *Journals of the Military Expedition of Major General John Sullivan
against the Six Nations of Indians in 1779* (Albany, N.Y., 1887), 63.
12. Cook, ed., *Journals,* 6.

wanted to live there, in spite of the risks of springtime floods. Skew'-do-wa, the site of modern Elmira, similarly meant *great plain*. Often place names referred to desirable local resources. Oquaga, a word of Mohawk origin, meant either *the place of hulled corn soup* or *place of wild grapes*. Ka-ri-ton'-ga, a word of probable Onondaga origin, meant *place of great oaks*; colonists termed the same area Cherry Valley, although one later observer recalled that the region had once been filled with oak trees.[13] Colonists might have altered the environment differently than Indians had, but they too relied on place names to instruct them about local resources.

Flora and Fauna

Like topography and climate, indigenous plants and animals, as well as species introduced by settlers, greatly influenced daily life in the eighteenth century. Forests, now regrown and towering over vast stretches of the region, were crucial for economic development. They provided timber for building houses and boats, fuel for heating and cooking, and eventually an enormously valuable export product. Animals too figured prominently in economic development. Many residents, especially the Indians, relied on indigenous animals for food, although settlers and some Indians later turned, at times, to domesticated livestock. Travelers seeking furbearing animals encouraged Indians to hunt them, a practice that transformed the regional economy and environment. Local stocks of fish and birds were also vital sources of food.

Thick forests covered many of the mountains and most of the valleys between the peaks. Although it is impossible to determine the exact composition of these forests, travelers' and surveyors' records, used in conjunction with studies of unexploited stands and forest succession, provide vital data for estimating their character. They were probably a mixture of hardwoods with large numbers of conifers. Dominant species included beech, hemlock, red and sugar maple, black and yellow birch, white pine, and chestnut. Some eighteenth-century accounts indicated that certain areas were dominated by particular species, most commonly beech, hemlock, and sugar

13. Donehoo, *Indian Villages and Place Names*, 259, 138; Beauchamp, *Aboriginal Placenames*, 43, 28, 173.

maple. Valley residents, some extremely knowledgeable about tree species, referred to certain places by the dominant vegetation in the area: Oak Creek ran south of Lake Otsego; "Pine swamp" described the area north of the confluence of the river's two branches. Those who came to claim areas full of hardwoods and white pines realized the profits to be made from exporting timber to outside markets; land stocked with sugar maples provided residents with food and, by the end of the century, substantial revenue as well.[14]

Eighteenth-century residents and travelers left clues revealing their perceptions of these dense stands of trees. Travel from town to town, confined to waterways or preexisting, perhaps ancient, Indian paths, took valley inhabitants through vast forests. Observers termed areas of dense forest "swamps," reflecting the perpetual moisture of ground covered by vegetation which never received enough sunlight to dry it completely. Travelers who wandered off well-trod paths occasionally became lost and disoriented. When Crèvecoeur traveled from Wyoming to the West Branch along an overland path in the mid-1770s, his party walked through a "huge pine swamp which had been partly consumed by some accidental fire; immense trees burnt at the roots were overset," he wrote, "one over the other in an infinite variety of directions, some hung half way down, supported by the limbs of those which still stood erect. Others had fallen flat to the ground and had raised an immense circumference of earth which adhered to their roots." The entire scene baffled Crèvecoeur. "In short," he concluded, "there was no penetrating through such a black scene of confusion; it was a perfect chaos."[15]

In general, however, eighteenth-century valley residents and travelers found that the forests covered not a heart of darkness but a world of plentiful resources. The forests were not dense everywhere. Open meadows appeared throughout the region, most probably cleared by fires or possibly by flooding. Valley residents knew how to

14. Stephen H. Spurr and Burton Barnes, *Forest Ecology*, 3d ed. (New York, 1980), 562–563; H. J. Lutz, "The Vegetation of Heart's Content, a Virgin Forest in Northwestern Pennsylvania," *Ecology* 11 (1930), 1–29; G. E. Nichols, "The Hemlock–White Pine–Northern Hardwood Region of Eastern North America," *Ecology* 16 (1935), 403–422. For eighteenth-century accounts see, for example, Samuel Harris, Jornel and field Notes . . . don for Robt Lettis Hooper and Compy, October–November 1774, Wallis Papers, Reel 6, HSP; John Lincklaen, *Travels in the Years 1791 and 1792 in Pennsylvania, New York and Vermont* (New York, 1897), passim; Bartram, *Observations*, passim; William Ellis to Samuel Wallis, August 2, 1793, Wallis Papers, Reel 6.
15. Bourdin and Williams, eds., "Crèvecoeur on the Susquehanna," 573.

thin forests, either to obtain fuel or to clear fields. Even those who just wanted to get rid of the trees and used fire to clear their fields benefited from the forests; the ash from the trees was marketable to pot and pearl ash works, and the fires themselves provided nutrients to the soil, thereby improving agricultural yields.

Human intervention altered the local ecosystem, but other forces, at work for many centuries, also influenced the valley environment. In particular, the retreat of the glaciers, which marked the landscape in distinctive ways, changed the composition of faunal stocks in the valley. When the ice receded and the regional environment warmed, a dramatic shift occurred in the regional animal population, from mammals that live in boreal or colder habitats to those adapted to a temperate climate. This shift probably began around 9300 B.C. and was completed around 7300 B.C. By the end of the transition period the fauna inhabiting the region was the same that Indians and colonists observed in the eighteenth century, the progeny of generations of animals that lived in the upper valley for upward of nine thousand years.

The remains of some animals of the transition period provide a precise record of ecological change in the valley. When the glaciers retreated, caribou, northern bog lemming, yellow-cheeked vole, and the northern flying squirrel lived in the area, all species familiar to habitats farther north. When these boreal species vacated the area, others, more suited to the temperate climate, soon inhabited the valley: southern flying squirrel, southern bog lemming, porcupine, pine mouse, cottontail rabbit, white-tailed deer, and elk. Palynological evidence similarly points to this same transition period, from roughly eleven thousand to nine thousand years ago, when the vegetation familiar to eighteenth-century residents replaced other species unable to cope with the shift in climate.[16]

The new temperate environment provided a range of habitats ideal for many species of fauna. Beavers, the favorite species in the fur trade, lived throughout the upper valley. The hundreds of small streams in the area provided excellent sites for these furbearers' dams, allowing young beavers to find locations for new colonies with minimal effort and risk; because of the ease of finding suitable lodge

16. John E. Guilday, "The Climatic Significance of the Hosterman's Pit Local Fauna, Centre County, Pennsylvania," *American Antiquity* 32 (1967), 231–232.

and dam sites, the indigenous beaver population of the valley became substantial.[17]

Other animals and fish found the upper valley an ideal habitat. These included elk, wolves, wildcats, otters, panthers, minks, martens, foxes, fishers, bears, raccoons, and muskrats. Flocks of passenger pigeons frequented the region. Travelers and early residents also reported a variety of fish species living in the river, streams, and lakes. Whitefish, lake herring, and probably lake trout, walleye, shad, largemouth bass, and smallmouth bass lived or spawned in the valley. Fauna, it appeared to eighteenth-century observers who at times attributed human faculties to other species, also believed that the region was a valley of opportunity.[18]

People and Environment in the Eighteenth Century

Valley residents knew they inhabited a plentiful world, but daily experience taught them that their existence remained precarious. Making a living, or possibly a profit, meant finding safe lodgings and reliable transportation through the region. Those who did not understand the valley environment were often destroyed by it: traders drowned in the ice-laden river; soldiers succumbed to illnesses exacerbated by climatic conditions; individuals failed to take precautions against bears and wolves. Valley residents did not believe, as earlier Europeans had, that the forests were inhabited by horrific beasts that would set upon and kill unprepared wanderers; terrifying man-beasts may have roamed the darkened forests and heaths of the Old World but did not thrive along the Susquehanna's banks.[19] But survival demanded that people strike a bargain with the

17. On the relationship between beavers and their habitat see Morrell Allred, *Beaver Behavior* (Happy Camp, Calif., 1986).

18. These species were all recorded in James Irvine's Invoice of Four Bundles of Peltry & Furrs, Commissioners of Indian Affairs, 1756–1765, Gratz Collection, Case 14, Box 10, HSP. Similar lists of species are in William Cooper, *A Guide in the Wilderness, or the History of the First Settlements in the Western Counties of New York, with Useful Instructions to Future Settlers* (1810; rpt. Freeport, N.Y., 1970), 28–31, and in Lewis Evans, "A Brief Account of Pennsylvania, 1753," in Gipson, *Lewis Evans*, 117–120. On fish see Harman and Sohacki, "Limnology of Otsego Lake," 91; Bourdin and Williams, eds., "Crèvecoeur on the Susquehanna," 570; Cook, ed., *Journals*, 20, 53, 82; Cooper, *Guide*, 9.

19. On the creatures inhabiting the forests of early Europe see Lisa M. Bitel, *Isle of the Saints: Monastic Settlement and Christian Community in Early Ireland* (Ithaca, N.Y., 1990), chap. 1.

natural world, and those who failed to do so generally paid a high price.

Local inhabitants could greatly change the landscape, as they did with fire, but they were still subject to nature's threats. They certainly recognized that the region was much more livable than other parts of eastern North America. Valley residents fared immeasurably better than settlers in places such as Jamestown, where colonists experienced devastating killing periods because of their inability to adapt to the local ecosystem.[20] Still, in spite of the benefits of the temperate climate, those careless or inattentive to matters of daily need, such as the procurement of food and secure shelter, faced the very real prospect of death. This specter always hung over the communities struggling to survive in the upper valley.

Over the course of the century the groups that occupied the upper Susquehanna Valley sought to create stable settlements. At times they succeeded, at times they failed. In the process of adapting their economy and society to local ecological realities they modified their work patterns, especially when certain activities, such as the fur trade or lumbering, depleted particular natural resources.[21] By 1800 the inhabitants of the area had learned to alter the regional environment and to extract valuable resources in efficient ways. The environment of the upper Susquehanna Valley, which had once dominated and practically controlled the lives of those who lived there, had begun to lose its elemental dominance, or so residents believed. Such a profound shift demonstrated the successful efforts of local inhabitants to understand the natural world they inhabited; having struck a bargain with nature, they realized that their investment in time, capital, and in some cases human life, was paying substantial dividends.

This economic success, most evident in the marketing of extractable resources such as coal and lumber, had disastrous ecological consequences. Once lumberers had thinned the woods, the many species of birds and animals that had depended on forest resources lost much of their habitat and either died or, more likely, migrated

20. Carville Earle, "Environment, Disease, and Mortality in Early Virginia," in Thad Tate and David Ammerman, eds., *The Chesapeake in the Seventeenth Century* (Chapel Hill, N.C., 1979), 96–125; Karen Ordahl Kupperman, "Apathy and Death in Early Jamestown," *JAH* 66 (1979), 24–40.

21. On the transition from wood to coal in the American industrial revolution, see Richard Wilkinson, *Poverty and Progress: An Ecological Perspective on Economic Development* (New York, 1973), chap. 8.

to areas where forests remained. When loggers shipped lumber down the river, or when by-products of coal mining leached into regional watercourses, vast stretches of the river and its tributaries, once brimming with fish, became, for a time, biologically dead. Drastic ecological consequences also resulted more directly from expansion of specific economic activities. The overfishing of certain aquatic species led to their depletion; furbearing mammals fell victim to hunters. When the people of the upper valley entered the industrial age and extensively employed the physical resources of their region to drive the machines of the modern world, their landscape looked less and less like the world of 1700.

2 The Susquehanna Indians

Indians had lived in the upper Susquehanna Valley for at least two thousand years before Europeans knew of the region's existence. When Europeans extended their territories in the wake of Christopher Columbus's expeditions, they transformed the lives of valley Indians.

Reconstructing the economic world of these Indians in the eighteenth century thus poses problems. First, the Indians who had lived in the region in the seventeenth century, the Susquehannocks in particular, suffered a demographic catastrophe and therefore had a minimal impact on the Indians and Europeans who moved into the region after 1700. Second, descriptions of the Indians' economy survive in the writings of European and colonial travelers, explorers, missionaries, and settlers. These individuals were not trained ethnographers; their descriptions of the Indians reflect prevailing early modern European attitudes and often emphasize the interaction between the natives and the newcomers rather than focus on the Indians exclusively. Third, these observers were, unknowingly, agents of a transformation of the Indians' world. Tribes that had existed for centuries collapsed within decades from European diseases. Surviving Indians created alliances with other Indians and also competed with different tribes for access to the Europeans' goods. Still,

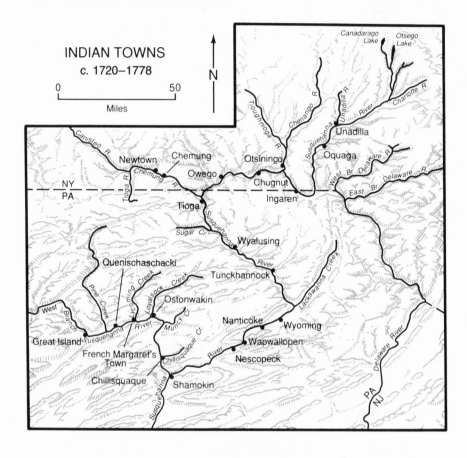

reconstructing the traditional economy of the Susquehanna Indians remains a valuable pursuit. Without an understanding of the Indians' economy, tracing the myriad ways the fur trade altered their world becomes meaningless.

Fortunately, the Indians left important material evidence about their economy. Pieces of pottery, mussel shells, fluted points from arrows and spears, and chipped and carved animal bones found in their graves and other archaeological remains all provide insight into the Indians' traditional economy.

Taken together, the evidence of archaeologists and travelers hints at the complexity of the Indians' world. Indians in the region farmed, hunted, and fished for food. They constantly modified the natural environment to meet their needs. But in comparison to the later extractive nature of the fur trade, monoculture, and lumbering, valley Indians adapted to their physical world in ways that did not seriously threaten their resource base. In addition, their economic behavior fit larger cultural and religious ideals in ways never fully comprehensible to contemporary Europeans.

The Indians of the Upper Susquehanna Valley

As we are learning from an abundance of recent historical research, the early modern period was an age when the movement of peoples reshaped the society and economy of the Western world. Internal migrations rearranged the social structure of England when people formerly tied to small, rural villages left for larger communities, many eventually moving into port cities, especially London. Thousands of people from Scotland migrated across the Irish Sea to Ulster, and many thousands of English people joined them. But such migrations went beyond the English-speaking world. Throughout Europe people moved, often over very long distances, to escape the ravages of war or for the promise of better fortune. Thus German-speaking Protestants fled the Rhine Valley; some found homes in western Russia and northern Prussia, while others ventured to England, Ireland, and America. A related migration involved the forced relocation of hundreds of thousands of people from west and central Africa to the Western Hemisphere.[1]

The movement of various peoples, Indian and European, into the upper Susquehanna Valley was but one part of this larger demographic phenomenon. Indeed, the peopling of the region in the colonial period mirrored the larger changes in the Atlantic world. The Susquehanna's eighteenth-century Indian population, like many other mobile peoples, had no deep ties to the region. These migrants settled in the area because European migration forced them to leave their previous territories; they chose the valley because of

1. Bernard Bailyn, *The Peopling of British North America: An Introduction* (New York, 1986); D. W. Meinig, *The Shaping of America* (New Haven, Conn., 1986), vol. 1, *Atlantic America, 1492–1800*, pt. 1; James Horn, "Servant Emigration to the Chesapeake in the Seventeenth Century," in Thad Tate and David Ammerman, eds., *The Chesapeake in the Seventeenth Century* (Chapel Hill, N.C., 1979), 51–95; Philip D. Curtin, *The Atlantic Slave Trade: A Census* (Madison, Wis., 1969).

available resources and the possibility of enjoying them with little competition from colonists or other Indians.

During the early decades of English colonization in North America the Susquehannocks were the most numerous people in the valley.[2] Around 1550, a half-century before the first permanent English settlements in North America, the Susquehannocks inhabited a stretch of the upper valley between Wyoming and modern Binghamton. They occupied territory overlapping the southern parts of Iroquoia, the area claimed by the five, and after 1722 six, Iroquois tribes. Possibly under pressure from the Iroquois, the Susquehannocks began to move southward, establishing settlements along the southern reaches of the river in the late sixteenth and early seventeenth centuries, displacing any smaller groups of Indians who were then inhabiting those regions.

Captain John Smith encountered the Susquehannocks in 1608, when he traveled up the Susquehanna River. They fascinated him. "Such great and well proportioned men are seldome seene," Smith wrote in *The General Historie of Virginia, New-England, and the Summer Isles*, published in 1624, "for they seemed like Giants to the English, yea and to the neighbours, yet seemed of an honest and simple disposition, with much adoe restrained from adoring us as Gods. Those are the strangest people of all those Countries, both in language and attire; for their language it may well beseeme their proportions, sounding from them, as a voyce in a vault." He wrote that they wore bear and wolf skins, smoked tobacco out of pipes carved with birds, bears, and deer, and carried "Bowes, Arrowes, and clubs, suitable to their greatnesse." Smith claimed they could muster up to six hundred warriors. Their population may have exceeded six thousand in the 1640s and was probably greater when Smith encountered them. The Susquehannocks were an Iroquoian people, and their social, cultural, and economic practices resembled those of the tribes in the Iroquois Confederacy. They lived in wooden longhouses, typically sixty to eighty feet long, which held several families all related in some way to a single matriarch. According to Smith, the Susquehan-

2. The following discussion of the Susquehannocks, unless otherwise noted, is from Francis Jennings, "Susquehannock," in William Sturtevant, ed., *Handbook of North American Indians*, vol. 15, *Northeast*, ed. Bruce Trigger (Washington, D.C., 1978), 362–367; Paul A. W. Wallace, *Indians in Pennsylvania* (1961; rev. ed. Harrisburg, Pa., 1981), 10–13; and Barry C. Kent, *Susquehanna's Indians*, Anthropological Series 6 (Harrisburg, Pa., 1984), 25–108.

nocks lived in palisaded villages "to defend them from the Massa-womekes their mortall enemies."[3]

After the Susquehannocks moved out of the northern valley in the late sixteenth century, they never found peace. They fought with the Iroquois over beaver territory and with the Delawares over trade relations with Europeans. Seeking help against the Iroquois, they established peaceful relations with colonists in Maryland in the mid-seventeenth century. But when the people of that colony later sought better relations with the Iroquois, they repudiated their alliance with the Susquehannocks, prompting these Indians to move farther south to an abandoned Piscataway settlement at the confluence of the Potomac River and Piscataway Creek. Unknowingly, the Susquehannocks had migrated into a troubled region, where Indians and backcountry settlers were competing for territory. Colonists from both Maryland and Virginia repeatedly attacked the Susquehannocks, prompting the Indians to seek safer territory.

Desperate for a new place to settle, the Susquehannocks accepted an invitation to move back to the Susquehanna Valley from an unlikely source: the Iroquois. Weakened by disease and competition with other Indians during the so-called Beaver Wars, the Iroquois needed to bolster their ranks with friendly Indians, and they believed that the Susquehannocks would meet this need. But during the move back, the Susquehannocks became dispersed, some merging with Iroquois bands and others into Delaware communities. Some periodically raided Indian tribes friendly to Maryland and Virginia until these tribes established tributary relationships with the League Iroquois.

In the late seventeenth century some Susquehannocks established their own town at Conestoga in the lower Susquehanna Valley north of the Maryland border. But even here the Indians found little comfort. During the French and Indian War a band of Pennsylvania vigilantes, known as the Paxton Boys, killed the remaining twenty Indians, eight of them children, still living at Conestoga.

The southward migration and eventual decline of the Susquehannocks during the seventeenth century left much of the Susquehanna Valley empty of human settlement. Other Indians no doubt traveled

3. Philip L. Barbour, ed., *The Complete Works of Captain John Smith*, 3 vols. (Chapel Hill, N.C., 1986), 2:106. See also William Strachey, *The Historie of Travell into Virginia Britania* (1612), ed. Louis B. Wright and Virginia Freund (London, 1953), 47–48.

in the region, and many probably established temporary hunting lodges during seasonal journeys. The situation changed in the early eighteenth century, when many displaced Indians moved to the region. Once again, the influence of European traders and colonizers lay behind these migrations. But the Iroquois also played a decisive role in the peopling of the upper valley with Indians in the early eighteenth century.

By 1700 the Iroquois were a far less potent military threat than they had been earlier. Hostile conflicts with other Indians—possibly the Susquehannocks in the 1670s, more certainly the Illinois and Miamis—had taken a severe toll on the Iroquois. At the same time, the members of the League Iroquois found themselves caught in the struggle between France and England for control of peltry. By 1700, the Iroquois were in a far weaker position than they had been a quarter of a century earlier.[4] To maintain control over desirable territory and, perhaps more important, to seize the great transportation and commercial opportunities offered by the Susquehanna River, the league actively encouraged other displaced Indians to migrate to the region. Once there, the Iroquois hoped, these tribes would accept the league's claim of sovereignty over the valley, exchanging an earlier but precarious independence for the protection of the league from future colonial aggression.

During the early eighteenth century, the Iroquois consolidated their territorial claims over the Susquehanna Valley by negotiation rather than military conquest, allowing displaced groups of Indians to settle in the upper valley while the League Indians maintained their claim to the region. The Iroquois wanted the valley settled to stave off colonists who were seeking land. They also hoped that a resident population of Indians along the river would help them create a stable trade system in the region. Many displaced Indians accepted the Iroquois' offer and found a refuge in the Susquehanna Valley.

These Indians shared a common fate: all had to find new places to live because the expansion of the British Empire across the Atlantic had displaced their villages. The intertwined histories of the Indians who moved to the valley during the eighteenth century help illuminate these broad demographic developments. The Conoys' experi-

4. Daniel Richter, "War and Culture: The Iroquois Experience," *WMQ* 3d ser., 40 (1983), 544–551; Kent, *Susquehanna's Indians*, 45–46.

ences proved typical. In the early seventeenth century they lived near Piscataway Creek between the Potomac River and Chesapeake Bay. The Conoys were just one of a group of tribes inhabiting the region along both sides of the Chesapeake; taken together, these tribes had perhaps more than twelve thousand members in the early seventeenth century. But the Conoys, like many other eastern tribes, soon faced hard times. The southward migration of the Susquehannocks forcibly displaced the Conoys, who migrated to an island in what is now Washington, D.C. The Conoys established friendly relations with colonists in Maryland, a move that seemed to promise security but eventually angered both the Iroquois and the Susquehannocks. But the decline of the Susquehannocks, in addition to a friendlier relationship between the Conoys and Iroquois developed in treaties in the 1680s, improved the Conoys' relationships with these northern Indian tribes while their relationship with colonists deteriorated. These changes prompted their northward migration.

At the end of the seventeenth century and continuing into the early eighteenth century, the Conoys began their migrations and almost immediately faced hardship. At a settlement on present-day Heater's Island an epidemic swept among them in 1704. Later they moved north into Pennsylvania and along the southern reaches of the Susquehanna River, just beyond the Maryland border. Some settled at abandoned Susquehannock town sites, where they did not have to clear forests to make fields. But here too colonists interfered with the Conoys. In the words of a 1743 message from Old Sack, one of their sachems, to Governor George Thomas of Pennsylvania, "now the Lands all around them being settled by white People, their hunting is spoiled." That year, under advice from the Iroquois, many Conoys moved farther up the Susquehanna to Shamokin, although six years later some were still living farther south, on an island at the confluence of the Susquehanna and the Juniata. By the mid-1750s many Conoys had moved to Otsiningo, at the confluence of the Susquehanna and Chenango rivers. During these migratory decades, which stretched from the end of the seventeenth century to the mid-eighteenth century, not all of the Conoys remained together. Some never left Maryland, and others migrated directly to Otsiningo without establishing settlements elsewhere in the valley.[5]

5. Wallace, *Indians in Pennsylvania*, 111–112, Old Sack quoted on 112; Christian Feest, "Nanticoke and Neighboring Tribes," in Sturtevant, ed., *Handbook of North American Indians*, 15:240–243, 245–246.

The Conoys' migrations were but one part of a larger movement of Indians from the Chesapeake region to settlements farther north in the Susquehanna drainage basin. The Conoys' movements resembled those of the Nanticokes, who in the early seventeenth century inhabited villages along the eastern shore of the Chesapeake around the mouth of the Nanticoke River. They eventually established an alliance with the Iroquois, and many migrated to the Susquehanna Valley in the eighteenth century. By the 1740s groups of Nanticokes from Broad Creek had established towns at the confluence of the Susquehanna and Juniata rivers and at Wyoming. Some other members of the tribe moved to the area around the Pennsylvania–New York border. While members of the tribe made seasonal journeys to Chesapeake Bay for seafood, the Nanticokes continued to move northward. In the early 1750s they moved to Otsiningo, joining the Conoys along the southern edge of Iroquoia. In 1753 the Nanticokes became nonvoting members of the League Iroquois.[6]

The Tutelos came from even farther south than the Conoys and Nanticokes. They had been living along the present border between North Carolina and Virginia, near the Roanoke River. In the seventeenth century they found themselves facing not only land-hungry colonists but also other hostile Indians, the Susquehannocks. When the Susquehannocks moved south, they tried to take the Tutelos' territory. The Tutelos, in response, allied with two hundred backcountry Virginia colonists to ward off these hostile Indians. After they succeeded in this struggle, the colonists severed their alliance with the Tutelos and attacked their earlier ally, valuing the Indians' stock of beaver pelts more than friendly relations. The Tutelos again emerged victorious, but this contest also took a toll on them. They began to migrate, first westward toward the headwaters of the Yadhin River in the mountains and then eastward to the Roanoke and Meherrin rivers. In the 1720s they turned their sights northward, making peace with the Iroquois and migrating to the Susquehanna Valley. By 1744 some were resident at Shamokin and, by the end of that decade, another group settled at the confluence of Catawissa Creek and the Susquehanna; soon after, other Tutelos settled near Tioga.[7]

6. Wallace, *Indians in Pennsylvania*, 112–113; Feest, "Nanticoke and Neighboring Tribes," 240–246.

7. Wallace, *Indians in Pennsylvania*, 116–117.

The Tuscaroras migrated even farther than the Tutelos. They were living in central North Carolina, particularly along waterways leading to Pamlico Sound, when they felt the impact of European expansion. In the 1660s they fought with colonists and, in spite of their efforts to maintain peace, lost land to settlers; duplicitous traders, purveyors of alcohol, and slavers victimized their communities. In 1713–1714 one group of Tuscaroras, numbering perhaps fifteen hundred, fled the hostilities that devastated their homeland and migrated north toward Iroquoia, hoping to find stability. Less than a decade later the Tuscaroras became the sixth tribe of the League Iroquois; members of the tribe maintained communities in the upper Susquehanna Valley into the 1760s.[8]

Other displaced Indians joined the migration to the upper Susquehanna Valley. Among these were bands of Shawnees, who began to move north along the Susquehanna from Chesapeake Bay, where they had settled in the early 1690s. The tribe originated farther west, in the Ohio country, but dispersed after hostilities with the Iroquois in the 1660s and early 1670s. Some moved west to Starved Rock in Illinois; others went south to the Savannah River. One group, with perhaps 170 members, migrated to the mouth of the Susquehanna River in northern Maryland. In the late 1690s and the early 1700s this band moved into Pennsylvania; colonists had forced other Shawnees out of Carolina, and they moved north to join the Pennsylvania group. In Pennsylvania groups of Shawnees established communities with other Indians, especially groups of Delawares. Some Shawnees settled at Shawnee Flats near Wyoming; others went to Tioga, where they lived with displaced Mahicans, and another group settled near the mouth of Fishing Creek. Some established villages on the West Branch of the Susquehanna, at Chillisquaque, Conaserage (now Muncy), and Great Island (now Lock Haven).[9]

The Delawares were the last major group to migrate to the valley. Pressure from land-hungry colonists in the Delaware Valley made preservation of their traditional territory impossible. The Delawares

8. Douglas W. Boyce, "Iroquoian Tribes of the Virginia–North Carolina Coastal Plain," in Sturtevant, ed., *Handbook of North American Indians*, 15:282, 287; David Landy, "Tuscarora among the Iroquois," ibid., 518–520.

9. Wallace, *Indians in Pennsylvania*, 125–128; Charles Callender, "Shawnee," in Sturtevant, ed., *Handbook of North American Indians*, 15:630–631; Kent, *Susquehanna's Indians*, 78–91.

lost their lands through a series of sales rather than warfare, although provincial leaders acted fraudulently in some of these transactions, especially the notorious "Walking Purchase" of 1737.[10] By the end of the 1730s few Delawares remained in eastern Pennsylvania. Most moved to Shamokin and Wyoming. After the deaths of two prominent sachems at Shamokin, some Delawares continued their migration north along the Susquehanna to Wapwallopen.

The Delawares moved to the upper valley after establishing an alliance with the Iroquois. The exact nature of the Delaware-Iroquois relationship has been a subject of much dispute among historians. In treaty negotiations, the Iroquois referred to the Delawares as "women." Provincial leaders in the eighteenth century assumed this meant that the Iroquois had defeated the Delawares in battle and prevented them from taking up arms again; since only men were warriors, the term *women*, from this perspective, signaled emasculation and inferiority. The Indians, however, did not necessarily share this interpretation. To them the term could have referred to the Delawares' role as peacemaker between warring Indians. It also could have been meant to describe the Delawares' agricultural economy. Among northeastern Indians women characteristically were responsible for peacemaking and agriculture. Regardless of the precise meaning of the appellation, the Delawares who migrated to the upper valley entered into the political world of the Iroquois, and the Six Nations sometimes used their authority to limit the Delawares' economic choices.[11]

Many of these migrant Indians, rejecting earlier practices of living in tribally homogeneous villages, inhabited multitribal communities in the upper valley. Great Island had Delaware and Shawnee residents; French Margaret's Town and Ostonwakin were home to Indians from several tribes. The Iroquois established a town along the West Branch in 1727 and sent Shickellamy, one of their leaders, there. When local Indians abandoned his town in 1738, Shickellamy did not leave the Susquehanna; he moved to Shamokin. This town,

10. On the "Walking Purchase" see Francis Jennings, *The Ambiguous Iroquois Empire* (New York, 1984), 330–339, 388–397.

11. Kent, *Susquehanna's Indians*, 99–104; Ives Goddard, "Delaware," in Sturtevant, ed., *Handbook of North American Indians*, 15:221–223; Wallace, *Indians in Pennsylvania*, 138–140. On the Iroquois use of the term *women* applied to the Delawares see Jennings, *Ambiguous Iroquois Empire*, 45–46, 161–162; and Jay Miller, "The Delaware as Women: A Symbolic Solution," *American Ethnologist* 1 (1974), 507–514.

founded in 1718, became a center of the fur trade and was also tribally diverse: one-half of the residents were Delaware, the remainder were Tutelo and Iroquois. By midcentury, Wyoming had Delaware and Mahican residents; a Nanticoke town was so close that two missionaries thought it part of the same settlement.[12]

Otsiningo, also known as Chenango, was probably the most tribally mixed village, or cluster of villages, in the eighteenth-century Susquehanna Valley. From the mid-1720s to the late 1770s Indians from eight tribes inhabited the region along the Chenango River between its juncture with the Tioughnioga to its confluence with the Susquehanna in present-day Binghamton, an area stretching roughly fourteen miles from north to south. In the 1720s and 1730s Conrad Weiser found Onondagas and Shawnees living there. Two Moravian missionaries traveling through in the early 1750s found members of these tribes still present, as well as Oneidas, Tuscaroras, and Nanticokes. Later observers noted the presence of Mahicans, Conoys, and, by the late 1770s, Cayugas. Although the tribal composition of the region changed over the decades, every traveler's account indicated that members of at least two tribes and sometimes as many as five inhabited Otsiningo.[13]

Although intertribal politics influenced their choice to settle the region, the Indians of the upper Susquehanna Valley were not mere pawns in an Iroquois attempt to control the area. The Delawares, Shawnees, and other Indians who migrated to the upper valley in the early eighteenth century found its resources extremely desirable.

12. Jonathan Edwards, ed., *Memoirs of the Rev. David Brainerd, Missionary to the Indians on the Borders of New-York, New-Jersey, and Pennsylvania: Chiefly Taken from His Own Diary* (1822; rpt. St. Clair Shores, Mich., 1970), 233; William Beauchamp, ed., *Moravian Journals Relating to Central New York, 1745–1766* (Syracuse, N.Y., 1916), 103, 55, 96; [J. C. F. Camerhoff], "Bishop J. C. F. Camerhoff's Narrative of a Journey to Shamokin, Pennsylvania, in the Winter of 1748," ed. John W. Jordan, *PMHB* 29 (1905), 175–178; Barry Kent, Janet Rice, and Kakuko Ota, *A Map of 18th Century Indian Towns in Pennsylvania*, reprint from *Pennsylvania Archaeologist* 51 (1981), 8–11 and map; Laurence M. Hauptman, "Refugee Havens: The Iroquois Villages of the Eighteenth Century," in Christopher Vecsey and Robert Venables, eds., *American Indian Environments: Ecological Issues in Native American History* (Syracuse, N.Y., 1980), 129–132. According to Bartram, Shickellamy was born to French parents in Montreal but adopted by a group of Oneidas; see Wallace, *Indians in Pennsylvania*, 181.

13. Dolores Elliott, "Otsiningo, an Example of an Eighteenth Century Settlement Pattern," in Robert E. Funk and Charles F. Hayes III, eds., *Current Perspectives in Northeastern Archaeology: Essays in Honor of William A. Ritchie*, Researches and Transactions of the New York State Archeological Association 17 (1977), 93–105.

The Indians established their towns along one of the branches of the Susquehanna or one of its major tributaries. Such locations facilitated travel and trade in the region and allowed the Indians to fish to supplement their diet. Periodic flooding of the river, especially during major spring runoffs, made the lands surrounding these towns much more fertile than the slopes of the region's hills and mountains. The Indians were better able to adjust their communities to flooding than were the colonists. For them, land was not individually owned but kept as a tribal trust; village members could rebuild flooded homes on dry ground. Because they built their houses for seasonal dwelling, the Indians were also accustomed to moving and rebuilding. No laws dictated that their houses had to have stone chimneys, a time-consuming addition to build, nor did existing legal customs fix an individual's property to a specific place on a year-round basis. The Indians also settled in areas frequented by traders, who used the river for transporting goods whenever possible.

Colonists recognized the Iroquois' claims to the upper valley, but some of the refugee Indians who moved there ultimately became dissatisfied with the League Indians' policies and decided to leave the valley. In the 1740s, a powerful association of Indians along the Ohio River developed, and many eastern traders dealt with them directly rather than through the Iroquois. The rise of the Ohio tribes prompted some groups, including many Shawnees and Delawares who then lived in the valley, to move westward and so escape the influence of the Iroquois. In spite of these departures, the Iroquois believed that the upper valley would continue to attract displaced Indians. Thus League Indians refused to sell the land around Shamokin and Wyoming because, as the Mohawk Chief Hendrick informed colonial officials in 1754, "We reserve it to settle such of our Nations upon as shall come to us from the Ohio, or any others who shall deserve to be in our Alliance." Noting the "Abundance of Indians" moving "up and down," the Iroquois intended to "invite all such to come and live here, that so We may strengthen ourselves."[14]

Still, emigration from along the Susquehanna threatened the Iroquois' control over the upper valley. League Indians knew that if more of the refugees emigrated, the confederacy would be unable to keep the valley free of colonists, and this region too would become a

14. Richard Aquila, *The Iroquois Restoration: Iroquois Diplomacy on the Colonial Frontier, 1701–1754* (Detroit, Mich., 1983), 239; Chief Hendrick quoted in Wallace, *Indians in Pennsylvania*, 157.

borderland where the Indians' villages would be constantly threatened by colonial land seekers.

The Indians' Economy

In the early eighteenth century Susquehanna Valley Indians took advantage of local resources in a variety of ways. They burned parts of some forests to plant fields, keeping timbered areas for hunting reserves. Although the Indians came from different tribes, they shared common ideas about the need to preserve areas for wildlife, and no group's field-clearing efforts ever seriously threatened the region's forests. The dense forests provided ample supplies of building materials and fuel. During the spring, Indians fished in the river, its tributary streams, and lakes.

Like other eastern Indians, those in the upper valley relied on maize, beans, and squash to meet their nutritional needs. As soon as they relocated their villages in the region they planted large fields of corn and supplemented their crops with cultivated legumes and fruits growing wild or in orchards left behind by earlier Indians. The extent and quality of their cultivated crops greatly impressed colonists who later traveled through the region. Indeed, as late as the 1770s, in spite of numerous encroachments on their lands and a demographic catastrophe, Indians in the valley tended extensive fields of healthy crops. When Continental army soldiers marched through the upper valley during the revolutionary war to destroy the Indians' fields, they were amazed by the extent and quality of the Indians' agriculture. Their journals reported oversized vegetables in vast quantities. Indeed, soldiers at times had to delay their military campaigns to burn the Indians' fields. One soldier described 150 acres of "the best corn that Ever I saw," in addition to abundant stocks of other fruits and vegetables. Another reported cornstalks eighteen feet tall with individual cobs up to one and one-half feet long. Such yields, one soldier wrote, could not "be equalled in Jersey"; he saw, as well, one hundred acres of assorted vegetables which were "in such quantities (were it to be represented in the manner it should be) would be almost incredible to a civilized people."[15]

15. Frederick Cook, ed., *Journals of the Military Expedition of Major General John Sullivan against the Six Nations of Indians in 1779* (Albany, N.Y., 1887), 27, 44–45.

Among valley Indians women performed most of the agricultural work while the men used their energies for hunting. Colonial observers found this gender division of the labor force common among eastern Indians. "The Women are the Butchers, Cooks, and Tillers of the ground," George Alsop wrote about the Susquehannocks in the mid-seventeenth century. "The Men think it below the honour of a Masculine, to stoop to any thing but that which their Gun, or Bow and Arrows can command." Similar gender distinctions prevailed among other valley Indians, including the Delawares, Shawnees, and members of various tribes of the League Iroquois.[16]

In spite of their agricultural skill, valley Indians had to solve the problems facing all agrarian peoples in the early modern period. Maize cultivation, for example, drained the soil of vital nutrients. Some of the Indians' agricultural techniques, however, prolonged soil fertility; they avoided the monocultural practices of colonists and often planted legumes in the same fields with corn, even training beans to grow up cornstalks. In addition, periodic flooding helped slow the pace of soil exhaustion. Most valley Indians probably moved every fifteen to twenty years when local supplies of fuel became scarce, which most likely occurred before their fields became exhausted.[17]

Pests, the great bane of farmers on both sides of the Atlantic, also plagued the Indians. The Mohawks set up scarecrows to fend off the numerous crows that ate their plants, but other pests could not be easily eliminated. At Tioga, John Bartram wrote in 1743, "I observed for the first time in this journey that the worms which had done much mischief in several parts of our Province by destroying the grass and even corn for two summers, had done the same thing here, and had eat[en] off the blade of their maize and long white grass, so that the stems of both stood naked 4 foot high." Although the worms were mostly gone by the time he arrived, he found enough specimens to confirm his fears. "I saw some of the naked

16. Quoted in Kent, *Susquehanna's Indians*, 42. Alsop's testimony on certain matters has been disputed by historians, but his information on a gender-based division of labor is consistent with anthropological accounts of eastern woodlands Indians. See, for example, Anthony F. C. Wallace, *The Death and Rebirth of the Seneca* (1970; rpt. New York, 1972), 23–25.

17. E. L. Jones, "Creative Disruptions in American Agriculture," *Agricultural History* 48 (1974), 516. On maize exhaustiveness see William Cronon, *Changes in the Land: Indians, Colonists, and the Ecology of New England* (New York, 1983), 150.

dark-coloured grubs half an inch long, tho' most of them were gone, yet I could perceive they were the same that had visited us two months before," he wrote. "They clear all the grass in their way, in any meadow they get into, and seem to be periodical as the locusts and caterpillar, the latter of which I am afraid will do us a great deal of mischief next summer."[18]

Violent storms also threatened to devastate villages and fields. Flooding occurred when the snow in the hills melted too quickly for the ground to absorb it or when there was a major rainstorm. Near Shamokin, for example, Bartram observed the long-lasting effect of a particularly devastating flood when the Susquehanna flowed well above its banks. "A great flood came down this branch a few years past and drove abundance of sand over this ground a great depth among the trees," he wrote. "It rose 20 feet perpendicular, washing away many yards of the bank, which was composed of gravel and sand, and doubtless had been raised to that heighth by former inundations, for the wood ground 30 rod from the river is several feet lower than the bank." Earlier, according to the naturalist, there had been an Indian town at this site. Peach and plum trees and grapevines still grew there, but any crops, as well as habitations, must have been washed away in the deluge.[19]

Even though the Indians knew how to cultivate and store nutritional foods, they still faced shortages at certain times. In early April 1737, Weiser stopped at Otsiningo, then inhabited by Onondagas and Shawnees, which he had visited in 1726. "The family with whom we lodged had not a mouthful to eat," he wrote in his journal. "The larger part of this village had been living for more than a month on the juice of the sugar tree, which is as common here as hickory in Pennsylvania." The misfortunes of these Indians drove Weiser to share his limited provisions with them. "We shared our small stock of provisions with sundry sick and children," he wrote, "who stood before us in tears while we were eating." When Weiser and his traveling companion consumed this sugar juice, they found that it "sus-

18. Jones, "Creative Disruptions," 516–517; John Bartram, *Observations on the Inhabitants, Climate, Soil, Rivers, Productions, Animals and Other Matters Worthy of Notice. Made by Mr. John Bartram, in His Travels from Pensilvania to Onondaga, Oswego and the Lake Ontario, in Canada* (1751; rpt. Barre, Mass., 1973), 49–50. See also William A. Starna, et al., "Northern Iroquoian Horticulture and Insect Infestation: A Cause for Village Removal," *Ethnohistory* 31 (1984), 197–207.

19. Bartram, *Observations*, 39.

tained life" but "did not agree with us." He wrote in his journal: "We became quite ill from much drinking to quench the thirst caused by the sweetness of the sugar. My companion Stoffel became impatient and out of spirits, and wished himself dead."[20] Local Indians responded to the situation with less anxiety, no doubt realizing that starvation was not common but, rather, a seasonal phenomenon. Most likely, Weiser happened upon Otsiningo at a time of the year when food supplies were low or before the spring fish runs.[21]

Most valley Indian groups farmed from spring to autumn, but after the harvest they turned their attention to the winter hunt. Like many eastern woodlands tribes, they maintained temporary hunting and fishing lodgings. Colonists traveling during the winter along overland routes through the forests saw hunting camps, often inhabited by whole families. "About November the best Hunters draw off to several remote places of the Woods, where they know the Deer, Bear, and Elke useth," George Alsop wrote about the Susquehannocks in the mid-seventeenth century. "There they build them several Cottages, which they call their Winter-quarter, where they remain for the space of three months, untill they have killed up a sufficiency of Provisions to supply their Families with in the Summer." Others cooked and ate the animals where they killed them or at their hunting camps; they often left behind what they could not eat on the spot.[22]

Indian hunters could track game more easily in snow, but they did not confine their hunting to the colder months. In August, Bartram observed an Indian shooting an elk at a salt lick, apparently a favorite place to find fresh game. Inhabitants of the valley knew the locations of local salt licks and realized their allure for game animals. "The soil, I suppose," Bartram wrote, "contains some saline particles agreeable to the deer, who come many miles to one of these places."

20. "Narrative of a Journey, made in the year 1737, by Conrad Weiser, Indian Agent and Provincial Interpreter, from Tulpehocken in the Province of Pennsylvania to Onondaga, the head quarters of the allied Six Nations, in the Province of New York," trans. H. H. Muhlenberg, *Pennsylvania Historical Society Collections* 1 (1853), 15–16. On storage practices see Arthur C. Parker, "Iroquois Uses of Maize and Other Food Plants," in William N. Fenton, ed., *Parker on the Iroquois* (Syracuse, N.Y., 1968), 34–36.

21. See Cronon, *Changes in the Land*, chap. 3.

22. Quoted in Kent, *Susquehanna's Indians*, 42; Robert Albion and Leonidas Dodson, eds., *Philip Vickers Fithian: Journal, 1775–1776, Written on the Virginia-Pennsylvania Frontier and in the Army around New York* (Princeton, N.J., 1934), 81.

Certain local vegetation also attracted particular species of game. For example, Bartram found an area covered with gooseberries. "All the trees were crowded with wild pigeons, which, I suppose, breed in these lofty shade trees." The Indians knew the locations of these breeding and feeding spots where they could find game birds.[23]

Some valley Indians also maintained seasonal residences on islands, either in the river or the many lakes in the valley, where they could catch fish and gather shellfish. On Deowongo Island in Canadarago Lake, for example, archaeological analysis of the Indians' trash heaps revealed the broken bones of many animals and fish presumably taken for food. These included bones from deer, bear, beaver, woodchuck, snapping turtle, green frogs, and various fish. Archaeologists have uncovered more netsinkers, used to weigh down nets, than any other tools, indicating the importance of fishing for the residents. The island also contained postholes indicating the existence of a typical Iroquois longhouse. Despite these signs of habitation, the island had no hearths, pits, or burials that would have indicated a more permanent settlement. Such remains demonstrate that the island was a seasonal residence, probably a fishing site.[24]

Economic Culture and Religion

Religion and culture influenced the economy of many valley Indians as much as climate and geography did. They practiced religious ceremonies associated with their farming and hunting, often to propitiate the divine powers that they believed controlled these parts of their economy. Unfortunately, only fragmentary evidence of these religious practices survives. Still, anthropological literature combined with travelers' accounts demonstrates beyond any doubt that the Indians of the upper valley believed that their economy and their religion were inextricably bound together.

Many Indians throughout the Americas believed that economic success was intimately related to their spiritual world. In eastern North America, groups of Indians developed complex rituals associ-

23. Bartram, *Observations*, 81, 45, 53; William N. Fenton, "Northern Iroquoian Culture Patterns," in Sturtevant, ed., *Handbook of North American Indians*, 15:297–298.

24. William A. Ritchie, *The Chance Horizon: An Early Stage of Mohawk Iroquois Cultural Development*, New York State Museum Circular 29 (Albany, N.Y., 1952).

ated with their economy. For many, especially those who lived in northern regions and relied on hunting for a major portion of their necessary food and clothing, this meant carefully propitiating the "bosses" or "keepers" of the animals they hunted. These spirits, often depicted as powerful, oversized animals, governed animal behavior in the Indians' territory. If the Indians paid proper homage to the game bosses through ritualized expressions of devotion, the keepers would reciprocate by informing Indians, through visions, of the locations of animals to be hunted. Since the Indians had demonstrated their fidelity to these spirits, thereby fulfilling the human part of the religious contract, the bosses would instruct the animals to be killed.[25]

In the Northeast, as elsewhere, the Indians believed that supernatural powers controlled the physical world. Thus, to preserve stability, they honored the various spirits that controlled, among other things, the weather, animals, and plants. The Iroquois devised a series of rituals, described by Anthony F. C. Wallace as a "calendar of thanksgiving," to express their appreciation to these spirits and intended, in large measure, to keep these powers pleased and thus willing to provide for the Indians. Delaware hunters appeased the *manëtuwàk* or spirits that controlled the animals they hunted. They developed distinct rituals for hunting bear, deer, otter, and opossum and took extreme care to tend to the hunted animal's remains so as not to offend the animal's *manëtu*.[26]

Some Indians in the upper valley in the eighteenth century demonstrated their belief in the power of such rituals. Bartram recorded evidence of their beliefs during his 1743 journey. One group of Indians offered Bartram and his traveling companions some venison, according to long-standing rules of hospitality that travelers be given a "double share" of food during a feast. After their repast, the cartographer Lewis Evans, one of Bartram's companions, gave his deer bones to the Indians' dog. The Indians, however, quickly sought to prevent this apparent insult to the deer spirits. "Tho' hungry Dogs are generally nimble," Bartram recalled, "the *Indian*, more nimble,

25. See Calvin Martin, *Keepers of the Game: Indian-Animal Relationships and the Fur Trade* (Berkeley, Calif., 1978); and for critiques of Martin's work and other interpretations of various tribal beliefs, Shepard Krech III, ed., *Indians, Animals, and the Fur Trade: A Critique of "Keepers of the Game"* (Athens, Ga., 1981).
26. Wallace, *Death and Rebirth of the Seneca*, 50–59; Herbert C. Kraft, *The Lenape: Archaeology, History, and Ethnography* (Newark, Del., 1986), 163–169.

laid hold of it first and committed it to the fire, religiously covering it over with hot ashes. This seems to be a kind of offering, perhaps first fruits to the Almighty power to crave future success in the approaching hunting season, and was celebrated with as much decency and more silence than many superstitious ceremonies."[27]

Bartram also described the rituals of the winter bear hunt. "As soon as the bear is killed," he wrote, "the hunter places the small end of his pipe in its mouth and, by blowing in the bowls, fills the mouth and throat full of smoak; then he conjures the departed Spirit not to resent the injury done his body nor to thwart his future sport in hunting; but as he receives no answer to this, in order to know if his prayers have prevailed, he cuts the ligament under the bear's tongue; if these ligaments contract and shrivel up, being cast into the fire, which is done with great solemnity and abundance of invocations, then it is esteemed a certain mark (as it rarely fails) that the *manes* are appeased." Such rituals demonstrated the ubiquitous links between the Indians' quotidian and spiritual worlds.[28]

Violations of ritual practices offended game spirits, with drastic implications for the Indians. Thus, Bartram learned, deer spirits once became offended by Indians fighting with each other at a popular salt lick. "In the squabble one lost his life," Bartram wrote, and "this made the deer keep from thence for many years."[29]

Bartram learned that valley Indians believed that their agriculture had spiritual origins as well. "An *Indian* (*whose wife had eloped*) came hither to hunt," one said when Bartram's party had just passed one branch of the Susquehanna, "and with his skins to purchase another here, he espied a young squaw alone at the hill; going to her and enquiring where she came from, he received for answer that she came from heaven to provide sustenance for the poor *Indians*, and if he came to that place twelve months after, he should find food there." This Indian, the narrator informed Bartram, "came accordingly, and found corn, squashes and tobacco, which were propagated from thence and spread through the country." Bartram believed this a "silly story" yet admitted that the tale was "religiously held for truth among [the Indians]."[30]

27. Bartram, *Observations*, 42–43.
28. Ibid., 43.
29. Ibid., 45.
30. Ibid., 54.

Bartram did not recognize the importance of the rituals he described. Unable to see beyond the cultural blinders shaped over centuries in a Christianized Europe, he could not have realized that the survival of the Indians' coherent, non-Christian religious identities in the wake of demographic catastrophe, constant migrations, and relentless missionizing efforts helped them maintain their indigenous cultural practices. To be sure, some valley Indians did convert to Christianity; Moravian missionaries at Wyalusing converted perhaps two hundred Indians with whom they lived from 1763 to 1772 before the community and its missionaries moved westward.[31] But colonial observers found that valley Indians still migrated during parts of the year, still resided in predominantly Indian communities, and still performed ceremonies intended to appease the spirits governing crops and game animals.

The survival of these customs and attitudes into the mid-eighteenth century demonstrates the preservation of the Indians' cultural identity as well as the continuing vigor of their economy. The Indians' hunting and agricultural ceremonies were another adaptation to their physical world. Although they altered the landscape when they cleared forests for fields, building supplies, and fuel and were able to procure game and fish, they believed that nature's bounty was not unlimited; offending the spirits could lead to scarcity, drought, and economic collapse.

In spite of demographic catastrophe, migration into a new area, and the difficulties of creating new communities with Indians from other tribes, the vast majority of the Indians of the upper valley chose to retain their old mores rather than adopt colonial ways. Their ceremonies might have perplexed and at times annoyed the colonists who observed them, but these rituals indicated the Indians' ability to maintain positive relations with the spirits that governed the world around them. But as the eighteenth century wore on, not even the keepers of the game could prevent traders and colonizers from seizing control of the Indians' economy and channeling the Indians' energy toward the demands of a far more exacting deity: the European market.

31. "Reverend John Ettwein's Notes of Travel from the North Branch of the Susquehanna to the Beaver River, Pennsylvania, 1772," ed. John W. Jordan, *PMHB* 25 (1901–1902), 208. The Quaker John Woolman described his meeting with the Christian Indians of Wyalusing in his journal; see *The Journal of John Woolman* reprinted in volume 1 of *The Harvard Classics* (New York, 1909), 275–279.

3 Indian-Colonist Trade

Traveling through the upper Susquehanna Valley in the early 1740s, Count Nicholas Louis von Zinzendorf, a Moravian missionary from Saxony, likened Shamokin to one of Europe's great trading centers. Here the Indians "have their Rendevous," he wrote, "and it is in some measure like the Hague in Holland." While the Indians of Shamokin never enjoyed the wealth of the Dutch, the missionary's comparison revealed how fundamental trade was in the valley Indians' world.[1]

The trade between colonists and Indians in the first half of the eighteenth century was one part of the extension of a transatlantic commercial empire. As that empire expanded, the people, commodities, animals, and parasites that together made up the colonizing forces of British imperialism transformed the upper valley, which in the eighteenth century became part of the marchlands of the empire. No longer terra incognita to the English, the numerous tributaries of the Susquehanna became trade avenues through the mountains, and the furs transported on the bateaux traversing these channels reached a market on the other side of the Atlantic.

1. William C. Reichel, ed., *Memorials of the Moravian Church* (Philadelphia, 1870), 1:133.

This change occurred with few overt manifestations of violence. Cooperation, not conflict, characterized the relationship between European traders and valley Indians. These peoples worked together to create an intercultural commercial economy in the region capable of transporting peltry across hundreds of miles of often hazardous natural terrain.

But even as the Indians embraced trade, the exchange system began to deteriorate, destabilizing their communities. By midcentury, Indians seeking European goods had overhunted the region's pelt-producing animals. In addition, European diseases and alcohol posed a deadly threat to the Indians' settlements.

The new economy of the valley, based on procurement of certain natural resources for an external market, bound the Indians into a western European commercial system. Traders responded to European demand for furs by encouraging Indians to gather as many pelts as possible with little thought about the far-reaching ecological and economic consequences of the fur trade. Such commercial behavior had decidedly political overtones because it altered the relationships among the Indian groups of the backcountry. These shifts could not have come at a worse moment for the valley Indians, who by 1750 found themselves not only in a declining economic position but also in competition with a growing colonial population for their lands.

Hospitality and Trade

Migrating Indians were not alone in finding the upper valley desirable. At the same time that refugee Indians were clearing fields and village sites, colonial traders turned their gaze toward the region. They were not disappointed. Traders used the major waterways and paths to transport their wares to the Indians, sticking to well-established routes through the often forbidding mountains and thick forests. Along these routes they received help from groups of Indians who provided essential travel services and extended hospitality.

Valley Indians engaged in trade long before 1700. Archaeological evidence indicates that the West Branch was an avenue for exchange as early as 500 B.C.; Indians moving along this branch of the river brought flints and pipes into eastern Pennsylvania, thereby extending the material culture of aboriginal Ohio Valley groups eastward across the Appalachian Mountains. During much of the seventeenth century, valley Indians carried on extensive trade with various European groups. In the early years of the century John Smith found that the Susquehannocks were already engaged in trade and possessed European goods. When he and some of his party encountered a group of Tockwoghs, an Algonquian-speaking tribe living near the mouth of the Susquehanna River, he found a vivid example of intertribal exchange. The Tockwoghs possessed "many hatchets, knives, and pieces of yron, and brasse," two of Smith's associates wrote, "which they reported to have from the Sasquesahanockes."[2]

By 1638, the Susquehannocks were exploring exchange relationships with English, Dutch, and Swedish traders. During the latter half of the seventeenth century, however, these trade relationships largely broke down. Depletion of peltry supplies, overt hostilities between the Iroquois and the Susquehannocks, and warfare between the Susquehannocks and colonial Chesapeake settlers all contributed to the decline in trade. Still, in spite of the hardships that beset the Susquehannocks in this period, they continued to trade with English colonists along the Susquehanna River. Conestoga, a Susquehannock and Seneca town founded around 1690, remained a commercial center until 1740, when depletion of fur supplies and westward migration of colonists undermined the town's economy. Much of the seventeenth-century trade along the Susquehanna took place in the lower valley; by about 1700 no trade centers such as Conestoga existed in the upper valley.[3]

When English colonists traced the Susquehanna on contemporary maps, they believed that the river was ideal for trade. It provided a natural transportation corridor through a mountainous region where overland travel was often impossible. William Penn decided that the province's second city ought to be situated along its banks. Because the river flowed near the Schuylkill, any goods coming from the Susquehanna Valley could be readily transported to Philadelphia with only one relatively short portage. Since Penn's lands included much of the river and its tributaries, he felt that he held the key to

2. Barry Kent, Ira Smith III, and Catherine McCann, eds., *Foundations of Pennsylvania Prehistory*, Anthropological Series 1 (Harrisburg, Pa., 1971), 197–198; Francis Jennings, "Susquehannock," in William Sturtevant, ed., *Handbook of North American Indians*, vol. 15, *Northeast*, ed. Bruce Trigger (Washington, D.C., 1978), 364; Philip L. Barbour, ed., *The Complete Works of Captain John Smith (1580–1631)*, 3 vols. (Chapel Hill, N.C., 1986), 1:231.

3. Barry C. Kent, *Susquehanna's Indians*, Anthropological Series 6 (Harrisburg, Pa., 1984), 28, 35, 38, 43, 45–47, 58, 61.

great profits from the fur trade. It was "the *Common Course* of the *Indians* with their *Skins* and *Furr's* into our Parts," Penn wrote in 1690, "and to the Provinces of *East* and *West Jersey*, and *New York*, from the *West* and *Northwest* parts of the *continent* from whence they bring them." Penn also believed that the development of New York's fur trade would benefit his province "because their *Traffick* and *Intercourse* will be chiefly through *Pennsylvania*, which lies between that Province and the Sea." Penn did not sit idly by waiting for trade to develop in the area. Rather, he began to entice prospective settlers from the West Indies and Europe, and in 1697 he negotiated for a royal patent to the entire Susquehanna River, much to the dismay of New York officials, who thought they had already obtained crown approval for the region and had obtained a claim to the area from the Iroquois.[4]

The development of the trading center at Oswego on Lake Ontario in the 1720s demonstrated the acumen of colonial officials. While many traders in New York channeled their wares via the Mohawk to Albany, others based in Pennsylvania traveled along the Susquehanna. Traders and Indians going to Oswego used the river because it was part of a natural route from southern and eastern Pennsylvania to Lake Ontario. John Bartram later speculated that the Susquehanna trade system would extend, via the Allegheny, "through the *Hokio* [Ohio] into the *Mississippi* and its branches among the numerous nations that inhabit their banks."[5]

Valley Indians hoped to attract traders to their villages and estab-

---

4. William Penn, "Some Proposals for a Second Settlement in the Province of Pennsylvania" (1690), in Samuel Hazard, ed., *The Register of Pennsylvania* 1 (1828), 400; *Doc. Hist. NY*, 1:393–413; Gary Nash, "The Quest for the Susquehanna Valley: New York, Pennsylvania and the Seventeenth Century Fur Trade," *NY Hist.* 48 (1967), 3–27. Penn's interest in the Susquehanna and his efforts to attract migrants to the valley can be followed in Richard S. Dunn and Mary Maples Dunn et al., eds., *The Papers of William Penn*, 5 vols. (Philadelphia, 1981–1987); see especially his letter to Ralph Fretwell concerning Barbados Quakers, April 13, 1684, 2:546–547, his circular letter to Friends in Ireland, January 8, 1690/1, 3:291–293, and his Agreement and Lists of Susquehanna Subscribers, May 20, 1696, 3:671–678.

5. Cadwallader Colden, "Observations on the Situation, Soil, Climate, Water, Communications, Boundaries, &c. of the Province of New York" (1738), *Doc. Hist. NY*, 4:169–179; Francis Jennings, *The Ambiguous Iroquois Empire* (New York, 1984), 74–78; Jennings, "The Indian Trade of the Susquehanna Valley," *Proceedings of the American Philosophical Society* 110 (1966), 406–424; John Bartram, *Observations on the Inhabitants, Climate, Soil, Rivers, Productions, Animals and Other Matters Worthy of Notice. Made by Mr. John Bartram in His Travels from Pensilvania to Onondaga, Oswego and the Lake Ontario, in Canada* (1751; rpt. Barre, Mass., 1973), 33. See also Cadwallader Colden, "Memoir on the Fur Trade" (1724) in *NY Col. Docs.*, 5:726–733.

lished a hospitality network that, by providing them with food, shelter, transportation, and information, insulated traders, missionaries, and traveling Indians from the most dangerous aspects of the natural world. In this way, the valley Indians also protected their own access to European goods. The Indians and the few colonists inhabiting the region facilitated the movement of itinerants in many ways, providing information about routes and provisions. A trader named Armstrong, who lived eighteen miles above Harris' Ferry, urged the party of Moravian missionary J. C. F. Camerhoff to delay their journey because the river and streams on the way to Shamokin were overflowing, making the trip extremely perilous. Scaling a steep mountain the next day, Camerhoff noted that the party "too late realized that the warnings we had received from the settlers, of the dangers attending the crossing, were not exaggerated." In 1750, Indians at Onondaga implored Camerhoff and David Zeisberger to follow the traditional path to Tioga, even though it might be slower than going straight through the woods; if the party got lost, the Iroquois remarked, the Europeans would have presumed they had been murdered by Indians and caused trouble for the Six Nations.[6]

Local Indians also provided much-needed food for travelers. At a time of famine along the West Branch in July 1748, the missionaries Zeisberger and John Martin Mack visited Great Island. Their host gave them dried venison; in return they gave him and his wife some needles and thread. The transaction was not financial: the missionaries did not purchase the food. Rather, the structures of hospitality in the region demanded that hosts provide food for their guests and that travelers present gifts to their hosts when possible. The needles and thread were gifts, not payment for any particular service. When the missionary Bernard Grube's party asked for food at a small Shawnee town along the West Branch in August 1753, their hosts gave them a choice piece of bear meat, a luxury the party had not anticipated.[7]

6. [J. C. F. Camerhoff], "Bishop J. C. F. Camerhoff's Narrative of a Journey to Shamokin, Pennsylvania, in the Winter of 1748," ed. John W. Jordan, *PMHB* 29 (1905), 166–167, 170; "Diary of the Journey of Br. Camerhoff and David Zeisberger to the Five Nations from May 3–14 to August 6–17, 1750," in William Beauchamp, ed., *Moravian Journals Relating to Central New York, 1745–1766* (Syracuse, N.Y., 1916), 91.

7. [David Zeisberger and John Martin Mack], "An Account of the Famine among the Indians of the North and West Branch of the Susquehanna, in the Summer of 1748," *PMHB* 16 (1892–1893), 431; [Bernard Grube], "A Missionary's Tour to Shamokin and the West Branch of the Susquehanna, 1753," *PMHB* 39 (1915), 444.

Offering hospitality was a vital part of the valley Indians' relations with other groups. The custom of presenting gifts existed before the colonists' arrival, and colonial leaders incorporated the presentation of gifts into their meetings with Indians. Indeed, the offering of gifts was a necessary precursor in meetings between parties; ritual exchange of goods solidified alliances between friendly groups. John Bartram described prevailing customs during his journey through the valley in the early 1740s, when local Indians provided his party with ample food. At a hunting camp near Tiadaghton Creek four Indians gave them venison and invited them to "a feast at their cabin." Travelers, Bartram wrote, were "intitled to a double share" of food. At Shamokin he found similarly hospitable Indians. "As soon as we alighted they shewed us where to lay our baggage, and then brought us a bowl of boiled squashes cold," he wrote. "This hospitality is agreeable to the honest simplicity of antient times and is so punctually adhered to, that not only what is already dressed is immediately set before a traveller, but the most pressing business is postponed to prepare the best they can get for him, keeping it as a maxim that he must always be hungry. Of this we found good effects in the flesh and bread they got ready for us."[8]

The provincial negotiator Conrad Weiser often received help from valley Indians when he traveled through the region. Madame Montour, who had been born to French parents but had become the matriarch of a village along the West Branch, fed Weiser and his party during a food shortage in the winter of 1737. But Weiser noted that she did not feel compelled to give food to the "many hungry Indians about" in the area. Weiser also encountered Indians who did not share prevailing customs about hospitality. At Tioga, Weiser had to purchase food for his hungry party because Indians there did not offer sufficient food to sustain them; he had to pay twenty-four needles and six shoe strings for five one-pound loaves of bread from an elderly Indian woman. Unfortunately for Weiser, some of the bread was stolen five days later while the party slept at Otsiningo. Weiser's party solved their food problems when Indians at Otsiningo decided to take stored corn from a hut whose occupants

8. Bartram, *Observations*, 42, 35. Hospitality did not necessarily exist only to facilitate trade along the Susquehanna; it is but one form of gift exchange that has great significance in many societies. See, for example, Marcel Mauss, *The Gift: Forms and Functions of Exchange in Archaic Societies*, trans. Ian Cunnison (1925; rpt. Glencoe, Ill., 1954).

were away on a hunt. In spite of the food shortage—the Indians at Otsiningo had been subsisting largely on juice from sugar maple trees that were particularly abundant in the area—those present took only enough for their immediate needs. This action indicated the importance of feeding travelers in the valley; town residents had not broken into those huts earlier.[9]

In addition to offering food and information to help their guests along their journeys, hosts also helped people and commodities move through the area. Residents of Indian villages used canoes and bateaux to transport missionaries across swollen streams in midwinter. Conrad Weiser gave an Indian named Jenoniowana needles and shoe strings in exchange for a ride across swiftly flowing Chillisquaque Creek in March 1737. Travel could be life-threatening if colonists could not get help, especially during the winter and spring when the Susquehanna was most dangerous. Only two weeks after Weiser received assistance, a colonial trader drowned, apparently unable to obtain help from any valley residents, when his canoe tipped over on Muncy Creek. Weiser's party needed the help of Indians from five separate towns to shuttle them across the Susquehanna or one of its overflowing tributaries in March and April 1737. Knowledgeable about local hospitality customs, Weiser assumed that the Indians would fill his needs. At Madame Montour's village, after "repeated firing of our guns," he wrote in his journal, "two Indians came from the village to see what was to be done; they brought at our request a canoe from the village and took us across." At Tioga, "toward evening we were also safely ferried in a canoe over the great branch of the Susquehanna River." Although Weiser noted in his journal that he thanked some Indians for certain services, he apparently felt that transporting his party across half-frozen streams required no such formal declaration.[10]

Missionaries also frequently received aid from valley residents. A party from Shamokin rescued Camerhoff after he was stranded alone on the opposite side of the overflowing, ice-laden Susquehanna. The party of Moravian missionary Bernard Grube left their

9. "Narrative of a Journey, made in the year 1737, by Conrad Weiser, Indian Agent and Provincial Interpreter, from Tulpehocken in the Province of Pennsylvania to Onondaga, the head quarters of the allied Six Nations, in the Province of New York," trans. H. H. Muhlenberg, *Pennsylvania Historical Society Collections* 1 (1853), 8, 13–17.

10. "Narrative of a Journey by Conrad Weiser," 7–8, 13–15.

canoe at Muncy Creek, near Ostonwakin, "as the water began to grow rapid." When they returned two days later, the canoe was there for their return trip to Shamokin; only a blanket and some provisions were missing. Camerhoff and Zeisberger bought a canoe at Wyoming from local Nanticokes, which made their return journey much easier. When the party had to switch to an overland route at Ganatocheracht, a Cayuga town near Owego, their host offered to let them leave their possessions in his storehouse and took care of their canoe. Six weeks later, on their return trip, they found their canoe and goods intact, and nothing had spoiled. In exchange for this service, the brethren gave their hostess a blanket they had brought with them from Bethlehem "as a token of our appreciation of her faithful care of our goods."[11]

The Valley Trade System

The fur trade reoriented the economies of valley Indian villages. Although their hunting and agricultural pursuits were enhanced by the wares traders provided, the influence of trade went beyond specific commodities. Travelers' needs for food caused temporary shortages in towns along major travel routes. To obtain trade goods, Indians in the valley overhunted the indigenous furbearing animals, especially beaver, pushing animal population levels well below those necessary to maintain the trade. Perhaps most important, traders introduced alcohol and diseases that spread quickly through the valley, destabilizing the Indians' communities.

Valley Indians substituted wares such as guns and kettles, blankets and needles, for their traditional products. These commodities helped the Indians perform their daily tasks more efficiently. Though it was perhaps easier to hit a target with a gun than a bow and arrow, guns also altered the nature of warfare, making it easier to kill hostile Indians or colonists. Kettles made of metal replaced those of clay and wood. These new products were lighter and more resistant to damage and therefore very attractive to Indians who moved between summer villages and winter campsites. Iron from

11. [Camerhoff], "Journey to Shamokin in 1748," 170–172; [Grube], "Tour to Shamokin, 1753," 442, 444; "Journey of Br. Camerhoff and David Zeisberger to the Five Nations," 25, 32–34, 101.

traders, perhaps originally part of kettles, ended up on the tips of axes and fishing poles.

Adopting these European technologies meant that valley Indians then needed the services of people who could sell ammunition and maintain guns and axes. By the late 1740s, a colonial blacksmith at Shamokin, who came to the area with Moravian missionaries, was serving customers from all over the valley, from Wyoming to Onondaga; he had become indispensable to the valley economy. When a party of missionaries traveled through Shamokin in August 1753, they left behind a new smith along with the new missionary. Although the missionaries often criticized the behavior of traders, their smith got much of his work from Indians who came to the town to trade and were referred to him.[12]

Some local Indians sought to emulate the missionaries' farming practices. Shickellamy, the Oneida sachem who lived in Shamokin, wanted the local colonists to fence a field for him, thus creating the ultimate symbol of colonial property definitions in this refugee Indian community. When the missionaries told him they had barely enough time to fence their own field, Shickellamy refused to give in. He thus disregarded a recent warning from a traveling Indian who had come to Shamokin seeking the services of a smith. This itinerant had told Shickellamy that the missionaries were "like Piggons" and if he "Suffered a paire hear to reside theyd Draw to them whole Troopes & take from him all his Land." Yet Shickellamy's desire to live like the colonists, at least by fencing his field, overrode any fears that the town might be overrun by Moravians. He even wished that the Moravians would "Send hear more Brothers," presumably to fence his land.[13]

Valley Indians became accustomed to trade and sought to extend it beyond simple dealings with traders. Indians at Shamokin wanted to pay the smith in furs. "So far the smith has only taken deer skins [in] compensation for his work," Shickellamy informed the missionary Camerhoff in 1748. "Cannot he also take raccoon, fox, wild-cat and otter skins, at the market price?" The missionary replied that

12. Bartram, *Observations*, 65; "Journey of Br. Camerhoff and David Zeisberger to the Five Nations," 96; [Grube], "Tour to Shamokin, 1753," 441, 444; [Camerhoff], "Journey to Shamokin in 1748," 173–174; Joseph Powell, Shamokin (Sunbury) Pennsylvania Diary, 1748, Records of the Moravian Mission among the Indians of North America (microfilm), Box 121, folder 4, entry for April 11, Harvard College Library.

13. Powell, Shamokin Diary, entries for January 31, March 6, and March 9.

the smith was not a trader and that he accepted deerskins because he could use them to "make breeches, caps, gloves, &c., for his brethren. But as we love you, the smith may *sometimes* take otter, raccoon, and fox skins, when they are good." Not yet satisfied, Shickellamy pressed the Indians' case further: "Cannot the smith also take bear and elk skins for his work?" Once again, Camerhoff gave in. "He can take as many bear skins as are brought," the missionary replied, "for he and his brethren need them to sleep on." To solidify relations between the Indians and the missionaries, Shickellamy and Camerhoff also agreed on a set of rules to govern the town. One was the missionaries' agreement not to get involved in "any dispute between Indians and traders, nor interfere with their bargains." The missionaries also agreed to send all traders to Shickellamy when they arrived in the village.[14]

Shickellamy's attempt to govern trade relations in the town suggests more than a desire to regulate economic behavior. In refugee towns composed of Indians from different tribal groups, a charismatic leader could ameliorate potential problems before they threatened the harmony needed to keep these communities stable. Shickellamy derived some of his authority from being an Oneida in territory claimed by the Iroquois, but his prominence in the town owed primarily to his having gained the trust and often obedience of the residents and travelers who passed through. The resident Moravian missionaries dined with him frequently, sent all visiting traders directly to him, and relied on him to keep order. His authority was apparent when, on one occasion, he intervened in a dispute between Samuel Danyals, a Delaware, who was visiting Shamokin, and the Moravian blacksmith Antoine, who fixed his gun. Danyals initially refused to pay for the service, and Shickellamy advised the missionaries not to give the gun back to Danyals. But as the missionary Powell wrote in his diary, "it was not so in our hearts being unwilling to make him an Enemy." Shickellamy, however, would not tolerate the situation and forced Danyals to pay the smith.[15] Shickellamy's authority ensured that traveling Indians would behave in such a way as to maintain the town's position as a center of trade.

The Indians' incorporation of trade goods was most evident in their inclusion of such wares into important rituals. Funerary rites,

14. [Camerhoff], "Journey to Shamokin in 1748," 175–178.
15. Powell, Shamokin Diary, entry for February 12.

among the most sensitive in their ritual world, for example, had become modified by January 1748, when Indians included traders' wares among the grave goods for a young girl who died at Shamokin. Two missionaries observed the preparation for the funeral. The coffin contained items the village members thought she would need in "the new country," including "a blanket, several pairs of moccassins, buckskin for new ones, needle and thread, a kettle, two hatchets, and flint, steel and tinder." Local Indians told the missionaries that the girl would need these goods to "go at once to housekeeping" in her new environment; other burials in the area, possibly from the same period, also included trade goods.[16] Valley Indians apparently saw little difference between trade goods and traditional commodities. The latter clearly had become necessary in their economy.

Yet in spite of the lure of trade goods, valley Indians realized that trade posed problems for their villages. Shamokin particularly, because of its location at the confluence of the Susquehanna's two main branches, became a major center of hospitality and trade, which was not always pleasing to local residents. The constant flow of Indians and colonists through the town depleted food supplies. When the missionary Bernard Grube visited Shamokin in August 1753, he noted that it was "uncomfortable for Indians there, for if they plant they cannot enjoy it, so many strange Indians pass through the town whom they must feed." The resident Moravian missionaries found it difficult to feed the hundred or so itinerants who stopped there each year. Shickellamy reacted in a practical fashion: he and most of his family left. Shamokin residents realized that instead of the prosperity that usually characterized commercial centers and helped offset the crowding and inconveniences of a bustling town, trade had unexpected and unwanted social costs.[17]

Other villages also experienced hard times. David Zeisberger and John Martin Mack wrote in their journal that a number of Indians left the West and North branches of the river in the summer of 1748, many of them going to colonial settlements hoping to find

16. [Camerhoff], "Journey to Shamokin in 1748," 173–174; Kent, *Susquehanna's Indians*, 101. See Bruce G. Trigger, "Ontario Native People and the Epidemics of 1634–1640," in Shepard Krech III, ed., *Indians, Animals and the Fur Trade: A Critique of "Keepers of the Game"* (Athens, Ga., 1981), 24–25; and Christopher L. Miller and George R. Hamell, "A New Perspective on Indian-White Contact: Cultural Symbols and Colonial Trade," *JAH* 73 (1986), 311–328.

17. [Grube], "Tour to Shamokin, 1753," 444.

food. Famines struck repeatedly, even though the land was fertile and the river and streams teemed with fish. The Indians and missionaries were not surprised by these hardships; they felt that traders and their wares destabilized communities and disrupted economic rhythms. Periodic shortages of food probably occurred before the development of Indian-colonist trade along the Susquehanna; the Indians in New England sometimes suffered from seasonal shortages and reoriented their subsistence patterns to cope with the problem. But the fact that valley residents attributed hard times to trade indicated a shift in their view of the world around them.[18]

The fur trade also prompted Indians to reorient their economic practices, at times with disturbing implications. Ever since the early seventeenth century, Indians who devoted too much time to the fur trade had to trade for goods such as food that before they had gotten on their own. By the 1740s Indians traveling through the valley sought food, often flour, as well as trade goods. Some Indians found that Indians at Shamokin would not take skins in exchange for corn. Thus the hungry Indians had to go to traders, who were eager to obtain pelts, and trade their furs for brandy, which they took to Shamokin and traded with Indians there for corn. The search for food had pushed these traveling Indians to acquire liquor to use in trade with valley Indians, thus revealing two of the unsettling consequences of the fur trade: food shortages and demand for alcohol.[19]

In spite of the perceived and actual disruptions to their settlements, Indians continued to desire traders' goods. But the fur trade in the valley, as it was throughout North America, was inherently unstable. Indians in the valley overhunted and nearly destroyed the beaver population. Beavers were largely sedentary and thus easy targets for Indian hunters. Beavers limited the size of their colonies through specific sociobiologic habits: monogamy and adult-breeding exclusivity. The rates of natality, mortality, and dispersal from the colony depended on the interaction of environmental factors such as food supply, proper habitat, and disease. Because the supply of bea-

18. [Zeisberger and Mack], "Account of the Famine," 430–432; Laurence M. Hauptman, "Refugee Havens: The Iroquois Villages of the Eighteenth Century," in Christopher Vecsey and Robert Venables, eds., *American Indian Environments: Ecological Issues in Native American History* (Syracuse, N.Y., 1980), 134–135; "Diary of a Journey to Onondaga, Residence There, and Return from Thence, by the Moravian Brethren, Charles Frederick and David Zeisberger, from June 9, 1754 to June 4, 1755," in Beauchamp, ed., *Moravian Journals*, 199–200; William Cronon, *Changes in the Land: Indians, Colonists, and the Ecology of New England* (New York, 1983), chap. 3.

19. Powell, Shamokin Diary, entries for April 3, February 2–3.

ver was limited and they were easy to find, especially in winter, when they rarely strayed from their lodges and ponds, they stood a slim chance of surviving an era of growing consumer demand and few conservation ethics.[20]

The expansion of the fur trade led to the almost complete depletion of the beaver in many parts of the Northeast, including the Susquehanna Valley, by the middle of the eighteenth century. Travelers in the region recognized the extent of this ecological change: they found many old or abandoned beaver dams but few beavers. But the decline of the beaver did not end the fur trade in the area. Rather, when possible, the participants shifted from being primary producers (hunters) to middlemen, acting as go-betweens for western tribes and Anglo-American traders. The Iroquois proved particularly adept in this pursuit, establishing relations with Shawnees in the Ohio country to maintain their trade interests well after the decline of the beaver in Iroquoia.[21]

Traders turned to other pelts in addition to beaver, thus continuing the trade despite its devastating effect on game supplies. By mid-century the valley peltry trade had diversified. In 1763 the agent in charge of the store at Fort Augusta, located at Shamokin, took an inventory of four bundles of furs he was shipping to Philadelphia. In addition to 158 beaver pelts, the parcels contained the hides of 3 elk, 10 wolves, 54 "cats," 59 otters, 23 panthers, 9 mink, 7 martens, 36 foxes, 20 fishers, 4 bears, 271 raccoons, 292 muskrats, and one box of "Bears oyl."[22]

The decline in the beaver population was only one legacy of the

20. John Bishir, Richard Lancia, and Harry Hodgdon, "Beaver Family Organization: Its Implications for Colony Size," in G. Pilleri, ed., *Investigations on Beavers* (Berne, Switzerland, 1983), 105–113. Indeed, as Donald Worster has demonstrated, eighteenth-century Europeans took an "imperialist" view of the environment; people sought to exert control over the natural world and saw in nature's bounty materials that should be used for the benefit of mankind. See Worster, *Nature's Economy: A History of Ecological Ideas* (1977; rpt. Cambridge, Eng., 1985), chap. 2.

21. Samuel N. Rhoads, *The Mammals of Pennsylvania and New Jersey* (Philadelphia, 1903), 67–77; "Diary of Brother David Zeisberger's and Henry Frey's Journey and Stay in Onondaga from April 23d to November 12th, 1753," in Beauchamp, ed., *Moravian Journals*, 193; Jennings, "Indian Trade of the Susquehanna Valley," 409, 407; see also Sara H. Stites, *Economics of the Iroquois*, Bryn Mawr College Monographs, Monograph Series, vol. 1, no. 3 (Bryn Mawr, Pa., 1905), 79; and Thomas E. Norton, *The Fur Trade in Colonial New York, 1686–1776* (Madison, Wis., 1974), 13–26.

22. James Irvine's Invoice of Four Bundles of Peltry & Furrs, Commissioners of Indian Affairs, 1756–1765, Gratz Collection, Case 14, Box 10, HSP. The range of pelts received in trade can also be seen in Invoice Book of Skins from the Several Trading Houses &c, April 17, 1763–Dec. 8, 1763, Indian Commissioners Papers, HSP.

fur trade. Colonists traveling through the area brought rum and pathogens, which gravely weakened the Indians in the upper valley and destabilized their economy far more profoundly than the decline of traditional supplies of pelts.

Colonial traders realized that they could use alcohol to persuade the Indians to dispense with their goods at lower prices. In 1739 on a foray to western New York, William Johnson, who would later become superintendent of Indian affairs in the northern colonies, planned to build a trading post at Oquaga but quickly discovered that rum was "the only thing they mostly trade for." The missionary David Brainerd, interpreting Indian behavior from a devout Christian perspective, believed the Indians' intemperance was a sign of their paganism. In 1745 he thought the Indians in Shamokin were incapable of proper behavior. "The Indians of the place, are accounted the most drunken, mischievous, and ruffianlike fellows of any in these parts," he wrote in his journal. "Satan seems to have his seat in this town in an eminent manner." Other travelers echoed his sentiments.[23]

Alcohol abuse no doubt varied from place to place and from time to time, and some valley Indians were more prone than others to suffer its effects. Indians in major trade centers such as Shamokin, Wyoming, or Onondaga hosted traders more frequently than those in more isolated areas and experienced greater problems with alcohol as a result. Alcohol abuse was most intense during trade sessions, but these bouts disrupted seasonal work rhythms and thus had a potentially long-lasting effect on the Indians' economy. The best

23. Johnson to Peter Warren, May 10, 1739, *Johnson Papers*, 1:6–7; Jonathan Edwards, ed., *Memoirs of the Rev. David Brainerd, Missionary to the Indians on the Borders of New-York, New-Jersey, and Pennsylvania: Chiefly Taken from His Own Diary* (1822; rpt. St. Clair Shores, Mich., 1970), 233. See also "Rev. Gideon Hawley's Journey to Oghquaga (Broome Co.), 1753," in *Doc. Hist. NY*, 3:1043–1044; Bartram, *Observations*, 66, 33–35; [Grube], "Tour to Shamokin, 1753," 442; [Zeisberger and Mack], "Account of the Famine," 431; Hauptman, "Refugee Havens," 133–134. According to one scholar of the Iroquois, "drunkenness was perhaps the most serious social problem." See Anthony F. C. Wallace, *The Death and Rebirth of the Seneca* (1970; rpt. New York, 1972), 26. Much of the evidence for alcoholism among the valley Indian population comes from missionaries' diaries and travel accounts. These people were perhaps more sensitive to the Indians' use of alcohol than most of their contemporaries and might have exaggerated the extent of alcoholism to make a larger point about the Indians' apparent need of the teachings of the gospel. But evidence of nonreligious observers and Indian sachems also supports the missionaries' descriptions of the Indians' drinking.

pelts could be obtained in early spring, when the animals still had their heavier winter coats, and Indians pursued them extensively during these months. But these were also the months when crops needed to be planted. Although men traditionally hunted game while women farmed, women, too, on occasion, became inebriated.[24]

Local Indians complained that alcohol abuse interfered with necessary agricultural tasks. Missionaries and Indians alike linked the Indians' growing dependence on alcohol to apathetic behavior that resulted in limited crop yields. As several Nanticokes told two Moravian missionaries visiting Onondaga in July 1754: "It is quite evident that there are now so few Indians, where they had been so numerous formerly. The cause of this falling off is their use of too much rum. Let the Indians try to do without rum for but four years even, and they will be astonished at the increase of the population, and at the decrease of diseases and early death. All this is the result of rum drinking, which is also the primary cause of famine among them, caused by their not planting their crops at the proper time." Aucus al Kanigut, a Tuscarora chief from Oquaga, echoed these sentiments thirteen years later. His people had battled alcoholism in Carolina before moving to the valley, he told Sir William Johnson, and they had "lived but wretchedly being Surrounded by white People, and up to their Lips in Rum, so that they cou'd not turn their heads anyway but it ran into their mouths. This made them stupid, so that they neglected Hunting, Planting &c."[25]

Some valley Indians believed that dependence on alcohol would destroy their communities. Weiser learned about this fear during his 1737 trip when he stopped at Otsiningo. He had been to the town twelve years earlier and found that in the intervening years conditions had become desperate. The Indians were "short of provisions," he wrote in his journal, and "now their children looked like dead persons and suffered much from hunger." Local Indians told him that game had become scarce and that "the Lord and Creator of the world was resolved to destroy the Indians." They explained that one

24. On Indian women drinking at one trade center see Powell, Shamokin Diary, entries for February 23, March 20, and March 24. Not all Indian women in Shamokin drank, as Powell realized when some Indian women and children took refuge in the missionary's dwelling during a drunken melee in the town; see Shamokin Diary, entry for February 9.

25. "Journey to Onondaga by Frederick and Zeisberger," 199–200; Johnson's Journal of Indian Affairs, February 25, 1767, *Johnson Papers*, 12:273.

of their seers had had a vision, in which a god told him: "You in-
quire after the cause of why game has become scarce. I will tell you.
You kill it for the sake of the skins, which you give for strong liquor
and drown your senses, and kill one another, and carry on a dread-
ful debauchery. Therefore have I driven the wild animals out of the
country, for they are mine. If you will do good and cease from your
sins, I will bring them back; if not, I will destroy you from off the
earth." The Indians, according to Weiser, believed the seer's story.
"Time will show, said they," he wrote, "*rum* will kill us and leave the
land clear for the Europeans without strife or purchase."[26]

Some valley residents, associating excessive drinking with apathetic or indifferent behavior that threatened necessary economic
tasks, tried repeatedly to counter the Indians' attraction to liquor.
The party of missionary Gideon Hawley made temperance a prereq-
uisite for the establishment of a mission at Oquaga in 1753. Indians
elsewhere fought against alcoholism among the native population of
the valley. By 1748 Indians living at Otsiningo forbade the drinking
of alcohol in their town with favorable results: even though some
residents of the village planted their corn late because they arrived
after the customary planting time, their harvest was successful because they took good care of the crops. Patrick, a Nanticoke resident
of the town, noted that the Indians there had banned the importa-
tion of rum and warned traders that they would break the casks if
any tried to sneak alcohol into the area. He also told traveling missionaries that he thought the regional blacksmith would fare better
at Otsiningo than at Shamokin, which was frequented by many
drunken Indians.[27]

Indian leaders throughout the middle colonies tried to stop the
flow of rum into the backcountry. In 1758 Conochquieson, an
Oneida sachem, applied to Sir William Johnson "for having a stop
put to the selling of any Strong Liquors to our People, first it not
only disturbs us in our Meetings & Consultations where the drunken
People come in quarelling & very often have Weapons in their
hands, but it likewise carrys off many of our People both old &
young." The Oneidas as well as the Onondagas and Cayugas wanted
to continue to trade, but only for clothes and ammunition. Johnson,

26. "Narrative of a Journey by Conrad Weiser," 17.

27. "Hawley's Journey to Oghquaga," 1046; [Grube], "Tour to Shamokin, 1753,"
443; Zeisberger and Frey, "Journey to Onondaga, 1753," 193.

who had long since realized the problems the Indians had with rum, promised to act on their behalf to stop the alcohol trade, although his actions often demonstrated that he valued trade over the Indians' welfare. Other Indian leaders, seeing the way rum devastated their communities, similarly sought provincial assistance in their battle against intemperance.[28]

But in spite of Indian leaders' protests, colonial officials did little to stop the rum trade. New York and Pennsylvania passed laws prohibiting the distribution of alcohol to the Indians, but their effect was limited. New York's laws were short-lived, and by the 1750s the trading post at Oswego, the most important in the province, was exempted from its provisions. Pennsylvania legislators modified the province's strict 1701 law in the early 1720s to allow colonial officials to offer alcohol to the Indians when negotiating treaties with them; they believed alcohol was necessary in these transactions, presumably to gain the goodwill of the Indians. Later acts intended to prevent "abuses in the Indian trade" similarly exempted provincial officials.[29] Colonial government attempts to limit the distribution of alcohol to the Indians ultimately floundered in the face of overwhelming economic pressure from traders who knew they could get better terms and greater profits if they could ply the Indians with rum when dealing with them. In spite of the laws, traders in the upper Susquehanna Valley continued to supply their Indian clients with rum.

Traders in the valley, like their counterparts throughout British America, cared little about the Indians' welfare. They were in business to make a profit and demonstrated few qualms about taking advantage of the Indians' fondness for rum. They no doubt shared the views of Albany traders battling provincial legislation to limit the sale of alcohol to the Indians, who explained their position in a 1764 petition to the Lords of Trade. Admitting that some Iroquois sachems sought to prevent the sale of rum to the Indians, the traders noted that other Indians still desired liquor. The traders believed that cutting off the flow of rum to the backcountry would have devastating economic consequences. They found "a considerable de-

28. Johnson's Journal of Indian Affairs, December 9–12, 1758, *Johnson Papers*, 10:69, 73.

29. *Colonial Laws of New York*, 1:657–658, 685–686, 740–741, 751, 755, 3:1096–1098, 4:93; *Statutes at Large of Pennsylvania*, 2:168–170, 3:310–313, 5:320–330, 6:283–293.

crease in the Trade which they can ascribe to no other reason than such prohibition because when the Indians have nothing farther to provide for than bare necessaries, a very small quantity of Furs in Trade will abundantly supply that defect, Whereas when the Vent of Liquors is allow'd amongst them, it spurs them on to an unwaried application in hunting in order to supply the Trading Places with Furs and Skins in Exchange for Liquors." Sir William Johnson echoed their views. Without rum, he believed, "the Indians can purchase their cloathing with half the quantity of Skins, which will make them indolent, and lessen the Fur Trade."[30]

At the same time alcohol was ravaging Indian communities, European diseases also attacked them, taking a heavy toll. While distance between settlements could have impeded the movement of certain pathogens, the frequent travel between towns along the river spread bacteriological and viral agents throughout the valley. Colonial traders, missionaries, soldiers, officials, and settlers all brought Old World germs through the backcountry. Diseases also spread from one Indian group to another. Intertribal trade, visits between different groups, and the Indians' practice of capturing members of other tribal groups and bringing them back as slaves or adopted members of families all ensured the spread of pathogens.[31]

Settlement patterns facilitated the spread of infectious diseases among the valley Indian population. The Indians lived in a concentrated belt, establishing their settlements mostly along the two branches of the Susquehanna. Although the total population of the valley was not large, its concentrated nature encouraged the spread of viruses. Both summer and winter were potentially devastating killing periods. During the summer the river ran low and the temperature and humidity were often high, an ideal climate for diseases such as malaria or yellow fever, which were borne by mosquitoes, a pest frequently complained about in travelers' journals. Snow often came as early as October, and cold weather continued well into spring, creating a climate conducive to respiratory ailments. Indians weak-

30. "Petition of Merchants of Albany to the Lords of Trade," *Doc. Hist. NY*, 7:613, 615; Johnson to Lords of Trade, ibid., 665; Norton, *Fur Trade in Colonial New York*, 31–33.

31. See Alfred W. Crosby, *The Columbian Exchange: Biological and Cultural Consequences of 1492* (Westport, Conn., 1972), 35–58; and Henry F. Dobyns, *Their Number Become Thinned: Native American Population Dynamics in Eastern North America* (Knoxville, Tenn., 1983), 8–26.

ened by smallpox would have been especially vulnerable to pneumonia or influenza. Indeed, in 1675, 1746, and 1761 influenza epidemics struck northeastern tribes; the 1746 epidemic was accompanied by smallpox.[32]

Smallpox, the most devastating disease Europeans brought to the Americas, was tragically familiar to the Indians of the Northeast by the eighteenth century. In the 1630s the Hurons, Iroquois, and Susquehannocks lost at least half of their members to the disease. Later, outbreaks occurred almost every decade.[33] The ailment raged through most Indian towns in the upper Susquehanna Valley in the first half of the eighteenth century. The missionaries David Zeisberger and John Martin Mack noted that smallpox killed many Indians at Long Island, along the West Branch, in 1748. At Great Island, the disease was even more devastating: "In all of the huts there were cases of small-pox." In 1753 Bernard Grube's party encountered afflicted Indians at Shamokin and Quenischaschacki, a Delaware town sixty miles from Shamokin along the West Branch. Grube noted that a Shawnee and two Tutelo warriors had died of smallpox at that town shortly after a raid on the Catawbas in August.[34]

Indians had inherited neither immunities nor adequate medical knowledge to combat European diseases. Many Indians requested missionaries to bleed diseased victims in their towns. The missionaries did not realize what effect their actions would have, and many of the Indians they bled probably soon died because this treatment weakened them further. Missionaries, however, believed they cured some Indians through bleeding. Yet when no action was taken, the results were comparable. In 1747 an unidentified scourge decimated Shickellamy's family; his wife, one daughter-in-law, one son-in-law, and at least eight of his grandchildren all perished at Shamokin.[35]

Traders had not intended to destroy the Indians' communities; after all, their livelihood depended on Indians gathering pelts for

32. Dobyns, *Their Number Become Thinned*, 19; see also Crosby, *Columbian Exchange*, 43.

33. Dobyns, *Their Number Become Thinned*, 11–16. According to Dobyns, smallpox epidemics occurred in 1649–1650, 1662–1663, 1669–1670, 1677–1679, 1687–1691, 1715–1721, 1746, and 1755–1760.

34. [Zeisberger and Mack], "Account of the Famine," 431; [Grube], "Tour to Shamokin, 1753," 441–442.

35. [Camerhoff], "Journey to Shamokin in 1748," 174. Indians frequently asked missionaries to bleed them; see, for example, [A. G. Spangenberg], "Journal of a Journey to Onondaga in 1745," in Beauchamp, ed., *Moravian Journals*, 12–14.

them. But if local Indians could not provide the necessary pelts, the traders knew that they could move farther west and find others who would. Indeed, the decline of peltry stocks prompted traders to look beyond the Susquehanna by the mid-eighteenth century. But while the traders could move elsewhere and continue their operations, valley Indians had fewer options; they salvaged little from their years of procuring pelts for the Atlantic market.

The Legacy of the Fur Trade

During the first half of the eighteenth century, valley residents' attitudes and assumptions about life shifted in response to the fur trade and the changes it initiated. Indians moving to the region had helped create and sustain a principal highway of interior trade, but their efforts also prepared the valley for large-scale colonial settlement. By midcentury this transformation was largely complete, and the Indians soon had to face the legacy of the fur trade.

Perhaps the most subtle shifts in the Indians' world involved the changed relationship between their economic behavior and their religious sensibilities. Over the first half of the century, the Indians in the upper valley had seriously depleted local populations of furbearing animals. Yet their participation in the fur trade did not mean that they had turned against the deities that governed animals; no documents from the period suggest a religious basis to this assault. The seeming contradiction between active slaughter of animals to supply fur traders and continued propitiation of game spirits suggests that the fur trade made gradual inroads into regional animal populations. The Indians' religious beliefs survived after the passing of the furbearers, as was evident in the story of the Indian seer Weiser recorded in his journal in 1737. But though the Indians' deity associated declining peltry supplies with participation in the fur trade, it sought a more specific end—temperance—than a general halt to the trade. The Indians' gods, like the Indians themselves, had apparently accepted the presence of fur traders and sought only to confine hunters' consuming habits to socially acceptable articles.

Yet local Indians and the game bosses would never willingly have eliminated entire game populations. What drove Indian hunters to do so? Perhaps decline occurred through ambiguity rather than conscious hostility to the keepers of the game especially since depletion, quite possibly, came without clear signals. Since beaver dams could outlive their occupants by decades and bears and elk continued to roam the woods, the destruction of valley game populations might not have been apparent. After all, game bosses, not Indians, had always directed the movement of animals. Bears, beavers, and elk were not domesticated livestock that could be counted or enclosed in fences. Since game animals did not entirely disappear, the decline of furbearers was a gradual, and highly ambiguous, process. Thus for the Susquehanna Indians, as for Indians elsewhere, depletion in supplies of animals represented the inroads of new economic customs rather than a repudiation of prevailing religious sensibilities.

Still, the new market-oriented ethos of the fur trade had at least an unintended influence on religious practices. Fewer animals caught in the hunt meant fewer rituals involving carcasses. When practiced less frequently, these rituals could have become yet another reminder of a way of life that was slipping, almost imperceptibly, into the past.

The fur trade initiated changes well beyond the altered relationship between Indians and furbearers: the landscape took on a new appearance because of the actions of valley residents. The changes in the local environment were most evident in places such as Shamokin and Wyoming. There, in towns where residents frequently hosted traders and travelers, colonists learned about the region and its resources. Although much of the upper valley remained covered with thick forests, many of the colonists who traveled in the region saw cleared fields with prodigious agricultural yields. The colonists who settled in the valley often spread news of the region in pamphlets and personal correspondence. These writings gave readers the impression that the valley was perfect for new settlements. This environment was desirable, in part, because of the many changes Indians had made in the landscape, some of them unplanned effects of the fur trade, others by-products of the traditional subsistence activities of the Indians. Without being aware of it, the Indians had made the landscape more attractive to colonists.

When the fur trade took its devastating toll on the local beaver population, the old beaver dams fell into disrepair and eventually collapsed. When they broke, the soil that was exposed to the air was much different than it had been before the beavers built their dams; grass soon grew in these now-drained ponds. New settlers were eager to claim these areas; their cattle or sheep could forage in the fields and the colonists could plant crops without having to remove any trees. The newly exposed lands could not support forests for an indefinite period because certain fungi necessary for tree growth had been killed by the impounded water behind the beaver dams and could be reproduced naturally only over time. Thus though beavers had always thinned the forests to provide building materials for their dams, the subsequent collapse of their dams prevented rapid regrowth of the trees. The allure of these meadows persisted for decades; at the end of the eighteenth century speculators still clamored for what one termed a "Beaver Dam meadow."[36]

The various Indian groups that traveled and lived in the valley from 1720 to 1750 altered the environment far more than beavers had done building their dams or when their dams broke. Wood was the primary source of fuel for Indian villages throughout the Northeast, and the Indians thinned the forests around their towns. One early traveler noted that the length of time a village had existed could be ascertained by the size of the clearing around the village. Indians also reduced the forests when they cleared fields to grow corn and other dietary staples. Indians cleared land when they moved to find settlements with better trade connections, to find village sites where indigenous wood supplies were abundant, or to find refuge from westward-moving colonists or other Indian tribes. Such movement and the subsequent cutting or burning of new sections thinned the forest in precisely the same places most commonly visited by colonists, who usually traveled along water routes.[37]

The changes in the landscape involved a small percentage of the total acreage in the region, but their importance far exceeded their size. Clearings in the forest gave colonists an impression of a potential agricultural bounty, an image of what they would enjoy when they gained control of the region. Although trees soon would have

36. Cronon, *Changes in the Land*, 106; S. A. Wilde, C. T. Youngberg, and J. H. Hovind, "Changes in Composition of Ground Water, Soil Fertility, and Forest Growth Produced by the Construction and Removal of Beaver Dams," *Journal of Wildlife Management* 14 (1950), 123–128; Henry Drinker to William Cooper, December 26, 1789, Drinker Papers, Land Correspondence, Cooper folder, HSP.

37. Gordon M. Day, "The Indian as an Ecological Factor in the Northeastern Forest," *Ecology* 34 (April 1953), 330, 332–333, 337–338; Stites, *Economics of the Iroquois*, 22–23; E. L. Jones, "Creative Disruptions in American Agriculture," *Agricultural History* 48 (1974), 516; and see Percy Bidwell and John Falconer, *History of Agriculture in the Northern United States, 1620–1860* (New York, 1941), 8; Cronon, *Changes in the Land*, 48.

encroached on the untended fields, colonists moved in before the forests once again reached their climax stage. When colonists arrived, fields remained cleared or were covered by younger, thinner, and more easily removable trees.

Natural population increase in the mid-Atlantic region combined with the influx of large numbers of immigrants created tremendous incentives for gaining control of western lands. By midcentury the need to obtain more land and to populate it seemed clear. News of the desirability of the Susquehanna Valley for settlement was spreading through New York and Pennsylvania. John Bartram's *Observations*, published in 1751, described in detail the flora and fauna as well as the regional topography of Pennsylvania and New York. His private correspondence mirrored his published work. Writing to Cadwallader Colden in 1744, Bartram extolled the virtues of the region, where "rich plains" were at times half a mile across and covered with only "grass and weeds." Mountains rose adjacent to the river, but on the opposite bank were fertile plains, "rich low land," where the Indians had once established towns.[38]

By midcentury prominent colonists from more densely settled areas sought ownership of parts of the valley that they thought would be profitable sites for agricultural settlements. In 1751 Sir William Johnson began to pursue a clear title to an extensive tract along the Susquehanna in south-central New York. He correctly predicted that, when promoted, the region would lure numerous settlers. In 1754 the Susquehannah Company, based in Connecticut, began its campaign to settle large sections of the upper Susquehanna Valley in Pennsylvania, an effort that pitted the two colonies in conflict for decades.[39]

Ultimately, colonists promoting new settlements replaced traders in the valley economy. But whether they realized it or not, these land jobbers owed a great deal to the fur trade. At the beginning of the eighteenth century, no one could have predicted the long-term shifts that would occur in the region. Trade could take place in the upper valley only when Indians and colonists needed desired commodities from each other. The successful development of this trade hastened

38. Bartram, *Observations*; Bartram to Cadwallader Colden, April 29, 1744, Gratz Collection, Case 7, Box 21, HSP.

39. William Johnson and Company to Goldsbrow Banyar, May 6, 1751, *Johnson Papers*, 1:921–922. The efforts of the Susquehannah Company are chronicled in *SCP*. These developments are treated in chapters 4 and 5 below.

its own collapse by altering the regional environment, destabilizing the Indian populations along the river, and providing colonists with increased knowledge of and interest in settling the area. Thus, though relations between the different peoples in the valley were generally amicable, the economic and social ties that bound them together could not maintain the trade-based system they had worked so hard to create.

The early eighteenth-century history of the valley, like that of other colonized areas, demonstrates the central importance of the marketing of natural resources. In the pursuit of economic gain, early Americans reshaped the world they inhabited. Colonists rarely limited their economic pursuits because of potential ecological consequences; such ideas were completely foreign to them. Thoughts of production, not conservation, dominated their actions. Environmental change from 1700 to 1750—the depletion of the indigenous peltry stocks and partial deforestation—had two primary consequences. Decline in furbearers prevented the Indians from maintaining their position in the trade-based regional economy, a commercial system they depended on for necessary goods. Thinning of the forests made the upper valley more inviting to an expanding colonial population seeking lands to settle. These ecological changes undermined the entire intercultural economy of the region. Few of the colonists who later migrated to the upper valley were aware of these earlier developments. Many, sharing the hubris of European colonists everywhere, thought they were engaged in the initial attempt to make the valley yield its bounty.

But those colonists were sorely wrong. The region they settled in the latter half of the eighteenth century was no pristine wilderness. The landscape reflected not a lack of human activity but the impact of a particular economic system. That system, fueled by the European demand for peltry, fundamentally and permanently shifted the balance of power in the region. But though colonists gained the upper hand, they soon realized that the expansion of their settlements into the backcountry would be a far more complex affair than they had anticipated.

4 The Collapse of Intercultural Trade

Fur traders bringing their wares into the upper Susquehanna Valley served as the commercial envoys of the British Empire. Theirs were only the first efforts of colonists to make money in the area. After midcentury, fur traders moved on, and the trade fell into the hands of provincial officials and settlers. This trade, still important to the Indians, quickly became an economic sideshow for colonists, a way to make money but no longer the basis of the valley economy. Another goal motivated the colonists: they wanted land. Although their economic interests differed substantially from those of the traders, the settlers became the new agents of English imperialism in the backcountry. And in their attempts to gain western land, the settlers, like the traders, were more concerned with economic success than with helping the Indians maintain a stable economy. The acquisitive impulses of the empire transferred easily from traders to settlers.

The colonial population swelled during the middle decades of the century, prompting colonists to seek new lands for settlements in the upper Susquehanna Valley. But these seekers quickly found expansion into the western hinterland difficult because no single individual or group held the balance of power in the region. Groups of colonists competed for land, fighting among themselves for control of specific tracts. Indeed, the claims of some Connecticut settlers to much of the upper valley brought that colony to arms against Pennsylvania. Other colonists, more interested in pelts than land, sought to prevent new settlements in the valley; they wanted to protect the resident Indian population, hoping to encourage the Indians to gather the remaining peltry in the area. Valley Indians, often with the backing of provincial officials, resisted colonists' attempts to take their lands. Realizing that hostile Indians and French forces to the west were a threat to the expansion of colonial settlements, some provincial and crown officials actively supported valley Indians by providing them with trade goods and, on one occasion, building a town for them. When the French threat receded after the French and Indian War, however, many provincial officials joined forces with expansionist settlers, although disagreements between different groups over titles to vast areas impeded any unified colonial position on the settlement of these western lands.

After midcentury provincial officials and Indian leaders found themselves in the middle of intense battles for control of the upper valley. Each had to struggle with the ambiguous legacy of the earlier trade system. People involved in that economic network had improved overland routes through the region, spread information about its resources, and cleared portions of the forests, thus making the region more attractive to land-seeking colonists. By the end of the 1760s tribal sachems and provincial officials alike realized that only a firm boundary between their peoples would allow them both to maintain their own economies and live in peace, a goal they thought could be attained. By 1768, stability demanded segregation.

Colonial Population Growth and Western Lands

After midcentury valley residents found themselves coping with the most significant social and economic phenomenon of eighteenth-century British America: population growth from both natural means and immigration. The increased population put greater pressures on the people and resources of the backcountry than any other market force, including the fur trade. Many colonists believed that the solution to the problems of overcrowding and division of property holdings was to send people into the rural hinterland to establish satellite communities of the longer-settled provinces. Some of these colonists, especially those with little experience in dealing with Indians, vigorously sought western land, provoking angry responses not only from the Indians they encountered but from provincial officials as well. In spite of the resulting tensions, their efforts to establish colonial settlements in the backcountry dominated the economy of the upper Susquehanna Valley after midcentury.

The pressure for new settlements developed among colonists who realized the staggering demographic growth of their provinces. The British North American population, approximately 275,000 in 1700, increased by over 400 percent in the next fifty years. Immigration was the major source of increase in the middle colonies. The population of Pennsylvania grew from 20,000 in 1700 to 100,000 in 1740; by 1750, there were 150,000 people in the province and by 1760, 220,000. Although Pennsylvania's population grew more rapidly than that of other provinces because of its great appeal to immigrants, population growth characterized all of the middle colonies. New York's population grew from 63,000 in 1740 to 80,000 in 1750. New York, Connecticut, and Pennsylvania, the colonies with the greatest interest in the upper Susquehanna Valley, grew to rival, in a demographic sense, the earlier, more populous provinces of Virginia and Massachusetts.[1]

Even though immigrants usually avoided Connecticut because it was more densely settled than many other colonies, population growth was still a major social problem there. Connecticut's growth rate was less than that of the middle colonies, but its population also grew steadily during the first half of the eighteenth century. The colony had 55,000 residents in 1730, but only ten years later that figure was 70,000, and by midcentury it was 100,000; from 1750 to 1760 the population grew by 42 percent to reach 142,000. In just thirty years, a single generation, the population of this long-settled New England colony had more than doubled.[2]

In addition to seeing their world becoming more crowded, colonists could read about population growth and its implications. Printers published bills of mortality in urban areas, providing precise evidence of demographic change. Benjamin Franklin, perhaps

1. J. Potter, "The Growth of Population in America, 1700–1800," in Glass and Eversley, eds., *Population in History: Essays in Historical Demography* (Chicago, 1965), 638–639.
2. Ibid.

the most famous printer in the colonies, published important works on population growth in the early 1750s. In the 1750 edition of his popular almanac, *Poor Richard Improved*, he analyzed the growth of the New Jersey and Massachusetts populations in the 1730s and 1740s and discussed demographic statistics of Boston for 1742 and Philadelphia for 1748–1749. He found that the number of people in the colonies was doubling every thirty years and that this growth was "owing not so much to natural Generation, as the Accession of Strangers." Franklin then compared his findings of American population growth with Breslaw, the capital of Silesia, and found that its population was growing at a very slow pace.

The reason for the tremendous growth of the American colonies seemed clear to Franklin. "I believe People increase faster by Generation in these Colonies, where all can have full Employ, and there is Room and Business for Millions yet unborn," he wrote. In countries that had been settled longer, such as England, "as soon as the Number of People is as great as can be supported by all the Tillage, Manufactures, Trade and Offices of the Country, the Overplus must quit the Country, or they will perish by Poverty, Diseases, and want of Necessaries." Such conditions would also discourage marriages and thus hinder natural population growth.[3]

In Pennsylvania and New York the increased population led many to emigrate from densely settled to less populated regions. During the first half of the eighteenth century, Pennsylvania residents moved from earlier settlements to new parts of Bucks, Philadelphia, Lancaster, and York counties. In addition, many colonists traveled south out of Philadelphia after the early 1730s. This movement was so large that migrants from southeastern Pennsylvania and nearby areas became a majority of the population in the developing region of the upper Shenandoah Valley. But in spite of migration away from the more heavily settled areas, the population of Pennsylvania and New York continued to grow throughout the prerevolutionary period.[4]

3. *The Papers of Benjamin Franklin*, ed. Leonard Labaree et al. (New Haven, Conn., 1959–), 3:438–441; see also 5:182–183 and James Cassedy, *Demography in Early America: Beginnings of the Statistical Mind, 1600–1800* (Cambridge, Mass., 1969), chap. 7.

4. Alan Tully, *William Penn's Legacy: Politics and Social Structure in Provincial Pennsylvania, 1726–1755* (Baltimore, Md., 1977), 53–57; Robert Mitchell, *Commercialism and Frontier: Perspectives on the Early Shenandoah Valley* (Charlottesville, Va., 1977), 34–36; Lester Cappon, ed., *Atlas of Early American History: The Revolutionary Era, 1760–1790* (Princeton, N.J., 1976), 22–23.

While population growth stimulated the colonial economy, especially by expanding the market for British products and increasing the productive capacity of the work force, many colonists realized that this demographic boom could become a threat to their economic system as well. For colonists who embraced the conquering instincts of the empire, the settlement of western lands seemed the best way to solve the problems of overcrowding created by population growth. They defined this effort in economic terms, justifying it on the grounds that it served the needs of both traders and farmers.

None expressed these sensibilities better than Franklin. He articulated his views in "A Plan for Settling Two Western Colonies." "Our people, being confined to the country between the sea and the mountains," Franklin wrote, "cannot much more increase in number; people increasing in proportion to their room and means of subsistence." He feared that the French would settle the trans-Appalachian west and cut off British trade with the western Indians. The French would further destabilize the English colonies by luring many "of our debtors, and loose English people, our German servants, and slaves" to add to their numbers; they would also encourage the Indians to attack colonial settlements. Franklin felt that the establishment of two English colonies between the Ohio and Lake Erie would serve as a buffer, protecting both the existing colonies and the Indian trade. Settlement could proceed quickly in the Ohio country, he argued, because the English colonies along the Atlantic would provide people, supplies, and assistance in transportation. Franklin believed that these new colonies would lead to "the great increase of Englishmen, English trade, and English power." The acquisition and settlement of western lands not only fit imperial concerns but would also aid the "many thousands of families that are ready to swarm, wanting more land."[5]

Franklin's ideas about settling western lands represented a transition in colonial economic thought. Earlier, English colonizers concerned with expansion conceived of their projects in largely mercantilist terms: they looked to uncolonized territory for extractable resources that could enrich themselves and the empire. Such ideas motivated settlement projects from the sugar islands in the Caribbean to tobacco farms in the Chesapeake and fur trading posts in New England. By the mid-eighteenth century, however, the growing

5. *Franklin Papers*, 5:457–459, 462.

population prompted a reconsideration of the function of western lands. Some prominent colonists came to believe that the backcountry would be best used for new agricultural settlements. Since they anticipated making a profit from farming these lands and exporting cash crops, the shift in focus required little change in the colonists' prevailing economic sensibilities.

Colonists who wanted to establish settlements on western lands needed the permission of the provincial officials whose jurisdiction covered the area. Gaining this approval, however, was often complicated even for enterprising colonists. Pennsylvania and Connecticut both claimed the territory between 41° and 42° north latitude, which included most of the upper Susquehanna Valley. Some individuals and groups believed that Connecticut's claim, based on the sea-to-sea clause in its 1662 charter, was valid. Thus Samuel Hazard, a Philadelphia merchant, petitioned the Connecticut legislature for a grant to establish a colony on lands he believed belonged to Connecticut. Hazard hoped to avoid the contested region by establishing his settlement west of the boundary line determined in William Penn's original grant as Pennsylvania's western border. He wanted his territory to have an eastern boundary one hundred miles west of the western border of Pennsylvania and to continue westward until it reached a line one hundred miles west of the Mississippi River. Connecticut legislators, accepting Hazard's claim that he had enlisted 3,508 people to move to the region with thousands more ready to move there once he got the land, granted his request.[6]

Hazard's petition proved an easy matter for the Connecticut legislature. Since the lands he wanted lay beyond the Pennsylvania border, his petition did not create problems between Connecticut and any other colony. But the petitions of the Susquehannah Company for lands between 41° and 42° north latitude, which lay within Penn's grant, immediately plunged the Connecticut legislature into a conflict with Pennsylvania and eventually led the colonies to take up arms against each other.

The Susquehannah Company, based in Windham, Connecticut, was a joint stock company, similar to those that had colonized North America under British auspices. Its owners believed that the sea-to-

6. Petition of Samuel Hazard to the Connecticut General Assembly, May 2, 1755, *SCP*, 1:246–259; Resolution of the Connecticut General Assembly on the Memorial of Samuel Hazard, ibid., 280–282.

sea clause in Connecticut's charter entitled that colony to all of the land between these latitudes, with the exception of New York, which was established before Connecticut received its charter. The company, in petitions to the Connecticut legislature and the king, argued that Connecticut controlled the territory because it fell within land set aside in the charter and therefore did not have to respect Pennsylvania's claims. The provincial assembly, however, was less certain of the legitimacy of the claim and directed the company to petition the king, the only power able to adjudicate such matters. Still, prominent provincial officials in Connecticut, including Governor Roger Wolcott, approved of the company's actions, seeing in its efforts an opportunity to ease the crowding of the colony.[7]

The resulting controversy between Pennsylvania and Connecticut revealed the deep divisions within the empire over the issue of settling western lands. Pennsylvania officials believed their charter gave their colony the right to the territory; they repeatedly protested the Susquehannah Company's actions and even mustered troops to disperse some of the settlers. The crown, after weighing petitions from both sides, agreed with Pennsylvania officials and refused to acknowledge the legitimacy of the company's claims.[8]

The company's efforts also enraged the Indians of the upper valley. The company hired the Albany trader John Lydius to purchase the territory from the Indians. By the mid-eighteenth century, Indians and colonists had established procedures for the sale of Indian lands. Because these lands were considered tribal trusts, only the entire group claiming control of the lands had the power to alienate property. But Lydius ignored this principle; he never attempted to

---

7. Petition of John Humphrey and others to the Connecticut General Assembly, May 10, 1750, ibid., 1–2; Memorial of Hezekiah Phelps and others to the Connecticut General Assembly, October 3, 1751, ibid., 6–8; Memorial of Joseph Blackleach and others to the Connecticut General Assembly, May 20, 1752, ibid., 9–15; Memorial of John Whiting and others to the Connecticut General Assembly, May 10, 1753, ibid., 21–22; Memorial of the Inhabitants of Greenwich to the Connecticut General Assembly, May 14, 1753, ibid., 22–24; Petition of the Inhabitants of Suffield to the Connecticut General Assembly, May 1753, ibid., 24–26; Memorial of Nathaniel Giddings and others to the Connecticut General Assembly, May 1753, ibid., 26–28; Roger Wolcott's Approval of the Susquehannah Company Project, January 1754, ibid., 50–51; see Julian Boyd, "Connecticut's Experiment in Expansion: The Susquehannah Company, 1753–1803," *Journal of Economic and Business History* 4 (1931), 40–44; and Edith A. Bailey, "Influences toward Radicalism in Connecticut, 1754–1755," *Smith College Studies in History* 5 (1920), 181–183.

8. Order of the King in Council, June 15, 1763, *SCP*, 2:255.

meet with representatives of the Iroquois tribes claiming possession of the region he sought to purchase for the Susquehannah Company. Instead, as Little Abraham, a Mohawk chief, informed Sir William Johnson, Lydius "made some of our People Drunk, & then persuaded them to Sign a Deed for [the land], & prevailed upon Others who had no right to Dispose thereof, to follow their Example." The Pennsylvania government, aware of Lydius's actions through meetings with Indians, quickly moved to halt the company's efforts, in part because of the way he had obtained title to the land. They knew, as did other provincial officials familiar with the backcountry, that the Susquehannah Company's actions could have broken the Covenant Chain, the alliance between the Iroquois and English colonies, and if that alliance came apart, the Indians of the hinterland might side with the French and threaten the British fur trade and any British settlements in the backcountry. Many colonists agreed with Sir William Johnson, who in May 1763 wrote to Governor Thomas Fitch of Connecticut, imploring him to stop the company's efforts. Continued attempts to settle the area would, Johnson feared, "prove fatal to our frontiers."[9]

Still, as Pennsylvania officials feared, the Susquehannah Company refused to give up its plans to settle northern Pennsylvania. In spite of the king's repudiation of their claims, company members continued to plan their new settlements, waiting for the right moment to move west and establish their towns, fashioned on New England models, along the Susquehanna.

Intercultural Tensions and a Resurgence of Cooperation

In spite of pressure to gain new tracts for colonial farmers, many provincial officials actively worked to help valley Indians protect their communities. They did so for two reasons. First, these colonists wanted to profit from the remaining fur trade. Second, they were, until the mid-1760s, still fearful of the French presence to the west and believed that Indians friendly to the British would be a useful buffer should hostilities arise. While colonists had problems with

9. "Indian Proceedings, April 21–28 1762," *Johnson Papers*, 3:714–717; Article on Indian Affairs, *SCP*, 2:190–191; James Hamilton to Johnson, May 12, 1761, ibid., 93–94; Hamilton to Sir Jeffrey Amherst, May 10, 1761, ibid., 88–92; Johnson to Fitch, May 17, 1763, ibid., 217.

their own population increasing rapidly, the Indians faced a different crisis: they had suffered a demographic decline and had to find
a way to maintain social and economic stability. The intercultural
cooperation that had fueled the trade before midcentury now
guided the efforts of Indians and colonists to create a more varied
economy in the valley. At numerous treaty meetings between colonists and valley Indians, each party acted on its own economic concerns. And because some of these concerns overlapped, the peoples
of the upper valley generally continued to live harmoniously with
each other.

Colonists' concerns to maintain amicable ties with valley Indians
rested on fears generated by the occasional hostilities that had arisen
in the region. Of particular concern to colonial leaders was the Indians' practice of taking prisoners from colonial settlements. Provincial officials largely failed to understand that many Indians, such as
the Iroquois, took captives to replace deceased members of their
community. The cultural gap between Indians and colonists was evident when Lieutenant Governor James Hamilton of Pennsylvania
tried to make the colonists' views on the subject clear to a group of
Indians at Lancaster in 1762. "As we are of a different Colour from
you, so we have different customs," he argued. "It is a constant rule
with us White people, that upon making peace with those with
whom we have been at War, the prisoners on both sides are faithfully delivered up." Local Indians, for their part, claimed that some
prisoners had already been returned but had been promptly stolen
by colonial soldiers. "When I brought them by the English Forts they
took them away from me," the Oneida sachem Thomas King contended, "All along from Oswego to the Carrying Place, and so to
Niagara, till I got to Shamokin, they got them all from me, and I
believe they have made servants of them." The colonial officials denied the charges, but the debate revealed the underlying tensions in
the region.[10]

These tensions did not always remain hidden. In August 1761, a
colonist killed an Indian in Easton, Pennsylvania; in late 1763 the
Paxton Boys killed the peaceful Conestoga Indians at Lancaster, the
last identifiable descendants of the Susquehannocks. Both colonial

---

10. *PaCR*, 8:731ff., 744, 760–761; Peter C. Mancall, "Environment and Economy:
The Upper Susquehanna Valley in the Age of the American Revolution" (Ph.D. diss.,
Harvard University, 1986), 87.

officials and Indian leaders knew that these events threatened the amity that existed between the peoples of the backcountry and strove to limit the repercussions of this violence. Thus Lieutenant Governor Hamilton reassured backcountry Indians that the colonist responsible for the Easton murder would, if he was found guilty, "suffer the same punishment as if he had killed one of us, Which punishment, by our Laws, is Death." Similarly, after the murders at Lancaster, a group of Indians then staying in Philadelphia believed that reprisals against "the back Inhabitants" could be prevented if they could travel quickly up the Susquehanna to assure the Indians there that the perpetrators would be "brought to Justice."[11]

Colonial officials also worked to resolve tensions associated with a far larger threat: the potential spread into the upper valley of the conflict between France and Britain, which would have devastating consequences for intercultural relations in the backcountry. If the valley Indians joined the French forces, outlying British colonial settlements would be in danger of attack. Neither New York nor Pennsylvania could muster sufficient troops to protect the settlers in the backcountry. Rather than risk alienating valley Indians by allowing colonists to take their lands, Pennsylvania leaders chose to defend their frontier settlers by maintaining an alliance with the Indians.

To secure their frontier, Pennsylvania officials in 1756 built a town for the Delaware chief Teedyuscung and his community at Wyoming. While the town had had an Indian population earlier, the provincial government planned a colonial-style town for the site. Thus with £100 allocated by the provincial legislature, Governor William Denny sent fifty carpenters, masons, and other workers to the town to help the Indians plant fields, start a garden, and split wood for fences.

Near the end of the project, a group of Indians traveling through the region killed one of the masons. When some of the frightened workers decided it was time to depart, Isaac Zane, a colonial leader at the site, berated them. "I told them they did not consider the thing right for the poor frontears were continually in as mutch Danger as we now were," he wrote in his journal on May 31, "and it would be well for them to consider that they did not live above 30 to 40 miles from the frontears and if these Dwelt between you & the wilderness should move away then you should be the front and in as

11. *PaCR*, 9:657–658, 135–136.

great Danger as you are now and should it not be as mutch your care to make peace as those that Dwel on the front (tho you live a few miles farther in the setled country)." Zane did not indicate whether his speech had much effect on the men, although they continued to work on the town and apparently gave up any idea of abandoning the project.[12]

Protection of colonial settlers prompted provincial officials to enlist the aid of valley Indians, yet an older motivation—preservation of the fur trade—prompted them to meet with Indians on a regular basis. These meetings reveal the Indians' awareness of the colonists' economic goals. Earlier, when valley inhabitants were establishing trade connections, local Indian groups negotiated for better trade terms whenever possible. After midcentury valley Indians again worked together to improve their trading position, but the treaty negotiations reveal the Indians' increased market sophistication. This greater understanding of the colonists' commercial goals enhanced their bargaining power and thus helped the Indians maintain economic stability in spite of the continued problems their communities faced.

At treaty negotiations Indians and colonists frequently discussed the price and availability of trade goods. At an August 1761 meeting at Easton, the Indians complained to Pennsylvania officials about the trading practices of Sir William Johnson. "When we come to him for Ammunition," noted Joseph Pepy, an interpreter for the Iroquois and other Susquehanna tribes, "and bring our Skins, he does not give us the worth of our Skins, but only a handful of powder, and for that reason we think there is certain death upon us." Pepy declared that Johnson "shuts up his powder from us, and will not give us more than will serve us two or three days." The Indians proposed a solution to the problem: "We hope you will have pity on us," their spokesman Tokahaio announced, "& erect a Trading House at Diahoga [Tioga], that we may be able to buy our Goods cheaper." The Indians wanted many trade goods, especially powder and lead, but did not want any liquor to be sold at the post. If the Pennsylvania government abided by this plan, the Indians would spread information about the store "both far and near." Such an operation would also influence Johnson's trading practices. "If your Goods are sold

12. Joseph A. Coates, ed., "Journal of Isaac Zane to Wyoming," *PMHB* 30 (1906), 417–426.

reasonable," reasoned Tokahaio, "we suppose that General Johnson will also sell his goods cheaper than he now does."[13]

At a meeting at Lancaster the next August, Thomas King, negotiating for the Indians, again stated the Indians' willingness to trade wherever they could find the best price. He noted that the Indians expected to visit the stores at Shamokin and at Harris' Ferry. "We desire you may have no trading Houses higher up the Susquehanna than Shamokin," King told Pennsylvania Lieutenant Governor James Hamilton and the other provincial officials in attendance at the meeting. "Let the Indians come there or to John Harris's; if they want to Trade, let them come down to these Trading Houses." King then proclaimed: "If we have a mind to have Goods cheapest, we may go to John Harris's; We, therefore, desire you will let us know what prices you set upon your Goods." The Indians' repeated complaints about disreputable agents at provincial stores further demonstrated their concern for getting reliable trade terms.[14]

Negotiations over prices best reveal the Susquehanna Indians' understanding of the colonists' market economy. Responding to the Indians' complaints about prices, Hamilton noted that he had no power to set prices. "You know we dont make the Goods ourselves," he explained, "they are made in England, and the Transporting them over the Seas is dangerous in time of War and very expensive, so that they must come much dearer now than in time of Peace, and their prices change, as the risque and demand for them is greater or less, but I am told, that they are sold to you as cheap as they can be afforded." Near the end of the treaty negotiations the Indians, echoing Hamilton, made a simple request. "They further say," the meeting's official record noted, "that as the Governor has acquainted them that the War has occasioned a rise in the price of Goods, they hope the Governor will give Orders that they may be paid a higher price for their Skins and Furs in proportion." Whenever possible, the Iroquois and other Indians of the upper Susquehanna Valley sought to obtain the best prices within the existing trade system. The Indians did not attempt to alter the structure of the system nor did they reject the economic logic of the colonists. Their concern was

13. *PaCR*, 8:642–643.
14. Ibid., 754.

with maintaining the commercial network and bettering their position within that system.[15]

The Susquehanna Indians' understanding of the economics of trade went beyond the search for lower prices. In 1762 the Iroquois met with Pennsylvania officials to discuss a trading post planned for the West Branch of the Susquehanna. Hamilton told the Iroquois attending the Lancaster treaty meeting that supplying goods to trading posts in western Pennsylvania was very expensive; the overland journey to Pittsburgh, where the province had opened a store, "was so long and made the Expenses so very high, that we lost money by the Trade every Year, and that I knew of no Method by which we could supply them cheaper than by your suffering us to go up the West Branch of the Susquehanna river, with Boats or Canoes, & to build some small Store Houses to put our Goods & skins in, as we went up and came down that river." Hamilton added that the request for the store along the West Branch had come from the Delawares, "who desired a Trade with us, & I did it that they might have their goods cheaper."

But the Iroquois at the meeting refused to give permission for the new trading post. Kinderhuntie, a Seneca warrior, gave two reasons for the refusal. First, the Iroquois present at Lancaster were "chiefly Warriors," and the provincial officials' request could only be granted by the Indians' "Chief men" meeting in council. Second, Kinderhuntie did not want to help the Delawares. Expressing "wonder" that the Delawares had not informed the Iroquois of the request, the Seneca warrior said that although the Delawares lived on land of the Iroquois, they "are grown proud and will, I suppose, not own us for their uncles." Trade, provincial officials realized, was only one aspect of intercultural relations; they learned that the Iroquois used their control over the upper valley to limit the economic options of valley Indians.[16]

The Pennsylvania General Assembly, which since the late 1740s had attempted to prevent "abuses" in the Indian trade, regulated trade at Fort Augusta, a provincial post built at Shamokin. The colonial

15. Ibid., 768, 774; see Arthur Ray, "Indians as Consumers in the Eighteenth Century," in Carol Judd and Arthur Ray, eds., *Old Trails and New Directions: Papers of the Third North American Fur Trade Conference* (Toronto, 1980), 255–271.

16. *PaCR*, 8:766–767.

Commissioners of Indian Affairs appointed James Irvine to be the storekeeper at Fort Augusta and ordered him to follow a rigid set of guidelines to protect the province's trade interests. They forbade Irvine from trading with the Indians for himself or for other individuals; prevented him from employing anyone to assist with the trade who did not have the approval of the commissioners; and ordered him to keep a full record of his transactions and submit these records annually to the commissioners.[17]

Many Indians who lived in towns along the Susquehanna came to the fort frequently for supplies. In June 1757, for example, Indians from Tioga arrived to trade for flour, rum, powder, lead, and flints. But the store's wares did not please all of the Indians. In early September 1757, some Indians brought furs to the post but seemed, according to James Burd, one of the commanders of the forces stationed there, "much disappointed" with the store's supplies. Still, the trading center at the fort served the valley Indians' needs, and even if they were disappointed with the available goods, they brought large quantities of furs to the store. Although the near depletion of the beaver population must have impinged on their hunting for the fur trade, the Indians continued to bring beaver skins and a variety of other pelts to the fort into the early 1760s.[18]

Although Indians frequented the store, Irvine thought conditions there were far from ideal. He complained vehemently about the difficulty of finding trustworthy people to assist him, the lack of storage facilities, the absence of places for the Indians to sleep, and the lack of a smokehouse for venison brought by the Indians. Irvine also found the soldiers far from helpful. "What dependance can be Placed on Soldiers," he wrote to Joseph Morris in May 1763, "who are kept almost continually Drunk, and who, whenever Obliged to do anything for the advantage of the Trade, doe it with the utmost reluctance." Irvine apparently convinced provincial officials in Phila-

17. James Irvine's Bond & Securitys, June 6, 1763, Commissioners of Indian Affairs, 1757–1765, Gratz Collection, Case 14, Box 10, HSP.
18. "Journal of Col. James Burd While Building Fort Augusta at Shamokin, 1756–7," *P. Arch.* 2d ser., 2:796, 812; James Irvine, Invoice of Four Bundles of Peltry & Furrs, Commissioners of Indian Affairs, 1757–1765, Gratz Collection, Case 14, Box 10, HSP; and Shamokin Ledger B, June–December 1759, Shamokin Ledger, January 4–April 5, 1762, Fort Augusta Ledger A, April 8–November 24, 1762, Fort Augusta Ledger B, April 6, 1762–May 5, 1763, and Fort Augusta Ledger, May 6–August 10, 1763, HSP.

delphia that the trading operations at the fort had to be reorganized. The Commissioners of Indian Affairs, echoing Irvine's sentiments, wrote to Governor James Hamilton to order that the storekeeper's suggestions be implemented.[19]

The store at Fort Augusta preserved the valley Indian trade, but the fort itself did not fulfill the other goal of provincial leaders: it failed to make the region safe for hinterland residents. Colonial officials provided funds to create the fort in the mid-1750s to protect Indians and colonists living in the backcountry, but small groups of Indians continued to attack colonial settlements and some colonists preyed on both traveling and settled Indians in the less sparsely populated areas on the periphery of colonial settlement. The troops at Fort Augusta could not prevent such bushwhacking. When a party from the fort sought to track down hostile Indians after an attack, the troops were seldom able to locate the offenders in the dense woods and hilly terrain of the valley. Indeed, colonial officials' inability to understand the topography of the valley contributed to these problems. The fort was not situated atop one of the hills overlooking the confluence of the two branches of the river; it sat instead on a plain barely above water level, where potential enemies could look down on it from nearby hills, planning their raids on nearby Indians or colonists while the soldiers remained unaware of the danger.[20]

In addition, provincial officials failed to understand that local Indians viewed Fort Augusta with suspicion. Although many Indians traded there, the Iroquois were not pleased with its location. The fort lay along the major trail from Iroquoia to the homeland of the league's southern enemies, particularly the Cherokees. The Iroquois had originally agreed to the construction of the fort because of the hostilities between the English and the French; they believed it was built only for that purpose. "You said you would keep a Fort there as long as the War continued," Thomas King declared at Lancaster in 1762, "but that you did not want any of our Land there." The

19. James Irvine to Joseph Morris, May 26, 1763, Commissioners of Indian Affairs, 1757–1765, Gratz Collection, Case 14, Box 10, HSP; Commissioners of Indian Affairs to James Hamilton, n.d. [presumably 1763; form of letter identical to Irvine's letter to Morris], ibid.

20. On the problems experienced by soldiers at Fort Augusta see "Journal of Col. James Burd."

continued presence of the fort threatened relations between the Indians and the colonists, King argued. "For you to keep Soldiers there, is not the way to live peaceable," he noted. "Your Soldiers are very often very unruly, and our Warriors are unruly, and when such get together they do not agree, for as you have now made peace with all our Nations, there is no occasion for Soldiers to live there any longer." Hostilities between the Cherokees and Iroquois would continue, he argued, because the league had "been at War with them ever since we were created." But rather than accede to the Indians' requests, the provincial government asserted that tensions with the French prevented the removal of the soldiers from the fort. Seeking to maintain good relations with the Iroquois, these colonial leaders promised to order the soldiers to behave peacefully toward Indian warriors and hunters and expected the Indians to act peacefully toward the soldiers.[21]

In spite of the hostilities between provincial soldiers and Iroquois warriors and hunters, the Indians along the Susquehanna did not want the government to withdraw its agent from Fort Augusta. Indeed, even when Thomas King lamented the hostilities, he implored the Pennsylvania government to leave the store there. "I must tell you again these Soldiers must go away from Shamokin Fort," he declared at Lancaster, "I desire it, and let there only be Traders living there, you know who are the honest people; we desire that only honest people may live there, and that you will not be too hard with us, when they may buy our Skins and Furrs, and such things as we may have to sell. This will be the way for us to live peaceably together." In addition to trading opportunities, the Indians also wanted a blacksmith and gunsmith at Shamokin.[22]

Indians and provincial officials alike sought to maintain trade and hoped to keep it isolated from the tensions prevailing in this borderland. But occasional acts of violence marred intercultural relations. The Delaware sachem Teedyuscung died in 1763 when his cabin burned down at Wyoming under suspicious circumstances; the fire might have been set by disgruntled members of the Susquehannah Company in retribution for an Indian attack on company members

21. *PaCR*, 8:752–753, 768.
22. Ibid., 753.

at the town, although there is little evidence of their complicity.[23] The murder of the mason at Wyoming in the mid-1750s was more typical: a traveling band of Indians, possibly with no knowledge of the mason's work for the Indians at Wyoming, killed him for un-known reasons. His death demonstrated to colonists that this fron-tier was still potentially unsafe. Other attacks in the backcountry caused Indians and colonists to eye each other suspiciously, espe-cially during the French and Indian War.

Fearing conflicts between traveling Indians and colonists, Ham-ilton urged the Indians to use their old warrior path on their south-ward journeys, avoiding the colonial settlements between Harris' Ferry and "Potowmack." Hamilton's plea reflected the movement of colonists westward from the Philadelphia region, especially into southern Pennsylvania. But this population movement affected In-dians living in the upper Susquehanna Valley who traveled along the lower reaches of the river and nearby paths. South of Harris' Ferry, Hamilton noted, "the White people are settled very thick, so that should your Warriors now use that Path, frequent Differences be-tween them and the Inhabitants might probably arise, by means whereof the peace so lately established between us, may be endan-gered." Hamilton told the Indians that he had received "several Complaints of great mischief being done by the Indians" on their way to the treaty meeting and implored the warriors to "restrain your Young Men from committing any further Violence, or from taking any thing from the Inhabitants, in their return, for this must have a natural Tendency to raise ill Blood in the minds of the peo-ple." The Iroquois and other Susquehanna Indians, wanting to maintain peace with the colonists, agreed to use the path from Shamokin that ran along the "Foot of the Allegheny Hills" and away from the settlements.[24]

---

23. There is some dispute over whether Teedyuscung was murdered. Anthony F. C. Wallace and Francis Jennings claim he was deliberately killed; Paul A. W. Wallace believed the fire was accidental. See Anthony F. C. Wallace, *King of the Delawares: Teedyuscung, 1700–1763* (Philadelphia, 1949), 258–261; Jennings, "'Pennsylvania In-dians and the Iroquois," in Daniel K. Richter and James H. Merrell, eds., *Beyond the Covenant Chain: The Iroquois and Their Neighbors in Indian North America, 1600–1800* (Syracuse, N.Y., 1987), 90–91; and Paul A. W. Wallace, *Indians in Pennsylvania* (1961; rev. ed. Harrisburg, Pa., 1981), 183.

24. *PaCR*, 8:769–770, 772.

But though the Indians hoped to lessen contact between their warriors and colonial soldiers, they still wanted to trade with colonists. Thus they requested that the trader John Harris be well supplied. "We don't now desire a Store House should be kept at John Harris's for the Warriors," asserted the Onondaga chief Deogwanda, "but that he may be supplied with provisions & other necessaries for our Chiefs & old Men, as they pass to and fro *about* the good work of peace."[25] Indian leaders soon realized, however, that preserving peace in the backcountry entailed a redefinition of their relationship with colonists.

Toward Segregation

The defeat of the French and their Indian allies in the early 1760s was a watershed in the history of the upper Susquehanna Valley. Earlier only a few colonists lived in the region; Cherry Valley, located near the headwaters of the river, and Shamokin attracted only small groups of settlers. But after the French threat receded, colonists immediately began to plan settlements in the upper valley. Indeed, the movement of colonists into the region was an attractive way to ease the pressure of population on land farther east; the valley, with its fertile fields and numerous watercourses, had become well known because of the fur trade and was a logical place for settlement. But the efforts of colonists to migrate to the region displeased valley Indians, who wanted to retain possession of the area. Yet these Indians faced hard times; alcohol, diseases, and trespassing colonists all threatened their communities. By the mid-1760s many Indian and provincial leaders wanted to establish a boundary line separating their peoples.

In the early 1760s, in spite of the protests of Pennsylvania officials, the Susquehannah Company pressed its claim by trying to establish towns in the Wyoming region, sending two groups of settlers to the area. In 1762 ninety settlers arrived at Wyoming when most of the village Indians were attending a treaty meeting in Lancaster and quickly began to establish their settlement. According to the Pennsylvanian Daniel Brodhead, who went to the region "to discover the Pretences and Intentions of the Connecticut People," these set-

25. Ibid., 772.

tlers had cut fifteen tons of grass for their livestock; begun construction on three blockhouses for their defense; established connections with settlers in Minnisink, along the Delaware, and sent a party there to get flour; and sent another party to "New England to conduct 200 Families to their quiet Possession at Wyoming." The company members' optimism faded rapidly when the Wyoming Indians, along with a contingent of perhaps five hundred Iroquois and other Indian warriors, returned to the village. According to Brodhead, the Indians "ordered the Connecticut people to go away, and quit the Land, and said if they had not done so forthwith, the Indians would have killed every Man of them before they could have got into the Inhabitants." The company members, wisely sensing the danger, went back to New England.[26]

But the company did not give up. The following year it sent more settlers to Wyoming. This group fared even worse than the first. A party of Indian warriors found them at Wyoming and killed them. According to a report of some Pennsylvania soldiers who went there to chase off the Connecticut intruders, only the mutilated corpses of nine men and one woman remained. They had been "most cruelly butchered," the soldiers reported, "the woman was roasted, and had two Hinges in her Hands, supposed to be put in red hot, and several of the men had Awls thrust into their Eyes, and Spears, arrows, Pitchforks, &c sticking in their Bodies." The company attempted no further settlements in the region until after the Indians formally ceded much of the area in 1768.[27]

The Susquehannah Company's failures in the 1760s demonstrated more than the power of the valley Indians. The company's inability to people the Wyoming region showed how precarious was the expansion of settlements; colonists could not simply ride roughshod over the Indians in those areas.

But while the Susquehannah Company could not succeed, neither could the Indians. An epidemic had spread through Wyoming in 1762, killing, among others, Teedyuscung's wife. The following year Teedyuscung died in a fire. Their deaths prompted the other Indians at Wyoming to abandon the town and move to the West

26. "Narrative of Daniel Brodhead's Journey to Wyoming," *SCP*, 2:166–170. See *PaCR*, 8:730, for the number of Iroquois and other warriors at the Lancaster treaty meeting.

27. Extract from the *Pennsylvania Gazette* reprinted in *SCP*, 2:277; Joseph Shippen, Jr., to James Burd, October 21, 1763, ibid., 276–277.

Branch of the Susquehanna.[28] Throughout the valley, Indians continued to suffer from alcohol abuse. Some Indian sachems pleaded with colonial officials, especially Sir William Johnson, to stop the flow of rum into the backcountry, but traders still used alcohol to pay for furs from the Indians. The Indians also became much more aware of the dangers of colonial trespassers. They had rebuffed the Connecticut migrants who wanted to settle Wyoming in the early 1760s but knew they would not always succeed in repelling trespassers.

Both Indian and colonial leaders realized that they needed a genuine boundary line to separate the Indians from the rapidly growing colonial population. The Proclamation of 1763, which ruled that colonists must remain east of the crest of the Appalachian Mountains, was impossible to enforce and widely ignored. Colonists in Pennsylvania and New York had purchased extensive tracts of land from many tribes before the 1760s, but none of these early sales matched the amount of land that changed hands because of the Fort Stanwix treaty of 1768. The extent of the territory demanded serious commitment by both sides. More than twenty-two hundred Indians attended the conference to negotiate the sale, including leaders of the Iroquois, Shawnees, and Delawares. The colonial governments sent important representatives: Sir William Johnson, superintendent of Indian affairs, presided over the colonial delegation; Governor William Franklin and Chief Justice Frederick Smyth from New Jersey attended to press an earlier claim that involved their province; Thomas Walker, who named the Cumberland Gap and later explored other rivers on the western edges of colonial settlement, represented Virginia; Richard Peters and James Tilghman pressed the views of the Pennsylvania government. Deputy agents of Indian affairs George Croghan, Daniel Claus, and Guy Johnson—all of them knowledgeable about the backcountry—joined the colonial representatives. Never before had so many prominent people attended a land sale in the upper valley.[29]

At Fort Stanwix colonial leaders sought to purchase much of central New York and Pennsylvania, as well as additional territory to the south; they also wanted the Indians to relinquish any outstanding claims to already colonized areas. These officials were seeking a

28. Wallace, *Indians in Pennsylvania*, 156–158.
29. *NY Col. Docs.*, 8:112.

boundary line that would divide colonists and Indians throughout much of British North America. They felt that a carefully negotiated settlement with the Indians would be more enforceable than the Proclamation of 1763; they and the Indians both knew that colonists were trying to steal land from the Indians. "You know Brethren," Johnson told them at the meeting,

> that the encroachments upon your Lands have been always one of your principal subjects of complaint, and that so far as it could be done endeavors have not been wanting for your obtaining Redress. But it was a difficult Task, and generally unsuccessfull—for altho' the Provinces have bounds between each other, there are no certain Bounds between them & you, And thereby not only several of our people ignorant in Indian Affairs have advanced too far into your country, but also many of your own people through the want of such a Line have been deceived in the Sales they have made or in the limits they have set to our respective claims.[30]

Johnson used the Indians' experience with these land-hungry colonists to gain as much land as possible for the British. He pleaded with the Indians to push the northern edge of the boundary farther west than the Indians initially wanted, insisting that their preferred boundary line would interfere with lands at Oriskany already sold to colonists. The Indians' proposed line also approached colonial settlements, thus rendering "its duration very uncertain from the great increase of our people, whereas by giving them more room the Boundary would be so well known, and secured by Laws before there would be occasion to invade it, that people would act with extreem caution and rather go to other unsettled parts than attempt to transgress an agreement so well defended." The Indians eventually relented, although they wanted more money to compensate for the additional territory.[31]

The Indians agreed to part with the lands only after the treaty included provisions to protect existing Indian villages. While the Indian leaders stressed the need for a boundary line, they realized that it should demarcate only the limits of settlement, not halt all interaction between Indians and colonists. "Now we have made so large a Cession to the King of such a valuable and Extensive Country," an

30. Ibid., 118.
31. Ibid., 123–126.

unidentified Indian spokesman declared near the end of the treaty meeting, "We do expect it as the Terms of our Agreement that strict regard be paid to all our reasonable desires." He then enumerated the Indians' terms: "We do now on this behalf and in the name of all our Warriors of every Nation, condition that all our Warriors shall have the liberty of hunting throughout the Country as they have no other means of subsistence and as your people have not the same occasions or inclinations—That the White people be restricted from hunting on our side of the Line to prevent contensions between us."[32]

The Indians also wanted roads and water routes to remain open to them so they might continue to trade and negotiate with colonists in New York and Pennsylvania. The treaty reflected these concerns. When the dividing line followed the Susquehanna or one of its tributaries, it ran along a specific bank of the watercourse. This often worked to the Indians' advantage. Along the West Branch of the Susquehanna, for example, the boundary was along the south side of the river, giving the Indians claim to the water itself, an important source for fish and a prime area for catching game. Similarly, when the line followed Tiadaghton Creek and the North Branch of the Susquehanna from Awandae Creek to Owego, the Indians again controlled the water.[33]

Besides access to transportation routes, the Indians sought to maintain trade with colonists. "We were promised that when the war was over," one of the Indian speakers, referring to the French and Indian War, told the meeting, "we should have Trade in plenty, Goods cheap and honest men to deal with us and that we should have proper persons to manage all this." The Indians also desired "proper persons in our Countrys to manage affairs and smiths to mend our arms and implements."[34]

The final demand of the Indians concerned tribal settlements that would lie on the eastern side of the boundary line. The Indians refused to part with these towns and the areas that surrounded them. These lands, which included Wyoming and Great Island on the West Branch of the Susquehanna, were to remain the "sole property" of the Indians who were living on them, "at their disposal both now, and so long as the sun shines," although residents would have to

32. Ibid., 127.
33. Ibid., 135–137.
34. Ibid., 126.

abide by any previous deals granting parts of these lands to colonists. In addition, the Indians kept the territory between Owego and Oswego because, they claimed, this was "full of our Towns & Villages," and they could not "be expected to part with what lies at our Doors, besides your people are come already to close to us." The Indians reminded the colonists that the deed obtained by John Lydius in Albany in 1754 was invalid. The colonists agreed to these demands, realizing that the land the Indians reserved on the eastern side of the boundary line was a small fraction of the purchase. They no doubt assumed that these Indians would soon move away, leaving the entire region open for colonial settlement.[35]

The Indians at Fort Stanwix knew the treaty was necessary to protect their communities from land-hungry colonists. "We have been for some time deliberating on what you said concerning a Line between the English and us," their speaker told Sir William Johnson on October 28, "& we are sensible it would be for our mutual advantage if it were not transgressed, but dayly experience teaches us that we cannot have any great dependance on the white People, and that they will forget their agreements for the sake of our Lands." The fear of colonists' encroaching on their land forced the Indians to accept the payment offered for the territory, even if it was insufficient compensation for such a vast tract. "We now tell the King," one of their speakers said on November 1, "that we have now given to him a great and valuable Country, and we know that what we shall now get for it must be far short of its value." In addition to access to trade routes and hunting areas, the Indians received £10,460 7s. 3d. in cash for their lands. One representative from each of the tribes in the Iroquois Confederacy signed the treaty, thereby forever changing the lives of the Indians of the upper Susquehanna Valley.[36]

It appeared that at Fort Stanwix Indian and provincial leaders had reconciled their mutual interests and also achieved two important goals: the maintenance of the fur trade and the preservation of peace along the periphery of British North America. Those present believed that the treaty brought the promise of economic stability for competing parties; Indians could continue to hunt the remaining animals, and colonists could gain land for new farms.

35. Ibid., 123, 128, 136, 122.
36. Ibid., 120, 127, 136–137.

The treaty ushered in a new age in the upper valley. Several thousand colonists migrated to the area in the next decade, further expanding British settlement into the backcountry. These colonists, unlike the traders who preceded them, cared little about maintaining economic ties to the Indians. Like other colonists throughout eastern North America, the migrants to the upper Susquehanna Valley did not want Indian neighbors, but they soon discovered that the Indians were not yet ready to abandon the region altogether.

5 The Colonists' Economy

In the years following the Fort Stanwix treaty, several thousand colonists migrated to the upper valley. The vast majority of these settlers lived on farms. But they were not the yeoman settlers of lore, struggling independently against hostile Indians and uncooperative weather to clear their fields and reach self-sufficiency. Rather, they were part of an organized attempt to expand commercial agrarian settlements into the Appalachians.

Wealthy landlords directed much of the emerging valley economy, orchestrating it far more efficiently than the traders who had preceded them had organized their enterprises. From the late 1760s into the late 1770s the economy of the upper Susquehanna Valley resembled those of other newly colonized parts of British America. Most colonists farmed. Others milled grain for local consumption and lumber for buildings, ran ferries across waterways, cut roads through the forests, and transported goods from external sources to the valley and valley-produced commodities to external markets. Landlords and their agents organized new settlements, luring thousands of colonists into the region. Many of these migrants possessed limited wealth, and they realized that it made the most economic sense to become tenants of the wealthy; even those who could afford a freehold became customers of landlords' mills and stores.

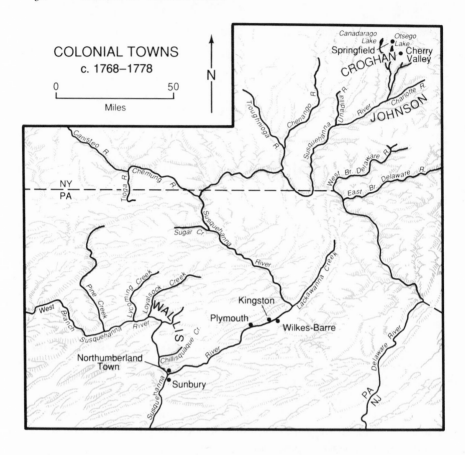

Crown and provincial officials provided valuable support to the landlords, many of whom had favorable political connections, often to colonial officials responsible for the distribution of western lands. Indeed, some of the most successful landlords held positions in provincial governments. Landlords also benefited from the decisions of local courts and, at times, settlers' committees. These courts and committees supported local economic development, seeking to protect property and all forms of investment.

Although many colonists battled over rights to specific parcels of land, they shared a common goal: to establish stable agricultural communities connected by water or overland routes to markets outside the valley so they could exchange the fruits of their labor for goods made elsewhere. Like the earlier fur traders, they sought to become part of a larger economic world.

Buying and Selling Land

After the Fort Stanwix treaty a group of wealthy investors purchased extensive tracts of land in the upper valley. Western land seemed to be a promising investment, the source of perhaps the greatest potential profit in the expanding colonial economy. To succeed, these would-be landlords needed to learn about the valley real estate market and to become experts, or hire people who were, in various tasks: acquiring titles from the provincial land offices in New York and Pennsylvania; settling outstanding Indian claims to their tracts; arranging the necessary surveys and patents for their lands; knowing when to buy and when to sell; understanding the region's geography sufficiently to know which lands were the best investments. Successful investors recognized that land had replaced peltry as the most important commodity in the region, and they struggled hard to gain control of tracts with access to the region's primary avenue of transportation, the Susquehanna River and its tributaries.

At first, would-be landlords had to contend with existing provincial laws limiting the amount of land any single person could acquire in the newly opened region. In both New York and Pennsylvania the allocation of land grants had been politically motivated since the early years. In New York, governors had used their control over land to enhance their sometimes precarious positions; granting patents of sizable tracts to political allies created a landed interest of powerful associates who the governors hoped would support their positions. But extensive land grants in New York throughout the early eighteenth century had led to protests and prompted the colonial government to vacate patents that were not settled within a certain time, usually three years. Similarly, to discourage engrossment of large tracts for speculative purposes, new laws dictated that no individual receive more than two thousand acres in a single patent; the limit was later reduced to one thousand acres.[1]

These laws did not prevent wealthy New Yorkers from obtaining large tracts in the upper Susquehanna Valley by using the names of other people to file for the patents and then transferring the rights

---

1. Ruth L. Higgins, *Expansion in New York, with Especial Reference to the Eighteenth Century* (Columbus, Ohio, 1931), 71–73, 75; Patricia U. Bonomi, *A Factious People: Politics and Society in Colonial New York* (New York, 1971), 203–205; Jack H. Christenson, "The Administration of Land Policy in Colonial New York" (Ph.D. diss., State University of New York at Albany, 1976).

to themselves. Sir William Johnson enlisted the help of twenty-five other people to fill out his patent along the Susquehanna in March 1770. Others did the same. George Croghan, an assistant superintendent of Indian affairs under Johnson and an avid land speculator, obtained a tract of forty thousand acres between Cherry Valley and the Susquehanna in the late 1760s employing the surveyor Alexander McKee and thirty-eight others to obtain the necessary patents. When a survey revealed that this area contained one hundred thousand acres, Croghan was undaunted; he soon had ninety-nine people willing to apply for the patents, which enabled him to gain control of the entire tract.[2]

The Pennsylvania provincial government had established even stricter provisions on allocations of land in the enormous territory obtained in 1768, limiting parcels to three hundred acres and imposing strict rules for surveying and payment, but some people still managed to gain enormous tracts. Among them, not surprisingly, were the heirs of William Penn, who were not bound by the existing legislation. They promptly reserved several manors in the upper Susquehanna Valley, totaling 72,548 acres, for their own use. A group of veteran officers from Henry Bouquet's French and Indian War campaign also received a substantial tract near the confluence of the river's two branches; when they divided the lands, each officer had far more than three hundred acres.[3]

Other colonists also evaded the laws. Some obtained multiple three-hundred-acre grants by using the same tactics as speculators in New York; once alleged purchasers received the lands, they transferred title to the person who had organized the acquisition. Thus Samuel Wallis, a Philadelphia merchant who was establishing an extensive estate and trading center at Muncy, filed sixty-four separate applications in the land office on April 3, 1769, the day it began to

2. Johnson to Banyar, March 10, 17, 1770, *Johnson Papers*, 12:787–788, 794; Albert T. Volwiler, *George Croghan and the Westward Movement, 1741–1782* (Cleveland, Ohio, 1926), 249, 251; Almon W. Lauber, "The Valleys of the Susquehanna and the Delaware," in Alexander C. Flick, ed., *History of the State of New York*, 10 vols. (New York, 1934), 5:110–113; Higgins, *Expansion in New York*, 71–75. The names of the patentees can be found in List of Patent Lands to be Sold for Arrears of Quit Rents, 3, typescript in the Office of the Montgomery County Historian, Fonda, N.Y.

3. "Draughts of the Proprietary Manors in the Province of Pennsylvania," *P. Arch.* 3d ser., 4, passim; "Minutes of the Proceedings of the Officers of the Pennsylvania Regiment, between 1764 and 1774 in relation to their obtaining a grant of land upon the west branch of the Susquehanna," *Pennsylvania Historical Society Collections* 1 (1853), 94–118.

receive requests for lands in the newly acquired parts of the upper valley. Wallis did not intend to keep all of these tracts for himself. In July 1771 he entered into an agreement with William Scull, a provincial surveyor, and John Scull, a merchant from Reading, to divide some of the lands with them, sharing the costs of the purchase and returning the necessary surveys.[4]

Johnson, Croghan, Wallis, and a few others dominated the real estate market in the region, but they did not try to retain possession of all of the land for themselves. Rather, they profited handsomely by obtaining large tracts for others with sufficient capital. Sarah Wistar, a single Philadelphia woman, employed Wallis to arrange a purchase of three thousand acres in the upper valley for her. The venture was profitable for Wallis, who received £10 for each hundred acres he passed on to Wistar.[5] Reuben Haines, a Philadelphia brewer and sometime associate of Wallis, agreed to purchase eighteen hundred acres of land in Northumberland County for Daniel Williams, a Philadelphia merchant; for the clear titles, Williams paid Haines £6 for every hundred acres. Williams also agreed to pay Haines £10 for every hundred acres he obtained in a fifteen-hundred-acre tract nearby. Haines knew that such arrangements were not always successful and was pleased when he was able to obtain lands for Williams and others. "Its an Easie Matter to make a contract," he wrote to Wallis in 1777, "but the Beauty is in the Accomplishing it."[6]

Wallis and Haines were recognized in Philadelphia for their knowledge of the valley real estate market and benefited from many contracts to obtain lands. Owen Biddle, a Philadelphia watch- and clockmaker, agreed to give Wallis a third of a twenty-eight-hundred-acre grant owed him by the provincial government; to receive these lands, Wallis had to find appropriate tracts and have them surveyed and returned in Biddle's name, tasks he soon accomplished. Haines arranged an even more profitable alliance with Thomas Willing and Robert Morris, two prominent merchants in Philadelphia, who

4. Agreement between Samuel Wallis, William Scull, and John Scull, July 11, 1771, Wallis Papers, Reel 6, HSP.

5. Articles of Agreement between Samuel Wallis and Sarah Wistar, February 26, 1773, Wallis Papers, Reel 6; Indenture between Wallis and Wistar, June 21, 1775, Wistar Papers, Case 14, Box 17, HSP; Reuben Haines to an unknown person, presumably Wallis, February 10, 1774, Wallis Papers, Reel 6.

6. Agreement between Daniel Williams and Reuben Haines, August 16, 1773, and Haines to Wallis, August 24, 1777, Wallis Papers, Reel 6.

would rise to fame during and after the Revolution. Haines organized the purchase of approximately thirty-four thousand acres in the upper valley for Willing and Morris, receiving £14 for every hundred acres he obtained near the West Branch of the Susquehanna and £16 for every hundred acres he acquired for them near the East Branch. Haines, recognizing the potential value of the lands, then agreed to purchase one-fourth of the lands from Willing and Morris.[7]

Those who succeeded in the real estate market often had favorable political connections in addition to good business sense and knowledge of how to avoid provincial laws. In New York many of those who prospered had contracts with Goldsbrow Banyar, the secretary of the province responsible for the issuing of patents. Banyar and Johnson corresponded frequently about land in the upper valley. Banyar helped Alexander and Hugh Wallace organize their valley holdings; he also managed George Clarke's lands in Cherry Valley. The Wallaces certainly benefited from their association with Banyar; their twenty-eight-thousand-acre patent along the Susquehanna, one of the most desirable tracts in central New York because of its proximity to the river, would have been unavailable to anyone who lacked connections to the provincial land office.[8]

Acquiring titles to land was only the first order of business for the landlords. Next they had to settle outstanding Indian claims to these lands. Valley Indians, no strangers to the colonists' thirst for land, knew the value of their holdings. Indeed, in 1764 one group of Indians in Cherry Valley had placed such a high price on a piece of good land that many prospective buyers could not afford to purchase it.[9]

Previous contact with valley Indians proved especially helpful to would-be purchasers. Sir William Johnson met little resistance from the Iroquois when he began to settle himself and his tenants on the tract of land he bought from the Indians along the Susquehanna. Indeed, he informed Banyar that he seemingly had more trouble

7. Agreement between Wallis and Owen Biddle, July 1773, and Agreement between Reuben Haines and Robert Morris and Thomas Willing, May 7, 1774, ibid.

8. Banyar to Johnson, December 15, 1760, *Johnson Papers*, 3:286. For the Wallaces' grant, see List of Patent Lands to be Sold for Arrears of Quit Rents, 7. For Banyar's involvement with Clarke lands, see Banyar Papers, Box 6, NYHS. Material from Banyar Papers is used courtesy of the New-York Historical Society.

9. Banyar to John Line, July 16, 1764, Banyar Papers, Box 6, NYHS.

obtaining a clear patent than he did getting the local Indians to approve of his purchase. But others had more troubled relations with the Indians. The Reverend John C. Hartwick had tried to purchase a tract south of Lake Otsego since the early 1760s but failed to pay the Indians what he had promised. The dispute had been going on for some years when a delegation of Indians from Canajoharie visited Johnson in February 1767 requesting his assistance to resolve the matter. In April of that year, another group from the same town returned to Johnson Hall "and Spoke much [against] Mr. Hardwick the Minister for taking underhand measures to get their land, and for not paying them the Consideration money for another tract formerly purchased of them." Two years later, the controversy remained unresolved; two Indians brought suit in New York against Hartwick for the still apparently unpaid purchase, although Hartwick's absence from the colony prevented the case from going forward.[10]

After obtaining patents and Indian titles to tracts in the valley, landlords set about their primary goal: to make a profit from the land. Landlords capitalized quickly on their investments when they purchased tracts and then promptly sold the land. Johnson entertained offers for parts of his Susquehanna holdings and sold some parcels. In February 1773 he sold a 147-acre tract in his Charlotte River patent to Henry Servis for approximately £67; the following year he sold James Strahon 177 acres in this same patent for £88 10s. Johnson informed New Jersey Governor William Franklin that, contrary to what Franklin had heard, the land in the upper valley "is perhaps as rich & Valuable for the Generality as any Land whatsoever, & this is allowed by some who have carefully viewed & are now Sollicitting me to dispose of it." Franklin, who had been in the region to attend the Fort Stanwix treaty meeting, shared Johnson's views. Within a short time he too obtained control of a large tract in the valley.[11] At times, profits came quickly. James Wilson, for example, purchased a 300-acre tract on the north side of Buffalo Valley for the token amount of 5s. in March 1772 from John Moore, the

10. Johnson to Banyar, March 21, Xcbr 22, 1769, November 5, 1770, *Johnson Papers*, 12:706, 767, 875; Journal of Indian Affairs, February 9, 1767, April 6, 1767, ibid., 269–270, 303; John Tabor Kempe to Johnson, March 11, 1769, ibid., 702–703.
11. Tryon County Deed Book 1, 257–258, 121–123, typescript in Office of the Montgomery County Historian; Joseph Chew to Johnson, June 20, 1770, *Johnson Papers*, 12:825–826; Johnson to William Franklin, June 12, 1769, ibid., 728–729.

original patentee; presumably Wilson had arranged the original allocation from the land office and the payment merely formalized the
conveyance from Moore. Two months after he acquired the title,
Wilson sold the tract for £200 Pennsylvania currency.[12]

Prospective purchasers tried to get the best possible prices for
their tracts. Josias Swart and John Becker attempted to buy a four-
thousand-acre tract on the west side of the Susquehanna from Johnson, believing they should receive more favorable terms than later
settlers. "It will be no disadvantage to You letting us have the lands,"
they wrote to Johnson in March 1772, "as it will be great encouragement to others to make purchase Once we break the Ice." Swart and
Becker knew that subsequent settlers would benefit from any improvements in the area. "The first Settlers on Any lands Should
have them on better terms than those that dont purchase untill they
See others Settled before them as they run A risque of living alone
for Sometime which woud lend very much to their disadvantage."[13]

To attract settlers, landlords sought access to the Susquehanna or
one of its major tributaries. Johnson's lands lay between other large
patents in the eastern section of the valley and the river; this location
gave him control over shipping and milling operations and thus
raised the value of his holdings. "Col. [Staats Long] Morris impor-
tuned me greatly to let him have as much of my Tract on the Sus-
quahana as lay between him & the River," Johnson wrote to Banyar
in October 1769. "As did all the others who have lands on either side
of that River & Adageghtengy Creek [Charlotte River], which I
promised they should [have] on paying me £10 per Hundred Acres
for my Indian purchase." He was also acutely aware of the struggle
between Pennsylvania and Connecticut over lands near the river in
Pennsylvania. "I could I am certain if patented," Johnson boasted to
Banyar in May 1769, "dispose of every foot of it in a Months time to
New England People, who have been lately about it, & wanted Sevrl.
Townships."[14]

The primary goal of those interested in the area was to gain possession of the best land. In the eighteenth century, the pursuit of
rich, arable land led many to acquire low-lying plots near rivers. In

12. Northumberland County Deed Book A, page number illegible, NCCH.
13. Josias Swart and John Becker to Johnson, March 18, 1772, *Johnson Papers*,
8:422–423; see also David McKinney to Johnson, December 5, 1770, ibid., 7:1031.
14. Johnson to Banyar, October 5, May 11, 1769, ibid., 12:754, 719.

the upper valley and elsewhere, those seeking such land were correct in believing them among the most productive in the region because periodic flooding of the river enriched the soil. In addition, land-owners whose tracts bordered on or included navigable waterways had the advantage of access to downstream markets; land adjoining any navigable watercourse thus attracted prospective purchasers. Johnson recognized the value of the tract owned by Banyar and the Wallaces; several people had applied to him for this land, thinking he owned it. "All seem more desireous of Settling along the Sus-quahana Banks," he wrote to Banyar in June 1770, "than any other part of the Country." Reuben Haines, who was bound by contracts to obtain "good Arable land" for others, was especially interested in obtaining clear title to lands along Toby's Creek and Tunckhannock Creek. "The Land on Tobys Creek is some of the best," he wrote in 1774, and he was "Determined to get some if not all Hook or by Crook."[15]

While investors realized that the best lands were those that lay along or near the Susquehanna and its major tributaries, woodland also commanded high prices. When James Whitelaw traveled from Philadelphia to Sunbury scouting lands for a settlement company in July 1773, he found that good land was still available in the valley, but it was expensive. Whitelaw's party spent time, he wrote, "inform-ing ourselves about the lands here and on the other parts of the Susquhanna, which had been much recommended to us by some people in Philadelphia but we found that there was no one place large enough for our purpose but plenty too large for our money, as wood land sells here from 20 to 50 shillings pr. acre."[16]

Although some colonists knew which land could be resold quickly and succeeded in their speculative ventures, others failed miserably and became bankrupt victims of their own greed. None collapsed more spectacularly than George Croghan, and his failure reveals much about the market in western lands. Johnson had appointed Croghan to the position of deputy commissioner of Indian affairs

15. Johnson to Banyar, June 28, 1770, ibid., 829–830; Haines to unnamed person, presumably Wallis, February 10, 1774, Wallis Papers, Reel 6. The wording in the contract comes from Haines's agreement with Daniel Williams, August 16, 1773, ibid.; similar wording also appeared in Haines's contract with Willing and Morris, May 7, 1774, ibid.

16. "Journal of General James Whitelaw, Surveyor-General of Vermont," *Proceed-ings of the Vermont Historical Society* (1905–1906), 134; Wallis Papers, Reel 6, passim.

for the Susquehanna River Indians, and Croghan knew the region well and had the necessary political connections to obtain patents to large tracts near the headwaters of the Susquehanna. After obtaining patents for two 9,000-acre tracts near Cherry Valley in February 1770, he purchased more land in the area: the 40,000-acre Skinner patent southeast of his planned Belvedere township near Cherry Valley; the 40,000-acre McKee patent southwest of Belvedere; the Butler or Tunaderry patent of 47,000 acres southeast of his Otsego patent; and the 1,893-acre Bowen patent at the headwaters of Schoharie Creek. Within four years Croghan obtained approximately 250,000 acres in the upper valley, becoming the largest landholder in the area. His associates quickly signed over their interest in his patents. No Indian group contested his claims, probably because he was well acquainted with the Indians and purchased his lands according to the accepted customs.[17]

Croghan controlled land that was well situated, with ready access to Lake Otsego, the Susquehanna, and the developing settlement at Cherry Valley. When Richard Smith traveled through the upper valley surveying the area for the Burlington Company of New Jersey, he found Croghan in the midst of developing his estate along the shores of Lake Otsego. He had, Smith wrote, "Carpenters and other Men at Work preparing to build Two Dwelling Houses and 5 or 6 Out Houses." Croghan also had powerful friends and business associates, and he kept well informed about the workings of colonial governments.[18]

But Croghan's speculations in the upper Susquehanna Valley differed dramatically from those of other large landholders: he purchased land solely on credit, and his estimates of the worth of some properties were wrong. Croghan believed he would make great profit in Vandalia, a settlement proposed to stretch from the Ohio River to the Greenbriar River and including much of modern West Virginia, and he mortgaged his other holdings to obtain land there. But the Vandalia settlement failed, and Croghan's creditors demanded payment, forcing him to sell his assets, including his one-

17. Volwiler, *Croghan and the Westward Movement*, 251–252.
18. [Richard Smith], *A Tour of Four Great Rivers*, ed. Francis Halsey (New York, 1906), 36.

quarter of a million acres in the upper valley. By April 1775 he no longer owned land along the Susquehanna.[19]

Croghan's failure demonstrated that it was not always easy to make a profit in land speculation. Those who succeeded understood the relationship between their capital and their desires. They knew that success depended on the ability to manage their estates, not merely to accumulate land titles. Like fur traders who encouraged local Indians to overhunt peltry supplies and the valley Indians who hunted the animals, Croghan failed to understand the long-term consequences of his actions. Overly optimistic about his prospects, he realized too late that success in western land development did not always go to those who gained the most land. He could have learned a valuable lesson from other speculators, who, instead of concentrating solely on real estate investments, focused their energies on obtaining the commodity most needed for success: labor.

Landlords and Tenants

The landlords who prospered were those who attracted people to their holdings. For these investors, claiming the land was only the first step in creating an agrarian economy in the upper Susquehanna Valley. Land was useless without people to work it. Settlers would "improve" the land, modify the natural environment, and make it more suitable for farming.[20]

The economics of tenancy in the backcountry were understood by landlords and tenants alike. All realized that the landlords' lease arrangements had to be attractive because prospective settlers could purchase land in much of the backcountry. Thus landlords had to compete with one of the basic and well-known aspects of the colonial economy: the very real possibility that most adults could acquire a freehold. Indeed, land prices were so reasonable that even newly arriving immigrants, escaping burdensome tenancy in Britain, could

19. Volwiler, *Croghan and the Westward Movement*, 241, 279–287. The sale of Croghan's lands continued for years; see the notes of judgments and mortgages on Croghan's estate, Banyar Papers, Box 6, NYSH.

20. See William Cronon, *Changes in the Land: Indians, Colonists, and the Ecology of New England* (New York, 1983), 77–78.

buy land. Goldsbrow Banyar summed up the matter concisely. "In a Country where there is such Plenty of unsettled Lands," he wrote to the Reverend Samuel Dunlop in August 1761, "I am sensible People who can afford it would rather purchase than be burthen'd with a perpetual Rent even tho. low."[21]

Prospective tenants recognized their favorable position. Allan Mac-Donell, seeking lands for himself and others to lease, believed that landlords needed to court prospective tenants. MacDonell had heard about Johnson's lands, and in November 1773 he informed Johnson that tenants would be attracted if Johnson provided families with a year's "Maintenance," presumably a supply of seed, food, livestock, and necessary tools and shelter. "If their endeavours are found worthy," MacDonell wrote, they would then owe Johnson a cow and a horse or their value. In addition, prospective tenants wanted access to markets, sawmills, and gristmills. MacDonell sought land "in our Vicinity in order that such of our friends & Countrymen as will incline to follow our fate may sit down in our Neighborhood." It is unclear whether Johnson accepted all of Mac-Donell's terms, but he did attract tenants to his lands even before several legal questions involving the lands were settled. "I am daily Settling People on my long Tract alias *Adageghteinge*," he wrote to Banyar in November 1770, "but am at a great loss for the want of the Draft or Survey of it, which I wrote for Several times."[22]

The tenants on lands that Banyar managed also told him how to attract settlers. Peter Martin, a prospective tenant for George Clarke's lands in Cherry Valley, explained that they would want a gristmill, sawmill, meetinghouse, and school. In addition, Martin wrote to Banyar, tenants wished "that our Rentes may not be uncertain For if it should our Improvementes will be of much less value than at present." Both landlords and tenants realized that tenants

---

21. Banyar to Dunlop, August 28, 1761, Banyar Papers, Box 6, NYHS. All could understand Governor William Tryon's comments on observing the arrival of a shipload of immigrants from the Isle of Skye. Rather than being forced off estates because of rising rents, Tryon wrote to the earl of Dartmouth in November 1773, "these new Settlers purchase uncultivated Patented Lands on such easie terms as they can agree upon with the Proprietors." Prospering in their new settlements, Tryon continued, "they are encouraged to send invitations to their Countrymen to come over to them. . . . A Recommendation that very much promotes the Emigration to these Colonies" (Tryon to Dartmouth, November 2, 1773, CO 5/1104, f. 454).

22. Allan MacDonell to Johnson, November 14, 1773, *Johnson Papers*, 12:1041–1042; Johnson to Banyar, November 5, 1770, ibid., 875.

were in a favorable position and could find other landlords if they became dissatisfied, as Johnson learned through experience when several of his tenants moved to Pennsylvania in July 1769.[23]

In the effort to obtain and keep agricultural workers, landlords enhanced economic opportunities for their tenants. Johnson financed the cutting of a road from his settlements to the Schoharie so his tenants would have easier access to other colonial settlements. He encouraged one of his tenants to construct a gristmill, even though this effort would deprive Johnson of income he might have received from running his own mill.[24]

Nothing encouraged settlement more than favorable leasing terms. The leases offered to tenants reflected the landlords' desire for long-term economic stability, which could be achieved only if sufficient labor were available to work their holdings. According to Richard Smith, the valley landlord Augustine Prevost, son-in-law of George Croghan, gave "wages" ranging from 55s. to £3 per month to maintain several families living near his estate at Lake Otsego; the families presumably performed labor in exchange. On George Clarke's lands in Cherry Valley, tenants paid no rent for the first ten years; the next seven years cost 3d. sterling an acre; after seventeen years, the rent increased to 6d. sterling an acre. Clarke's tenancy terms changed only slightly over time. In the 1760s he offered his tenants free rent for seven years, then seven years at 3d. sterling, and then a full rent of 6d. sterling per year.[25]

Clarke's leasing tactics proved successful. By 1773, he had twenty-five tenants and 3,350 acres leased, almost all of the arable land in his Cherry Valley patent. Landlords in the upper valley recognized that they could not charge the higher rents demanded in more settled areas. None in the upper valley could have received the $15 to $20 annual rent charged to most tenants on Philipsburgh Manor in Westchester County in the same period.[26] Living in the backcountry,

23. Peter Martin to Banyar, September 22, 1762, Banyar Papers, Box 6, NYHS; James Tilghman to Johnson, July 20, 1769, *Johnson Papers*, 7:64.

24. Johnson to Banyar, June 28, 1770, *Johnson Papers*, 12:829–30.

25. [Smith], *Tour of Four Great Rivers*, 34; Copy of Agreements between Clarke, Lindesay and Samuel Dunlop, November 1738–October 1743, and Dunlop to Banyar, March 17, 1773, Banyar Papers, Box 6, NYHS.

26. Dunlop to Banyar, August 28, 1761, March 17, 1773, Banyar Papers, Box 6, NYHS; Beatrice G. Reubens, "Pre-Emptive Rights in the Disposition of a Confiscated Estate: Philipsburgh Manor, New York," *WMQ* 3d ser., 22 (1965), 440.

which entailed isolation from the comforts of society at least during the first years of settlement, was less appealing than taking up lands in more settled areas, where tenants and their families could attend church and school and find stores and artisans nearby to provide them with desirable goods. Landlords knew that moving to the valley had a high social cost for their tenants, and to keep the lands occupied they often demanded only minimal rents. Some leased their lands for as little as one peppercorn per year.[27]

Throughout the valley many people with less land than Johnson, Banyar, or Clarke but with as great a need for labor attracted people to their tracts. Turbutt Francis, who received 4,038 acres along the West Branch in 1774 in exchange for his earlier efforts to defend Pennsylvania from the French and western Indians, leased his lands to tenants who grew wheat, rye, and oats. By August 1775 James Potter had six people farming the two hundred cleared acres of his Penn's Valley farm, but, according to one colonial observer, they were not sufficient to tend the estate properly.[28]

Tenancy spread throughout the valley, almost always along the banks of the Susquehanna or one of its tributaries. Along Buffalo Creek, for example, many owners of no more than several hundred acres had tenants. Thomas and Sarah Lemmon's tenant, John Buchanon, contracted to perform services for them: building a house, clearing ten acres of field and two acres of meadow, and planting ten apple trees and twenty cherry trees. Others similarly worked their landlords' holdings. James Moore farmed twenty-five acres of Joseph Green's land; John Kilday cultivated ten acres of John Reed's tract; William Bennett and his son worked William Blythe's lands, running the gristmill and cultivating twenty acres. Some tenants, like Nicholas Leas, who lived on John Boal's land, and David Duncan, who lived on Ludwig Derr's property, did not cultivate land for themselves but kept livestock. Robert Cooper lived with William Bennett, a tenant of Blythe's; Cooper kept a horse and two cows and was apparently a sharecropper for Bennett. John Davis, a mason, lived with Abel Reese but did not have any livestock or cultivate any

27. See, for example, the agreement between Robert Adems and John Johnson et al., September 20, 1771, Tryon County Deed Book 1, 97–99, and the agreement between Christian Earnest and John Kline, Jr., September 1, 1774, ibid., 129–133.

28. Robert Albion and Leonidas Dodson, eds., *Philip Vickers Fithian: Journal, 1775–1776, Written on the Virginia-Pennsylvania Frontier and in the Army around New York* (Princeton, N.J., 1934), 88–89.

land for himself; presumably he exchanged his skills for food and shelter.[29]

Tenancy existed also in Wyoming, where the Susquehannah Company gained control of land long enough to establish a farming community. After the 1768 treaty, migrants came from Connecticut hoping to set up a New England–style town in which all residents owned land. According to Hector St. John de Crèvecoeur, who traveled through the area in 1774 and 1776, approximately 1,250 families occupied the territory following the signing of the Fort Stanwix treaty. In 1774 Crèvecoeur believed that the company's settlements demonstrated the superiority of America over Europe. "The equal partition of the lands," he wrote in his journal, "the ignorance in which we happily are of that accursed feudal system which ruins everything in Europa promises us a new set of prejudices and manners which I hope will establish here a degree of happiness to the human race far superior to what is enjoyed by any civilised nation on the globe." Two years later, the situation at Wyoming was even better. "I observed with pleasure that a better conducted plan of industry prevailed throughout, that many of the pristine temporary huts and humble log houses were converted into neater and more substantial habitations," Crèvecoeur wrote in his journal. "I saw everywhere the strong marks of growing wealth and population; it was really extremely pleasing to navigate up and down this river and to contemplate the numerous settlements and buildings erected at different distances from these shores."[30]

But Crèvecoeur failed to describe the profound distinctions between the landlords and tenants in the upper valley. He must have seen some settlers in Wyoming prospering, eating off fine porcelain with silver forks and spoons, sleeping on feather beds, and managing vast estates. Others, however, owned only a horse or cow and maybe a few rudimentary kitchen utensils. Indeed, according to in-

29. *ABV*, 34, 67–74. Tenancy among small landholders was not unique to the upper Susquehanna Valley; see, for example, Lee Soltow and Kenneth W. Keller, "Tenancy and Asset-Holding in Late Eighteenth-Century Washington County, Pennsylvania," *Western Pennsylvania Historical Magazine* 65 (1982), 1–15; James Lemon, *The Best Poor Man's Country: A Geographical Study of Early Southeastern Pennsylvania* (1972; rpt. New York, 1976), 94–96; and Lucy Simler, "Tenancy in Colonial Pennsylvania: The Case of Chester County," *WMQ* 3d ser., 43 (1986), 542–569.

30. H. L. Bourdin and S. T. Williams, eds., "Crèvecoeur on the Susquehanna, 1774–1776," *Yale Review* 14 (1925), 578, 570–572, 583.

ventories of estates, some possessed almost nothing. At his death, for example, Isaak Walker's most valuable possession was a coat worth £3, fully one-fifth of his entire estate; Japhet Utley owned two cows but little else. If there were, as Crèvecoeur remarked, "everywhere the strong marks of growing wealth and population," this most often reflected the landlords' successes and was not a fair evaluation of individual colonists' financial standing.[31]

Nowhere were the contrasts clearer than in Muncy Township near the West Branch of the Susquehanna. In the years before the Revolution, Samuel Wallis's holdings there might have been the envy of wealthy southern planters. In 1774, according to the most complete tax records for the area before the Revolution, Wallis owned 3,520 acres in the township, as well as land elsewhere in Northumberland County. His holdings constituted one-third of the assessed land in the township and equaled those of the total holdings of the bottom seventy-six (out of eighty-nine) resident taxables, only five of whom were listed as "poor." Wallis's economic dominance was even clearer, if a bit less dramatic, in that his property, valued at £243, was approximately the same as the bottom sixty residents combined; he had the most servants (eight), the most slaves (two), the most livestock (twelve horses and sixteen cows), and the most land under cultivation (fifty acres of grain). Compared to others in the township, including fifty-two who had no land at all, Samuel Wallis had become the dominant economic actor in the region in the years following the Fort Stanwix treaty.[32]

The Colonists' Economy

The establishment of agrarian settlements in the backcountry required far more than clearing fields. Like the Indians who inhabited the valley earlier, colonists' economic practices reflected prevailing cultural attitudes. Colonists migrating to the valley needed mills, stores, roads, and ferries. Landlords provided many of these necessi-

31. "The Records of the Probate Court of Westmoreland in the County of Litchfield, in the Colony of Connecticut. Liber A. from January 6, 1777, to June 16, 1783," *Proceedings and Collections of the Wyoming Historical and Geological Society* 18 (1923), 146, 186.

32. Muncy Township MS Tax Assessment, Northumberland County, Pennsylvania Board of County Commissioners Tax Records, LR 91.2, PHMC. See Table 2 in the Appendix.

ties, realizing that they would be more likely to attract settlers if such a move did not take them into what they believed was a primitive wilderness.

While the valley Indians' religious beliefs had taught them to propitiate the bosses of the game, the colonists who migrated to the region similarly held religious attitudes that influenced their economic behavior. For the colonists who took up lands near the Susquehanna, the Bible contained the simplest and most instructive lesson. These new residents took seriously the message of Genesis. "Be fertile and increase," their God had told Adam and Eve, "fill the earth and master it; and rule the fish of the sea, the birds of the sky, and all the living things that creep on earth" (Gen. 1:28). In the upper valley, such teachings constituted cultural approval for the new inhabitants' attempts to make the local environment suit the economic desires of colonists moving there, and none learned the lessons more clearly than the landlords.

Gristmills and sawmills, the landlords knew, attracted tenants. Nearby sawmills enabled settlers to get building supplies; gristmills would turn their grain into usable and marketable flour. The closer the settlers lived to mills, the less time they would waste in travel and hauling. Many valley landlords, anticipating the profits these businesses promised, built mills to serve the needs of their tenants and other nearby settlers. Augustine Prevost, Theobald Young, and the Harper family all erected sawmills on their New York patents. Johnson informed Banyar that one of the settlers on his Charlotte River tract was "going to erect a Grist Mill thereon, which will be a great inducement to the Settling them parts."[33] Prominent landholders in Northumberland County, including Ludwig Derr, John Aurand, and William Blythe, also built mills on their property. In the Wyoming region members of the Susquehannah Company built mills, although they did not finance them personally. In December 1773 the town of Kingston appointed two separate committees to view mill sites; when they found a proper site, they voted to "Build & Erect a Good Grist mill & Sawmill on Tobies Creek—and to Build them on the towns Cost." Crèvecoeur found that by 1774 company members "had already erected a good number of saw mills with

33. Peter Martin to Banyar, September 22, 1762, Banyar Papers, Box 6, NYHS; Lauber, "Valleys of the Susquehanna and the Delaware," 121; [Smith], *Tour of Four Great Rivers*, 34–35; Johnson to Banyar, June 28, 1770, *Johnson Papers*, 12:829.

which the settlement was supplied with all the boards and scantling they wanted." He noted that some settlers had already begun building rafts and sending "black walnut logs commonly 14 feet long, and 18 inch. wide" down the river to "the upper Pennsylvania settlements for a dollar a piece."[34]

Mills became the hubs of local commercial networks, but colonists also traveled to valley trading centers. Near the headwaters of the Susquehanna many colonists frequently visited Cherry Valley, a town John Lindesay founded in 1738. In 1742 seven families, thirty individuals in all and led by the Reverend Samuel Dunlop, migrated from Londonderry, New Hampshire. Dunlop actively recruited settlers, establishing an economic tie to George Clarke, the wealthiest landlord around Cherry Valley. Dunlop became the intermediary between Clarke and his tenants; the landlord arranged for the tenants to pay their rents to Dunlop, who would pass the money on to Clarke. But Dunlop eventually became mired in disputes with the tenants over the use of pasture land; he even refused to baptize one tenant's child when he was battling with the child's father over access to a field. Settlers in the area rebelled against Dunlop's misuse of his religious duties and refused to pay their rents to him, preferring to pay them to an Albany merchant instead. Banyar, who helped Clarke oversee his lands, quickly intervened in the dispute, resolving it in favor of the tenants. Still, Dunlop remained in the town and maintained his religious office.[35]

By 1769, Cherry Valley had forty to fifty families, most of them apparently Scotch-Irish; in the surrounding area, there were an almost equal number of Germans and other settlers. Six years later, the town had three hundred residents.[36] According to Richard

34. *ABV*, 60, 67–74; Minutes of a Meeting of the Proprietors in Kingston, December 6, 1773, *SCP*, 5:192–193; Minutes of a Meeting of the Proprietors in Kingston, December 21, 1773, ibid., 203–204; Bourdin and Williams, eds., "Crèvecoeur on the Susquehanna," 570; see Sung Bok Kim, *Landlord and Tenant in Colonial New York: Manorial Society, 1664–1775* (Chapel Hill, N.C., 1978), 164–169, 229–230.

35. Tenants of Cherry Valley to Banyar, September 20, 1762, Banyar to Dunlop, October 18, 1762, and Dunlop to Banyar, March 17, 1773, Banyar Papers, Box 6, NYHS.

36. Agreements between Clarke, Lindesay and Dunlop, Respecting Lands at Cherry Valley, November 1738–October 1743, Banyar Papers, Box 6, NYHS; John Sawyer, *History of Cherry Valley from 1740 to 1898* (1898; rpt. Cherry Valley, N.Y., 1976), 2–7; Lauber, "Valleys of the Susquehanna and the Delaware," 120.

Smith, who traveled through Cherry Valley in 1769 on his way to view the nearby Otsego tract, the town had three gristmills, one sawmill, and "divers Carpenters and other Tradesmen." Robert Wells, considered "one of the principal Freeholders" of the area even though he owned only two hundred acres, ran a store that provided necessary goods for settlers. He sold powder, shot, osnaburg (a coarse cloth for grain sacks or clothing), rum, and flaxseed. The latter was especially important in Cherry Valley because the settlers made "all their own Linen and some Woolen," despite the lack of a fulling mill. Wells's trade in rum was limited by the production on many nearby farms of cider that sold locally at 12s. per barrel, a price Wells could not match. Besides Wells's store, Cherry Valley had a pearl ash work that purified ashes from burned trees, a common product of field clearance, for use in soap and gunpowder. The manager of the pearl ash work paid 7d. and 8d. a bushel for ashes. A gunsmith, a blacksmith, and a shoemaker plied their trades in the town as well.[37]

Cherry Valley met the needs of many settlers, but residents farther south wanted nearby towns as well. The Pennsylvania provincial government, well aware of the need for a town in the upper valley in Pennsylvania, developed Sunbury at the confluence of the two branches of the Susquehanna, adjoining Fort Augusta. The town's plan reflected long-held notions in the province about the necessity of creating a well-organized city. Indeed, the plan for the town resembled Penn's plan for Philadelphia. Sunbury had a main street eighty feet wide, other streets sixty feet wide, and lanes and alleys twenty feet across. Provincial officials required colonists who obtained patents to land in the town to build "a Dwelling House twenty feet square at least, with a Brick or Stone Chimney," within three years or their titles became void. The Penns, apparently anticipating the development of a major inland trading center, perhaps along the lines William Penn had originally envisioned for the Susquehanna Valley, retained many of the lots for their own use.[38]

Sunbury developed according to plan. "Here they have laid out a new town," the surveyor James Whitelaw wrote in his journal in July

37. [Smith], *Tour of Four Great Rivers*, 30–33, 35; and see Higgins, *Expansion in New York*, 71–73, 75.

38. Rent Roll of the Town of Sunbury, June 1772, Cadwallader Collection, Box 30, HSP; *ABV*, 43. On the Penns' ideas about settlement see Lemon, *Best Poor Man's Country*, 50.

1773, "much after the plan of Philadelphia which is building very fast." Northumberland Town, across the river from Sunbury, became a shipping depot. "Here are a Number of Boatmen imployed in going up & down the River to Middleton," the onetime Virginia tutor Philip Vickers Fithian observed when he traveled through the area in June 1775. "With these & others from the Country this infant Village seems as *busy* & *noisy* as a Philadelphia *Ferry-House*." By 1775 Sunbury had one hundred houses, and various craftsmen plied their trades in the area. Valley residents could travel to Sunbury and Northumberland Town to get newspapers, go to church, and engage in trade.[39]

But even though Cherry Valley and Sunbury became magnets, drawing colonists to their smiths and stores, many valley residents lived too far away to make routine visits. To meet their needs they traveled to the nearby estates of wealthy landlords, which, in some instances, came to resemble small towns. Thus Muncy Farm, Samuel Wallis's plantation four miles above the mouth of Muncy Creek, served the immediate needs of local settlers, including Wallis's tenants. When the Moravian missionary John Ettwein traveled through the area in June 1772 with a party of Indians moving from Wyalusing on the North Branch to Friedenstadt on the Beaver River, they stopped and traded at Wallis's plantation. During their brief encampment, Wallis purchased fifteen young cattle, "some canoes, other bowls, firkins, buckets, tubs and diverse iron ware" from the Indians; in exchange he sold them flour. Wallis's authority extended beyond economic matters. When a trader's agent smuggled some rum into the Indians' camp, Ettwein wrote, the landlord took possession of the liquor "for safekeeping, until the trader should return." Wallis, always looking for a profit, sought to make money from diverse investments. In February 1776, for example, he purchased several hundred apple trees, presumably either to resell, to market the fruit, or to make cider, a popular drink in the backcountry.[40]

39. "Journal of General James Whitelaw," 134; Albion and Dodson, eds., *Fithian Journal*, 39, 40–66, and passim.

40. "Reverend John Ettwein's Notes of Travel from the North Branch of the Susquehanna and the Beaver River, Pennsylvania, 1772," ed. John W. Jordan, *PMHB* 25 (1901–1902), 209–210; Jacob Haines and Rudolph Haines to Wallis, February 1, 2, 1776, Wallis Papers, Reel 6.

Public Support of Economic Development

Landlords exerted authority over extensive parts of the upper valley, but they did not completely control the economic development of the hinterland. In the 1770s county courts and settlers' committees also became involved in supervising the valley economy. The upper valley during these years before the Revolution fell into two counties: Northumberland County, Pennsylvania, and Tryon County, New York. Each was vast; new counties were carved out of them after the Revolution. The records of these courts, especially those of Northumberland County, since the boundaries of the upper valley and those of the county were almost identical, reveal colonists' efforts to use public institutions to improve the economy. In the Wyoming region, where the Connecticut migrants had no court and avoided any dealings with the Northumberland County courts, residents turned to settlers' committees to support economic development. These courts and committees met the settlers' needs in two ways. First, courts and committees of settlers appropriated labor and finances to create a viable transportation system in the valley. Second, and less obvious, their decisions articulated a distinct view of economic development, especially the primacy of property rights, which provided much-needed security in this still thinly peopled borderland.

During the years after the Fort Stanwix treaty, valley residents constantly sought to improve local transportation routes so as to facilitate the movement of people and goods. Roads would enable these hinterland settlers to visit nearby relatives and acquaintances and travel to church, meetings, and court sessions. Easy access to well-cleared roads would also provide psychological benefits. Settlers in the process of clearing forests for their fields understood that overland travel through the region remained precarious, especially near the dense swamps in the area. If roads connected settlements, the inhabitants would not have to fear the "perfect chaos" that, as Crèvecoeur wrote, disoriented and threatened travelers in the woods.

Landlords occasionally employed colonists to cut roads through forests to connect their holdings to nearby towns, but local courts, at least in Pennsylvania, organized far more extensive road-clearing efforts. From 1772 to 1776 the Quarter Sessions Court of Northumberland County sat in Sunbury and heard many petitions from residents who wanted roads cut to connect them with major travel routes in the area. The petitioners, in the words of an August 1772 petition, "and the Publick labour under many Inconveniences for want of a Publick Road or highway from the Town of Sunbury to fall into the Road leading to Carlisle." Over the next few years the petitions became more elaborate. Settlers requested roads that would link the outlying inhabitants with Sunbury and major roads and also with nearby mills. In the years before the Revolution, the residents of Northumberland County used public funds to construct a network of roads that connected their properties to the region's major thoroughfares and towns. Settlers' petitions for roads indicated their need for public assistance to incorporate their holdings into the valley commercial system. In allocating funds for road clearing, the Northumberland County court, holding its sessions at the hub of commercial activity for much of the upper valley, demonstrated that local government would support the colonists' efforts to develop the economy.[41]

The members of the Susquehannah Company organized road clearing a bit differently, but they too sought public assistance from local governing groups. In October 1772 the proprietors of Wilkes-Barre decided to cut a road from the Delaware River to Pittstown. Two months later the company decided to tax the inhabitants of the settlement to pay the expenses of cutting the road, charging one dollar for "Each Settling Right on the East Branch of the Susquehannah River." The proprietors gave settlers the opportunity to work on the road, adjusting the pay scale to the difficulty of the labor. The most arduous task was to cut the road from the "westermost part of the Great Swamp"; those involved would receive 3s. each day. Those who worked between the Great Swamp and Wilkes-Barre would earn only 1s. 6d. per day. By early 1773 the residents of Kingston had undertaken similar clearing efforts.[42]

The numerous bends in the Susquehanna River and the large number of streams that fed into it made crossing over water a part

41. Johnson to Banyar, June 28, 1770, *Johnson Papers*, 12:829–830; Northumberland County Quarter Sessions Docket, 1772–1788, 12, 87–91, NCCH.

42. Minutes of a Meeting of Proprietors and Settlers in Wilkes-Barre, October 2, 1772, *SCP*, 5:40; Minutes of a Meeting of the Proprietors and Settlers in Wilkes-Barre, December 7, 1772, ibid., 57; Minutes of a Meeting of the Proprietors in Kingston, January 5, 1773, ibid., 64–65; Minutes of a Meeting of the Proprietors in Kingston, March 4, 1773, ibid., 71.

of most trips, encouraging settlers throughout the valley to provide ferries for their own use and for travelers. In May 1773 the settlers' committee in Wilkes-Barre decided to keep ferryboats on each side of the Susquehanna. The rates for crossing varied by season: in the summer a single man on foot could cross for one and one-half pennies while a horse and rider would cost 3d.; in the winter the rates increased to 2d. for a person and 4d. for someone with a horse. Town proprietors, concerned with the defense of their settlements and religious observance, ordered the ferry keeper to transport at no charge any guard on duty and "the People across on Sundays to Meeting." The settlers at Kingston decided that no resident should have to pay for ferry service. In December 1773 they agreed that "this town Does Now Look on the Ferries to be a Priveledge Belonging to this town" and that all of the residents "Shall be Carried over the River on free Cost."[43]

Residents of Sunbury and Northumberland Town also relied on ferries, but the need for them varied according to season. In the summer months, particularly in years with little rainfall, the water level around Sunbury often dropped to only two feet so residents could ford the river with relative ease. But at other times of the year, when the river was high, ferries were desperately needed. Beginning in 1772, the year colonial legislators established Northumberland County, a number of settlers obtained a provincial patent to run ferries.[44]

In addition to organizing road clearing and ferries, public institutions supported economic development in the region. Anglo-American legal traditions influenced court decisions, but valley judicial officials responded to local economic circumstances as well. Their decisions reveal colonial attitudes regarding the meaning of property and the society's role in supporting individual economic enterprise.

In Northumberland County settlers frequently turned to local courts to adjudicate disputes over property. The most prevalent legal actions were civil suits, generally brought for two reasons: debt and disputes over ownership of land. Considering the size of the

43. Minutes of a Meeting of the Proprietors and Settlers in Wilkes-Barre, May 25, 1773, ibid., 137–138; Minutes of a Meeting of the Proprietors in Kingston, December 21, 1773, ibid., 203–204.
44. "Journal of General James Whitelaw," 135; Albion and Dodson, eds., *Fithian Journal*, 38–39; *ABV*, 44.

county population, the number of cases was enormous. In the first session of the court held in August 1772 settlers filed only 33 suits, but in the next few years the number of cases increased markedly. From 60 cases filed in all of 1772, the number rose to 214 in 1773, 439 in 1774, and 542 in 1775. In the first two sessions of 1776, 180 cases were filed before the political crisis interrupted the court's activities.[45]

The few cases heard at the Northumberland County Orphan's Court similarly involved economic issues: the payment of an intestate's debts and the maintenance of orphans. In August 1773 the court authorized the sale of the lands held by Thomas McKee, who died intestate and approximately £1,200 in debt. The sale of McKee's 469-acre plantation, New Providence, on the Susquehanna River and an adjoining tract of 200 acres to William Dunbar for £725 Pennsylvania currency paid off much of McKee's debt. But this sum did not provide funds for his six children, nor did it adequately cover the cost "to maintain and Educate" McKee's minor child, as the court had ordered. In 1774, the Orphan's Court ordered the sale of lands held by John Jones, a Philadelphia tanner, and William McCoskey, both of whom died intestate; the proceeds went toward retiring their debts and providing for their children's maintenance. The court divided Simon Esper's estate for similar reasons. Proper care of minor children left without fathers concerned the court, but their maintenance was a secondary matter. Children received whatever remained in their father's estate after the payment of debts.[46]

The Quarter Sessions Court handled many more cases than the Orphan's Court but operated under similar assumptions. The court heard criminal cases involving assault and battery, theft, forgery, fornication and bastardy, and runaway servants. The court consistently punished violations against property more severely than crimes against people. Indeed, the severity of the sentence directly reflected the crime's threat to property. Such decisions stood in contrast to the decisions of contemporary English courts, which often meted out severe punishments for even trivial attacks on property.[47]

45. Northumberland County Appearance Dockets, August 1772–May 1774, August 1774–February 1776, and May 1776–February 1783, NCCH.

46. Northumberland County Orphan's Court Docket No. 1, April 1772–February 1785, 1–9, NCCH.

47. On contemporary English treatment of crimes see Douglas Hay, "Property, Authority and the Criminal Law," in Hay, ed., *Albion's Fatal Tree* (London, 1975), 18; and Leon Radzinowicz, *A History of English Criminal Law and Its Administration from 1750*, 4 vols. (London, 1948–1968), 1:3–15.

The court fined those convicted of assault and battery, which did not directly threaten the region's economic development, a small sum or warned them to behave more peacefully. In May 1773, for example, Martin and Michael Troster, each convicted of this offense, paid fines of 2s. 6d. When a violent conflict between James Buchanan and Leonard Groninger reached the court in May 1773, they were not fined but were ordered to return to the next session and, in the words of the court's decision, "in the mean time be of Good behaviour towards all his Majestys Subjects—But in Particular toward" each other.[48]

In contrast, colonists found guilty of crimes against property faced stiff penalties. In August 1775 Henry Shultits, James Murphey, and Mary Murphey were all convicted for receiving stolen goods; each was sentenced to two weeks in jail and fines ranging from 50d. to £2 10s. John Williams, found guilty of theft, had to make restitution, pay a £5 fine, "and occur on his Bare Back at the common Whipping Post, on the 3rd of October next twenty one Lashes."[49] Daniel Pettit found himself in a serious predicament after he was convicted of "altering a 5 Dollar Bill" in May 1776. Although his crime might seem minor—he had tried to make a five dollar bill resemble a nine dollar bill—he was sentenced to "stand in the public Pillory" at Sunbury for one hour on May 31 and then be imprisoned for one month. Again, though Pettit's punishment was severe, he fared better than counterfeiters elsewhere in the province and in England, who received the death penalty or physical mutilation for this crime.[50]

The court dealt unequivocally with cases of fornication and bastardy, which could drain public funds for the support of illegitimate children and unmarried women's maternity costs. The crime also carried a moral quality that distinguished it from other offenses. In

48. Northumberland County Quarter Sessions Docket, 1772–1788, 22, 23, NCCH; see also Herbert Fitzroy, "The Punishment of Crime in Provincial Pennsylvania," *PMHB* 60 (1936), 262–263.

49. Northumberland County Quarter Sessions Docket, 1772–1788, 81, 13, NCCH.

50. Northumberland County Quarter Sessions, 1772–1797, NCCH; Northumberland County Quarter Sessions Docket, 1772–1788, 107, NCCH; Hay, "Property, Authority and the Criminal Law," 19, 21, 33. A Pennsylvania statute of 1773, "An Act to Prevent Counterfeiting the Paper Money of Other Colonies," authorized the death penalty without benefit of clergy for the creation of counterfeit money but thirty-nine lashes, both ears cut off while sentenced to the pillory, a fine of £100, restitution to the aggrieved party in an amount double the value of the damages sustained, and court costs for those convicted of "altering the denomination" of any bills of credit. See *Pennsylvania Statutes at Large*, 8:339–340.

February 1774 Peter Weiser, Jr., and Eve Margaret Kesler were found guilty of fornication and bastardy. The court ordered Weiser to pay a fine of £10 and to pay Kesler £7 10s. for her "lying in Expenses and maintaining the Child to this Time." He also had to provide sufficient security for the child so that he would not drain funds from Penn's Township. Similarly, James Mackey and Mary Armstrong were found guilty of fornication and bastardy in February 1775 and received approximately the same punishment: Mackey had to pay a fine of £10 and then £2 to Armstrong for her maternity expenses, 2s. each week for the child's support, and "give security to indemnify the Township against the said Child's ever becoming a Township Charge."[51]

When indentured servant women became pregnant with illegitimate children they received even harsher punishments because their acts threatened the value of their masters' contracts. In February 1775 the court heard two fornication and bastardy cases involving indentured servants. Mary Mahon had one and one-half years added to the term of her contract at the request of Henry Starrett in exchange for the expenses he incurred because of her pregnancy. The father of Mahon's baby, James Cummins, was required to pay 2s. 6d. each week for the child's maintenance and a fine of £5. Catherine Hickey, an indentured servant of Robert Moodie, was less fortunate than Mahon. The father of her illegitimate child had left the area, and the court added two years to her term of service to make restitution to her master. Such verdicts were not unique to the valley; courts elsewhere in the colonies issued similar punishments for servants.[52]

Verdicts involving runaway servants similarly reflected the importance of indentured servitude in the area. In three cases, runaway servants, once caught, had extra years added to their sentences. In February 1774 Blayney Cochrane was sentenced to four additional years of service at the end of his contract to make restitution for the £7 7s. 3d. that William Maclay spent trying to capture him and also, in the words of Maclay's petition, for the "Damages arising from his absence & Loss of Time &ca." Other servants received additional

51. Northumberland County Quarter Sessions Docket, 1772–1788, 37, 66, NCCH.
52. Ibid., 62, 68; Fitzroy, "Punishment of Crime," 264; David H. Flaherty, "Law and the Enforcement of Morals in Early America," *Perspectives in American History* 5 (1971), 230–232, 239.

terms of service ranging from one year and eight months to two and one-half years.[53]

The Orphan's Court and the Quarter Sessions Court did their best to protect the rural economy of Northumberland County. In all their actions, from authorizing roads to preserving property in the form of servant contracts, the courts publicly extolled the importance of economic concerns. The message to potential settlers was clear: all forms of investment would be protected.

In the Wyoming region settlers' committees and town meetings served as courts and publicly controlled much of the developing agrarian economy. In December 1772, for example, the settlers in Wilkes-Barre, apparently worried about a food shortage, prohibited the sale "to any Person or Forrinor or stranger any Indian Corn Rye or wheat to Carry Down the River out of the Limits of this Purchase." Anyone who violated this decision before May 1, when the provision expired, would lose the grain and pay a fine of 10s. To enforce the new regulation three settlers were appointed to inspect "all such Persons that shall sell or Carry of or Down said River any sort of Grayn." Worried about depletion of nearby forests, the settlers tried to limit the cutting of any timber on the company's common lands along and near the Susquehanna River; anyone "not able to Give a satisfying account that said Timber was not Cut on the Propriators or Common Land it shall be Liable to be Seised & Sold for the use & Benefitt of said Propriators &c."[54] Such regulations also prevented erosion, thereby protecting the fertile lands near the river.

The residents of Kingston joined together in settlers' committees to adjudicate disputes and establish regulations governing access to specific resources. In March 1773 they divided fencing rails among four residents of the community who were fighting over possession of them. Two months later the town's residents agreed to establish a pound on Timothy Pierce's land and appoint him the pound keeper responsible for the livestock kept there. They further allocated land for two "Generall fields in this town (viz) from mr Peter Harrisses

53. Northumberland County Quarter Sessions Docket, 1772–1788, 36, NCCH; and see the cases of John Hambright (ibid., 58) and William Hawthorn and James Cassedy (ibid., 69).

54. Minutes of a Meeting of the Proprietors and Settlers in Wilkes-Barre, December 18, 1772, SCP, 5:60; Minutes of a Meeting of the Proprietors and Settlers in Wilkes-Barre, December 28, 1772, ibid., 63.

Southward to Plymoth Line Shall be one Intire field and Abrahams Plain to be another Intire field by it self." The settlers' committee also decided how long town residents could leave their livestock in the common pastures.[55]

Kingston residents controlled various economic tasks, ranging from the inspection of fences to horse branding. They appointed three men to a committee to check local roads to make sure they were passable. They authorized two separate committees to view potential mill sites and then voted to build a gristmill and sawmill on Toby's Creek "on the towns Cost." They decided that town residents should not be charged for ferry services. In addition, like their Wilkes-Barre neighbors, the Kingston proprietors limited the cutting of all timber on common and undivided land except when roads had to run through these lands.[56]

When the Connecticut legislature, which still claimed jurisdiction over the Susquehannah Company settlers, allowed the creation of the town of Westmoreland in 1774, public efforts to control the local economy became better organized. In March of that year members of the town convened to choose local officers. Besides appointing selectmen, constables, tax collectors, and a treasurer, the settlers appointed people to positions that involved direct participation in the organization of the local economy: twenty-two highway surveyors, fourteen fence viewers, and four "Sealers of Weights and Measures." At the town meeting the next month other economic issues were addressed. The settlers established a local tax, authorized pounds for stray livestock, appointed Obadiah Gore and his son "raters and Branders of Horses," and designated a tree for the "town sign post" to hold notices of meetings, stray animals, and other public information. Finally, the townspeople voted "that the Hogs are allowed to go at large on the Commons."[57]

In addition to these mundane concerns, the settlers around Wyoming, like those in Northumberland County, had to contend with

55. Minutes of a Meeting of the Proprietors of Kingston, March 4, 1773, ibid., 71; Minutes of a Meeting of the Proprietors and Settlers in Kingston, May 3, 1773, ibid., 129.

56. Minutes of a Meeting of the Proprietors in Kingston, December 6, 1773, ibid., 192–193; Minutes of a Meeting of the Proprietors in Kingston, December 21, 1773, ibid., 203–204.

57. Minutes of a Meeting of Westmoreland, March 1, 1774, ibid., 6:144–146; Meeting of the Town of Westmoreland, April 12, 1774, ibid., 209–210.

criminal activity that threatened the local economy. In October 1773 Asa Brown and eight others destroyed an eel weir in the Susquehanna between Exeter and Pittston "in a Turbulent & hy handed manner," according to John Jenkins and John Grant. Brown and his associates apparently stole the eels and "mad[e] to them selves a Booty to the Great Damage of the owners." To Susquehannah Company members, Brown's gang's actions seemed particularly reprehensible because most of the group were "Transient Persons & Common Disturbers of the Peace." Questioned about the matter, Brown boldly defied the authority of the settlers, supporting the claims of Pennsylvania to the region instead of those of the company. According to the men who served Brown his warrant, he "bids Defiance & Rules on this Ground & Says, they may Kiss his ass in be Damned &c for what he Cared for them." The proprietors and settlers of Wilkes-Barre, finding him "an Enemy to our Company by publickly Declaring himself as one," banished him from their territory.[58]

Protecting investments, whether they were servants' contracts or eel weirs, served an important function in the backcountry. Such efforts by courts and settlers' committees gave local colonists a sense of security; even though the region remained thinly peopled, it was no lawless borderland. Valley settlers, from wealthy landlords to their tenants, wanted to recreate colonial society in the hinterland. They migrated to the upper valley to find land, not to flee society. Even a group of squatters known as the "Fair Play" settlers, who seized land beyond the Fort Stanwix boundary, created a social system based on colonial ideals.[59] All of these colonists wanted to extend

58. Petition of John Jenkins and John Grant to the Settlers' Committee, October 11, 1773, ibid., 5:171; Warrant for the Arrest of Asa Brown, October 11, 1773, ibid., 172; Minutes of a Meeting of the Proprietors and Settlers in Wilkes-Barre, October 26, 1773, ibid., 173–174.

59. Although the so-called Fair Play code has never been found, depositions and oral histories given later indicate that an extralegal committee of settlers supervised the region along the West Branch, striving to keep the land settled. To improve a piece of land, the prospective settler had to be accepted by those who lived in the immediate vicinity; if any improvement was abandoned for more than six weeks, the property would become available for others. See John Linn, "Indian Land and Its Fair Play Settlers, 1773–1785," *PMHB* 7 (1883), 422–424; Deposition of William King, Family Deeds, Special Collection, LCHS; John F. Meginness, *Otzinachson; or, A History of the West Branch Valley of the Susquehanna* (Philadelphia, 1857), 160–168. Most of King's deposition is reprinted in Linn, "Indian Land and Its Fair Play Settlers," 422–424. For the most thorough study of the Fair Play settlers see George Wolf, *The Fair Play Settlers of the West Branch Valley, 1769–1784: A Study of Frontier Ethnography* (Harrisburg, Pa., 1969).

the empire into the valley and to live like rural residents elsewhere in British North America.

Indians among the Colonists

To most valley colonists the future looked bright, but their Indian neighbors knew that economic stability was both precious and precarious. While colonists migrated to the upper valley and established a viable agrarian economy under the guidance of landlords, county courts, and settlers' committees, the Indians who remained in their towns according to the terms of the 1768 treaty faced difficult times. With the decline in peltry and the movement of many traders westward out of the valley toward areas with larger populations of fur-bearing animals, Indians devoted more attention to agriculture. Some continued to engage in trade whenever possible, but their daily economic concerns lay elsewhere, especially when contending with colonial interlopers trespassing on their lands.

Evidence of the Indians' economy from the late 1760s to the late 1770s is fragmentary, but travelers' accounts and surveyors' journals describe important aspects of their lives. Samuel Harris, a surveyor for the wealthy landholders Robert Lettis Hooper and Samuel Wallis, received help from one group of Indians near Tioga in late 1774. His party, short of provisions, obtained a bushel of beans, a hog, and some dried venison from the Indians. Harris's notes reveal that these Indians apparently maintained a mixed hunting-farming economy. The fact that they kept hogs indicates a shift in their diet and the adoption of colonial livestock to supplement indigenous food supplies. Finally, in providing these goods as a gift to a trespassing party of surveyors, the Indians maintained traditional hospitality practices.[60]

Other travelers provided more details on the Indians' economy. When Crèvecoeur visited a town he called Anaquaga, near Wyoming, in 1776, he found it a "considerable Indian town inhabited by the Seneccas." There were fifty houses there, "some built after the ancient Indian manner, and the rest of good hew'd logs properly dove-tailed at each end," he wrote; "they afford neat and warm habitations." Although the Indians had modified their architectural

60. Harris, Jornel and field notes . . . don for Robt Lettis Hooper and Compy, Wallis Papers, Reel 6.

styles, their horticulture remained traditional. Indeed, the Anaquaga Indians' crops impressed Crèvecoeur: "The low lands on which [the town] is built, like all the others are excellent, and I saw with pleasure [a] great deal of industry in the cultivation of their little fields. Corn, beans, potatoes, pumpkins, squashes appeared extremely flourishing." In addition, many of the local Indians had cows and horses, although he wrote that, unlike colonists, the Indians "seldom plough'd" with their livestock.[61]

Local colonists, Crèvecoeur noted, traveled periodically to the town. In addition to a Moravian missionary who preached to the local Indians, other colonists visited the town to see Indians, who were "famous for [their] medical knowledge." The Indians' secret formulas apparently worked wonders for a variety of ills. "Several were cured while I was there," Crèvecoeur wrote, "a woman in particular who had a running ulcer in her breast for 5 years before appeared perfectly well cured and the ancient wound entirely healed." Although the Indians tried to keep their medical techniques a secret, Crèvecoeur got one Indian woman drunk and elicited the details from her. "The good I have done with it will, I hope," he wrote, "compensate the method I made use of to procure it." In addition to agriculture, Crèvecoeur found that some of the Indians still traded for necessary goods. Unlike earlier Indians, who traded for metal products or alcohol, however, these Indians exchanged pelts for food. Indeed, when Crèvecoeur left the town he traveled to Wyoming with three Indians "who were going to exchange some furs for flour." Other Indians in the upper valley also traded with resident colonists. At Bald Eagle's Nest, off the West Branch, Philip Fithian saw young Indians bring fish to some colonists in July 1775; in exchange they received bread and venison.[62]

The success of the colonists' economy promised only more hardship for the Indians. Time and again, in spite of the Fort Stanwix treaty, colonists encroached on land set aside for the Indians, creating animosities throughout the region. For example, Samuel Harris's surveying party trespassed on the Indians' lands near Tioga. Rather than harming the party, however, the Indians provided them with tools to carve a canoe and a tree suitable for the purpose; without this assistance, the party later realized, they might not have survived

61. Bourdin and Williams, eds., "Crèvecoeur on the Susquehanna," 581.
62. Ibid., 581–582; Albion and Dodson, eds., Fithian Journal, 82.

their planned overland journey back through an early winter snow-storm. Indians sometimes followed surveyors through the woods, re-minding them each time they crossed the boundary line.[63]

Other groups of Indians acted less kindly toward colonial tres-passers who tried to settle beyond the Fort Stanwix boundary. The Fair Play settlers in particular aroused the ire of Indians along the West Branch of the Susquehanna. Rather than attacking these set-tlers, however, the Indians complained to provincial officials, who took their side and ordered the squatters to move back to the colo-nists' territory. Pennsylvania officials even authorized the death penalty without benefit of clergy for those who remained on the disputed lands. The Fair Play settlers, however, refused to leave, further adding to the Indians' growing discontent.[64]

The Valley Economy on the Eve of the Revolution

Within a decade after the signing of the Fort Stanwix treaty, thou-sands of colonists had migrated to the upper valley. But even while this part of the king's domain became more and more integrated into the Atlantic economy, economic stability remained fragile.

The best evidence for the instability of life in the valley can be found in the journal of Philip Vickers Fithian, a remarkable ob-server of colonial life. His recollections about his years as a tutor in Virginia describe subtle aspects of gentry society in the Chesapeake; its dances and dinners come alive through his writing, and we see through his eyes a world of carefully nuanced hierarchies and social rituals.[65] Fithian traveled through much of the upper Susquehanna Valley in the mid-1770s and deftly described an entire social uni-verse, leaving perhaps the best available image of the colonists' pre-war economy.

Fithian arrived in Sunbury and Northumberland Town in June 1775, when the Anglo-American political crisis was becoming threat-ening. After reading Philadelphia papers at the end of June, he be-lieved that "All things yet look dark & unsettled." Along the banks of

63. Harris, Jornel and field notes, Wallis Papers, Reel 6; Will Cockburn to Banyar, September 10, 1773, Banyar Papers, Wallace and Misc. Patents, NYSL.
64. PaCR, 10:94–95.
65. See Rhys Isaac, The Transformation of Virginia, 1740–1790 (Chapel Hill, N.C., 1982), esp. chap. 4.

the Susquehanna, however, all things were not bleak. Northumberland Town, Fithian wrote, was surrounded by boats and "without Doubt in a few Years, will be grand & busy." He stayed with the wife of the surveyor-general William Scull, and her household greatly impressed him. "She has a pleasant, & valuable Garden, the best by far in Town," he wrote, "in it a neat, & well designed Summer-House." Fithian especially liked the parlor, "with many Pieces of good Painting—Four in special, which struck me much; large heads, from ancient Marbles, of *Hypocrates, Tully, Socrates,* & *Galen.*" A few days later, she showed him her husband's library. He borrowed a copy of the "Critical Reviewer" and wrote, "It is charming to see Books in the Infancy of this remote Land."[66]

Fithian soon ventured beyond his hosts' lodgings and ambled about the area, taking note of the crops in the fields and the types of labor employed. Traveling along the West Branch, through fields kept by tenants of Colonel Turbutt Francis, he saw "Wheat & Rye, thick & very high: Oats I saw in many Places, yet green, & full as high, in general through the field, as a six railed Fence! Pokes, & Elders higher than my Head, as I sat on my Horse!" Nearby he saw others reaping rye and observed free-ranging cattle, horses, and sheep grazing in fields and forests.[67]

Everywhere Fithian traveled he found people harvesting their grain, and he often joined them at their work. Throughout the West Branch valley fertile fields were bursting with healthy crops. In spite of the mosquitoes and fleas that plagued him in the evening, the region's bounty impressed him. After traveling for two weeks along the West Branch, Fithian described the great potential of the valley. "My Wonder ceases," he wrote in his journal, "that the Indians fought for these happy Valley's." He also recognized the great development boom then under way. Returning to Northumberland, he met a party traveling to a settlement about fifty miles up the West Branch. "Two Waggons, with Goods, Cattle, Women, Tools &c, went through Town to Day from East-Jersey, on their Way to Fishing Creek up this River, where they are to settle," he wrote. "Rapid, most rapid, is the growth of this County."[68]

But if the valley was quickly gaining population, the times were troubled. When he returned to Sunbury on July 20, the day of the

66. Albion and Dodson, eds., *Fithian Journal,* 40, 45–47, 49.
67. Ibid., 50–51.
68. Ibid., 54, 58, 62.

Continental fast, Fithian preached to an overflowing crowd, many of them fearful of the looming crisis. He too had worries, but his were for his future travels: "I must now away up this Long River sixty Miles higher," Fithian wrote, "among quarrellsome Yankees, insidious Indians, & at best lonely Wilds!"[69]

In spite of his fears, Fithian continued on his journey. On his first stop, at Chillisquaque, he attended a funeral for a small child who choked to death on some rye his father was carting back after the harvest. He continued to see prospering colonial farms and plump cows and horses grazing on meadows "said to be anciently Indian-Towns." He ran into an Indian trader and later encountered two Indians carrying pelts they wanted to trade. Farther on, as he traveled west, he found Indian hunting camps, one with a half a deer, still fresh, hanging from some branches. At Bald Eagle's Nest and in Penn's Valley colonists were clearing land and growing wheat, rye, oats, and flax. Nearby he encountered a smith, with Indian clients, who shoed Fithian's horse.[70]

Fithian longed to return to Northumberland Town and Sunbury. The farther he traveled, the more foreboding the situation appeared to him. Even the surrounding environment seemed to be more hostile. Some of the creeks, overflowing in winter, were practically dry, and some settlers could not find sufficient lumber to meet their needs. But more threatening still were the signs of savagery Fithian detected. Some of the Indians looked fierce, with "the outside Rim of their Ears slitted," and others wore silver in their noses and ears. "The Trees near their Camps," he wrote, "are painted with Red & Black Colours many wild & ferocious Animals—in the most furious gestures." What a contrast, he must have thought, to the paintings of classical authors adorning the Sculls' library.[71]

Fithian occasionally recognized the Indians' contribution to the valley economy, either by providing business for traders or smiths or by clearing fields later settled by colonists, but by the end of his travels, he distrusted the Indians. He summed up his feelings when he was at Bald Eagle's Nest. "I am at the farthest Frontiers of this Colony," he wrote, "& among the wild-natured Savages, I am in Fear—indeed I am—" Even the colonists' successes paled in his final

69. Ibid., 64–65. The term *Yankees* refers to settlers living in Pennsylvania with titles from the Susquehannah Company.
70. Ibid., 67, 70–71, 81, 85–87.
71. Ibid., 83–84.

estimation. "For all this Settlement I would not live here; for two such Settlements—not for five hundred a Year—nothing would persuade me—!"[72]

Fithian's views were at times extreme, but his writing was not fiction. Some colonists continued to trade with Indians, but many feared and resented them. The Indians had even greater reason for suspicion and hostility; they lived in a border region, on the edge of an expanding colonizing power. They too were fearful of their neighbors, especially when colonists' free-ranging livestock browsed on Indian food supplies, when settlers turned more and more of the forests into fields, and when colonists trespassed on Indian lands.

Still, few valley residents realized that when delegates from the colonies traveled to Philadelphia and declared themselves independent of the king and his empire, that act would forever change their lives and economy. When the larger crisis reached the backcountry, colonists and Indians who had eyed each other suspiciously across smiths' shops and traders' stalls found themselves at war. Most Indians allied themselves with the king, but few valley settlers joined the loyalists, thus giving the revolutionary war in the hinterland racial overtones it lacked in other regions. When hostilities spread into the backcountry, Indians and colonists alike found that the communities each had created in the valley could not survive.

Fithian believed that the Indians were savages. In the years after his journey, valley residents would discover that no group had a monopoly on savagery.

72. Ibid., 83.

6 The War in the Valley

Throughout the eighteenth century the Atlantic commercial world had shaped the valley economy. When the Anglo-American commercial system shifted in the revolutionary era, so did local economic rhythms along the Susquehanna and its tributaries. The spread of the revolutionary conflict into the valley was not surprising in light of the earlier European demand for pelts and the subsequent settlement of the region by colonists seeking new territory. Still, when military hostilities spread through the region, few colonists or Indians could have expected the conflict to undermine the world they had created.

Valley residents of all political alliances felt the brutality of the conflict when the hostile armies, along with local recruits, campaigned in the region. Soldiers following orders burned almost every farm and town, killed livestock, and prompted widespread emigration from the region. Local histories of the upper valley vividly describe "the great runaway" of the late 1770s, emphasizing that the revolutionary conflict had far-reaching implications for valley residents and for people who resettled the region in the 1780s and later.[1]

1. See, for example, Helen H. Russell, "The Great Runaway of 1778," in Charles F. Snyder, ed., *Northumberland County in the American Revolution* (N.p.: Northumberland County Historical Society, n.d.), 83–98.

The military conflict ushered in a new age of commercial development, eliminating many vestiges of the earlier economy.

The war had vastly different meanings for colonists and Indians. Most colonists sided with the rebels and organized their economy and society through committees of correspondence; these committees, authorized by the Continental Congress, became the political infrastructure of the Revolution, especially in the backcountry. Almost the entire valley Indian population supported the crown, hoping that such an alliance might stem the flow of settlers into the hinterland.

War and the Organization of the Settlers' Economy

Preparations for war placed new demands on the region's inhabitants and their economy. The committees of correspondence in Tryon and Northumberland counties, often acting in place of the county courts, tried to provide support and personnel for the Continental army, supervise the distribution of strategic goods throughout the region, and preserve order against suspected threats. But in spite of their efforts, many settlers recognized that the preparation for military activity threatened vital components of the local economy.

The committees often dealt with economic issues. In 1776 and 1777 the Tryon County Committee, whose jurisdiction covered the upper valley in New York, assumed control over the maintenance of roads, tavern licenses, and adjudication of property disputes between settlers over such matters as ownership of livestock and orchards.[2] The Northumberland County Committee, with authority over settlers in the Pennsylvania parts of the valley, heard similar cases. In March 1777, for example, the committee ordered Henry Sterrat [Starrett?] to stop profaning the Sabbath by beating his servants if they did not "Maul Rails &c" on Sunday. The committees also assumed jurisdiction over the allocation of goods within the region. In September 1776 the Northumberland County Committee authorized the division of newly arrived salt from Philadelphia, intended for the use of county inhabitants who had not received any.

2. Maryly Penrose, ed., *The Mohawk Valley in the Revolution: Committee of Safety Papers and Genealogical Compendium* (Franklin Park, N.J., 1980), 119, 135.

The committee confiscated a quantity of salt in the possession of Aaron Levy and John Bullion, who would not sell it at the committee-approved price, giving it to William Sayers with instructions to sell it for 15s. per bushel, not to sell more than half a bushel to any single family, and to keep an account of his transactions. Bullion, the committee decreed, would be reimbursed for his portage costs and given one shilling for each pound to compensate him for his time.[3]

Control over grain yields became a hotly contested issue. The Northumberland County Committee heard of a number of farmers in Bald Eagle Township who would not sell their rye unless they received "Eighteen pence or two Shillings per bushell above the highest Market price that grain is giving in the County." If they did not receive this price, they would sell their grain outside the county. The committee ordered that distillers in the township purchase no more grain during the season and that "no grain be carried out of this Township till the Necessity of the poor is Supplied" or until the first day of May; "any person having grain of any kind to Dispose of and will not take the market price at Sunbury reducing a Reasonable Carriage or the highest price that it will be there when the grain is wanted we allow to seize on it and take it by force and pay them their money." The county committee referred the case to the local committee, over which it had jurisdiction, but worried that the Bald Eagle committee, in its attempt to provide for local settlers, might generate resistance among the grain farmers. Thus the county committee cautioned the Bald Eagle committee "against using too much Rigour in their Measures" and to "keep by moderation as much as possible and Study a Sort of medium between Seizing of property and Supplying the wants of the poor."[4]

These decisions by committees reflected the intentions of the Continental Congress and also indicated the persistence of older attitudes regarding the moral economy. Wartime profiteering, in the opinion of those serving on these committees, was unacceptable, and they authorized the seizure of goods being sold for more than the current market, or just, price in the valley's most important trading center at Sunbury. This position stood in stark contrast to the actions of local courts and settlers' committees, which before the war had

3. Northumberland County Committee of Safety Minute Book, 29, 7–8, 10, 5, HSP.

4. Ibid., 28–29. Some of the words in this manuscript copy are difficult to read; the text can be compared to the published edition in *P. Arch.* 2d ser., 9:361–362.

worked to protect the local commercial economy; these groups probably would have done little to prevent merchants from charging
whatever they wanted for their wares, expecting that the grain
sellers would lose customers if their prices were too high. But the
wartime committees, like the Wilkes-Barre committee that had prevented the export of grain in the winter of 1772–1773 because of
fear of a food shortage, took action because the merchants' behavior
threatened the entire community, and such a threat violated deeply
held beliefs about the proper functioning of the economy. Commercial exchange was tolerated, but striving for individual profit when
others were in distress was not acceptable behavior. The committee
members believed that the valley economy needed to be protected
from marauding soldiers and price-gouging merchants alike, and
their actions reflected this belief.

But the committees proved unable to preserve the stability of the
regional economy. They failed because local economic and military
needs were contradictory; each relied on a constant supply of labor.
If valley residents joined either the Continental or British army,
their families could not maintain their properties. If they remained
on their farms, the residents risked invasion by enemies. The local
militias could not protect the region because they could not muster
sufficient people to defend the large territory under their charge. In
more heavily populated areas such as New England, communities
could find militia recruits among the men who were not essential to
the local economy; in Peterborough, New Hampshire, and Concord,
Massachusetts, for example, marginal, often poor, members of the
community filled the recruitment quotas.[5] In the upper Susquehanna Valley the population had not reached the level at which
some could be spared to serve in the army.

The committees tried to address the feared loss of labor. In an
appeal to the Committee of Safety of Philadelphia, the Northumberland committee noted that the recruitment of soldiers from the area
could have devastating consequences; indeed, the county was already in danger from both the Indians and the members of the Susquehannah Company, and the petitioners questioned whether it was

5. See John Shy, "Hearts and Minds in the American Revolution: The Case of
'Long Bill' Scott and Peterborough, New Hampshire," in Shy, *A People Numerous and
Armed: Reflections on the Military Struggle for American Independence* (New York, 1976),
163–179; and Robert Gross, *The Minutemen and Their World* (1976; rpt. New York,
1982), 151–152.

"prudent to drain an infant frontier County of its strength of men" and whether "the safety of the interior parts of the Province would not be better secur'd by adding strength to the frontiers." Defense of their communities was of paramount concern to the settlers, yet recruitment damaged local economic interests. Did the assembly intend, the committee asked, to "distress one County by taking from it all the men necessary for the business of Agriculture as well as the defence of the same?" The local committee understood better than the state authorities the difficulties of forming a county militia in the thinly peopled hinterland and believed it "morally improbable" that they could establish "A well disciplined Militia." To meet their defense needs, the petition concluded, the state should raise two more companies and station them in Northumberland County "in order to be near and defend our frontiers should they be attack'd by our enemies of any denomination"; the petitioners promised that the local militia would assist these companies in any skirmishes.[6]

Petitions from groups of valley residents echoed the committee's position. In June 1778, 143 settlers who lived north of the Muncy Hills along the West Branch appealed to the Pennsylvania Supreme Executive Council for protection. They cited a recent attack along Loyalsock Creek when Indians murdered or captured 13 settlers and the lack of protection afforded by the 73 soldiers assigned "to cover a Frontier of at least Forty miles in length." The county militia was unable to defend the region adequately because the dispersed nature of settlement required troops to cover an extensive area; the militia was even less effective because its members were then "out in the midst of Harvest," an activity more important to them than preparing for war, and would thus be delayed in mustering. Only state troops stationed in the area would prevent settlers fearful of attack from abandoning their improvements.[7]

Many residents of the upper valley realized that military service was not compatible with their economic needs. Thus fifty-six residents of Penn's Township petitioned state officials in August 1779 to release them from militia duty so they could perform necessary agricultural work. "The most Part of the Back Inhabitants are of the

6. Northumberland County Committee of Safety Minute Book, n.p., entry for March 27, 1776; also in *P. Arch.* 2d ser., 9:341–342.

7. Ferdinand J. Dreer Collection, Northumberland County, HSP, folder titled June 10, 1778, August 2, 1787.

Minor Rank which most out of Want was obliged to Settle the Back Parts In hope to get a Living in the Willdernisse," they claimed, "and are all of us New Beginners which was Obliged to Begin with good and Charitable Peoples Money and therefore are not Capable to do our Duty for the Pressent Time in the Militia for it is Impossible for us to get our Living In this Dismal Time if not Released from the Militia." If not released from military service, the residents concluded, they would have to "Leave the County as Many of our fellow Cittizen has done."[8]

These settlers believed the state was responsible for defending the hinterland. The state, however, thought the backcountry residents should provide men to protect their settlements. The dispute echoed the earlier controversy between the crown and British colonists in North America over the raising of revenue to support British troops to defend the territory gained in the French and Indian War. The earlier dispute fueled tensions between Britain and its overseas colonies. In the 1770s, neither settlers in the upper Susquehanna Valley nor state authorities wanted a similar resolution to their conflict over troops. But into the late 1770s neither side was willing to change its views, and the result was catastrophic: the backcountry remained insufficiently defended and loyalists and Indians attacked hinterland settlements, often killing settlers who were tending crops in their fields instead of mustering to protect their communities. Unable to rely on the Continental army for their defense, settlers who were allied with the rebels and many others who wished to remain neutral moved their families into stockaded forts, leaving the maintenance of crops to adult males who traveled to their fields during the day, risking their lives to obtain the food they needed.

The Military Conflict

Even in their worst visions valley residents could not have imagined how devastating the war would be. Crown and rebel leaders, each for their own reasons believing it was important to control the backcountry of Pennsylvania and New York, waged intentionally de-

8. Petition from Penn's Valley to Committee of Safety to be Released from Militia Duty, August 21, 1779, Ferdinand J. Dreer Autograph Collection, Misc. Mss., HSP.

structive campaigns in the upper Susquehanna Valley. But the only large pitched battle that occurred was at Newtown on August 29, 1779. Instead, the combatants fought an unconventional war. They killed valley residents loyal to their enemies and ruthlessly destroyed their fields, livestock, and buildings. Soldiers on each side sought to destroy grain supplies, vital not only for residents but also for thousands of people outside the valley.

In 1778 the British, assisted by hundreds of Iroquois and other Indians and armed loyalists, devastated valley settlements. John Butler, who owned extensive property in the northernmost parts of the valley and was an interpreter at the Fort Stanwix treaty in 1768, led these forces, maintaining contact with British officials stationed in North America. Butler began to organize troops for his campaign as early as March 1777 and reported immediate success in raising soldiers from among settlers in western New York and the Iroquois; indeed, he expressed surprise at the likely prospect of raising as many as one thousand Indians for his force. At least seventy settlers on the Susquehanna volunteered to join his rangers, risking their family homesteads to serve the king. Loyalists came from a variety of social positions in the upper valley, ranging from those with much land, like Butler and the family of Sir William Johnson, to tenants of those landholders; John Johnson's tenants in particular supported the British.[9]

By the spring of 1778 Butler was making the final preparations for his campaign. He claimed to have recruited one hundred loyalists from "the back Settlements." In addition, he wrote to Sir Guy Carleton, the British general and governor of Quebec, "I have frequently sent out parties to the Susquehanna, from whence, after having destroyed their upper Settlements, they have brought in some prisoners, and about 170 Scalps." The Indians, Butler realized, knew the territory well, and they established an extensive surveillance network to monitor settlers' activities and those of Continental army troops.[10]

9. Butler to Carleton, March 31, April 8, 1777, CO 42/36, f. 116–117; Joseph Chew to an unnamed person, January 25, 1776, Add. Mss., 29,237, f. 22–23; cf. Sung Bok Kim, "Impact of Class Relations and Warfare in the American Revolution: The New York Experience," *JAH* 69 (1982), 326–346. For Butler's lands see List of Patent Lands to be Sold for Arrears of Quit Rents, 73, typescript in the Office of the Montgomery County Historian, Fonda, N.Y., and Dot Rolled Map 273:33, NYSL.
10. Butler to Carleton, April 10, 1778, CO 42/38, f. 112; Butler to Captain Francis

Butler's forces staged their most destructive raids in July 1778. Within four days his forces had routed the rebel soldiers based in and around Wyoming, the largest settlement in the upper valley besides Sunbury and Northumberland Town near Fort Augusta. On July 3, the day before the second anniversary of the Declaration of Independence, Butler's troops achieved their primary goal: the destruction of Wyoming. "Our fire was so close and well directed," Butler wrote several days later, "that the afair was soon over, not lasting above half an hour, from the Time they gave us the first fire till their flight[.] In this action were taken 227 Scalps, and only five Prisoners: the Indians were so exasperated with their loss last year near Fort Stanwix, that it was with the greatest difficulty I could save the lives of those few." After the battle Butler proceeded with his plans to destroy the settlers' property, promising to "harrass the adjacent country and prevent them from getting in their Harvest." Butler claimed that his forces attacked only people in arms and spared noncombatants; this position, maintained with the loss of a minimal number of Indians and British soldiers, earned him praise from Whitehall.[11]

The British and their Indian allies followed up the Wyoming attack with a devastating raid on Cherry Valley in November. According to Continental army soldiers who arrived shortly after the attack, a party of seven hundred Indians and British soldiers rampaged through the settlement in an apparently wanton display of force. Captain Benjamin Warren, a Continental army officer, estimated that forty women and children had been "butchered." "Such a shocking sight my eyes never beheld before of savage and brutal barbarity," he wrote in his journal. "To see the husband mourning over his dead wife with four dead children lying by her side, mangled, scalpt, and some their heads, some their legs and arms cut off,

---

Le Maistre, January 28, 1778, CO 42/38, f. 104; Butler to Haldimand, January 20, September 17, 1778, Add. Mss., 21,765, f. 9, 34–36; "Major Butler's Return of Scouts Employed 1779," February 12, 1779, Add. Mss., 21,765, f. 80–81; John McDonell to Butler, July 24, 1779, Add. Mss., 21,765, f. 122; Butler to Captain Mathews, August 2, 1779, Add. Mss., 21,765, f. 124. Butler to Haldimand, April 10, 1778, contains the same information as Butler's April 10 letter to Carleton, except that it notes only seventy scalps taken; see Add. Mss., 21,765, f. 21

11. Butler to Lt. Col. Mason Bolton, July 8, 1778, CO 42/38, f. 169–170; George Germain to Sir Henry Clinton, November 4, 1778, CO 5/96, f. 128–129.

some torn the flesh off their bones by their dogs—12 of one family killed and four of them burnt in his house." The mutilation of corpses probably resulted from the Indians' actions since the Iroquois often incorporated such behavior into rituals associated with war.[12]

The attacks on settlements along the Susquehanna and throughout much of the backcountry of Pennsylvania and New York prompted Continental army officials to take action. In addition to the loss of life, these officials recognized that the campaigns of the British and Indians had far-reaching economic implications. Thus New York governor George Clinton wrote to John Jay, one of New York's representatives to the Continental Congress, soon after the destruction of Cherry Valley: "The Public have lost by the Destruction of these settlements some of the principal Granaries in this State from whence alone the army might have drawn supplies sufficient, at least to have prevented their present want." In his view, the only way to guard the backcountry and protect their valuable agricultural supplies was to carry out "Offensive Opperations, thereby carrying the War into the Enemy's Country." Failure to mount a campaign into the British-controlled hinterland would have long-lasting economic consequences. "If the Enemy are suffered to continue their Depredations much longer," Clinton concluded, "the Consequence may be fatal, as this state will be disabled from furnishing any supplies to the army & hitherto they have depended upon it for Bread."[13]

In 1778, Continental army soldiers made sporadic forays into the valley. But because of the lack of an effective information-gathering network, these raids met with limited success. For example, an attack on the suspected rendezvous sites of the enemy at Unadilla and Oquaga, both on the Susquehanna, failed to find any military forces because Indians had abandoned their villages.

In 1779 the Continental army organized a more sustained campaign against the British and Indians, which became one of the most important to Continental army leaders, who gave General John Sullivan a substantial number of troops and supplies with which to carry

12. "Diary of Captain Benjamin Warren in 1778," ed. David E. Alexander, *Journal of American History* 3 (1909), 383. On Indian mutilation of enemies during war see James Axtell, "The Indian Impact on English Colonial Culture," in *The European and the Indian: Essays in the Ethnohistory of Colonial North America* (New York, 1981), 308–315.

13. Clinton to Jay, November 17, 1778, *Public Papers of George Clinton*, ed. Hugh Hastings and J. A. Holden, 10 vols. (Albany, N.Y., 1899–1914), 4:289–290.

it out. George Washington hoped that a massive force, organized at Wyoming and Lake Otsego and then meeting at Tioga, could destroy the Indian settlements in the backcountry, thereby weakening British control over the area. The help of the Indians was crucial for the British war effort in the hinterland; without the Indians, the crown's troops were too few in number to control the backcountry effectively. Washington thus sought to concentrate the Continental army's actions on the Indians. He wanted to "cut off their settlements, destroy their next Years crops, and do them every other mischief which time and circumstances will permit."[14]

In late August a force of four thousand Continental army soldiers, twenty-five hundred mustered at Wyoming under Sullivan and fifteen hundred gathered at Lake Otsego under General James Clinton, moved along the Susquehanna and met at Tioga. On their march these forces ruthlessly destroyed every Indian and loyalist settlement in the Susquehanna Valley. Except for one battle with British soldiers and Indians at Newtown on August 29, the soldiers encountered little resistance because the Indians and loyalists mostly abandoned their communities as the Continental army approached. Thus the soldiers marched through the heartland of the Iroquois around the Finger Lakes, burning every Indian settlement they found, caring little if any of these villages belonged to Oneidas and Tuscaroras, who were fighting for the Continental army. By the end of September, according to Sullivan, the soldiers had destroyed forty Indian towns and, more important, 160,000 bushels of corn.[15]

In spite of its apparent success, the campaign did not achieve one of its primary military goals: the British and Indians continued to make forays against settlers in the backcountry, often along the Susquehanna. Once Continental army soldiers left the area, the settlers in the valley became easy targets for British and Indian raiding parties. The destruction of the Indians' food supplies, contrary to the hopes of Continental army leaders, reinforced their commitment to the crown. Indians loyal to the king made at least thirty-five separate raids in the valley from 1780 to 1782. Most of these forays involved the murder or capture of valley residents, many of them noncombatants, and the further destruction of crops. In September 1780, for example, one party led by William Johnston, Jr., marched through

14. Donald R. McAdams, "The Sullivan Expedition: Success or Failure," *New York Historical Society Quarterly* 54 (1970), 62–65.
15. Ibid., 70–73.

the valley and destroyed wheat, rye, and livestock at Chillisquaque and Fort Jenkins. On other raids the Indians and British captured or killed valley residents.[16]

The Indians' War

Most valley Indians, along with most of the tribes in the Iroquois Confederacy, fought for the British because it seemed the only way to protect their territory. British officials appreciated the role the Indians played in the crown's campaign to control the backcountry. Guy Johnson, who became superintendent of Indian affairs in 1774 after the death of his uncle and father-in-law Sir William Johnson, praised the Indians' efforts. Indian warriors had, he wrote in 1781, "laid waste a Country abounding in Supplies for the Rebells, which has compelled the latter to contract their frontier, and confine themselves within little forts."[17] What he did not state, however, was that the Indians' military prowess had failed to achieve their primary goal.

By the time of the Revolution, valley Indians had become very familiar with the problem of land-hungry colonists. Although every tribal group present at the 1768 negotiations at Fort Stanwix accepted the terms of the treaty, their approval of the agreement waned as they watched colonists establishing homesteads and farms in their territory. They became especially alarmed when they realized that the map used at Fort Stanwix was inaccurate and that they had unknowingly sold a far larger tract than they had intended. As early as March 1775, thirty-two chiefs and warriors from five tribes resident on the Susquehanna at Otsiningo, Chugnut, Owego, and Tioga complained about this discrepancy to Guy Johnson. Reminding Johnson that Indian settlements on the colonists' side of the line were to be excluded from the Fort Stanwix agreement, the Indians informed him that a recent survey had run a line "in Such a manner along the Susquehanna as to Affect our Property Very much and as we Apprehend Contrary to the Intention of the Treaty." Johnson admitted the error but noted that it "was not the fault of Government it arose from the want of Information" and was partly owing to

16. Ibid., 76–81; John H. Carter, "Indian Incursions in Old Northumberland County during the Revolutionary War, 1777–1782," in Snyder, ed., *Northumberland County*, 373–380.

17. Guy Johnson to George Germain, October 11, 1781, CO 5/82, f. 248–249.

the Indians' suspicions, which had prevented colonists from taking a proper survey before the treaty negotiations. Johnson promised that he would settle the issue, although he did not specify how.[18]

During the war, the British claimed to understand the Indians' desire to reclaim their old territory and openly supported them. Butler, who had negotiated land sales with backcountry Indians before the war, knew of the Indians' hostility toward the colonists in the valley. At a meeting with all of the Iroquois tribes and the Delawares resident on the Susquehanna in early 1778, the Indians informed him that, following the lead of the Senecas, they would join the British forces. Frederick Haldimand, who succeeded Carleton as governor of Quebec and was commander in chief of the crown's North American soldiers, urged Butler to do all he could to keep the Iroquois solidly in the crown's interest. "Their Example," he wrote to Butler in April 1779, "will greatly influence the other nations to act in concert with them in opposing and repulsing the invaders of their property."[19]

In allying themselves with the British, most valley Indians probably shared the logic of several of the tribes in the Iroquois Confederacy: neutrality was impossible, and the British best served their interests. Local circumstances further influenced the Indians' decision. Earlier, the Pennsylvania government had supported them in their struggles with trespassing colonists in the Wyoming Valley and along the West Branch. The Indians also negotiated repeatedly with the Johnson family, representatives of the crown in the backcountry. When many valley colonists began to ally themselves with the rebels, thereby dividing the colonial population, valley Indians chose to support the British in hope of preserving their territory.[20]

The war put an end to the Indians' agriculture and hunting.

18. Proceedings of a Congress with the Chiefs and Warriors of the Cayugas and several Chiefs of the Six Nations Confederacy, February 28, 1775, CO 5/76, f. 114–117. The thirty-two chiefs from the Susquehanna arrived after the meeting began.

19. Butler to Haldimand, September 17, 1778, Add. Mss., 21,765, f. 34–36; Haldimand to Butler, April 18, 1779, Add. Mss., 21,765, f. 97.

20. Robert Albion and Leonidas Dodson, eds., *Philip Vickers Fithian: Journal, 1775–1776, Written on the Virginia-Pennsylvania Frontier and in the Army around New York* (Princeton, N.J., 1934), passim; cf. Barbara Graymont, *The Iroquois in the American Revolution* (Syracuse, N.Y., 1972), esp. 86–128. The Pennsylvania government's battles with members of the Susquehannah Company for control of the Wyoming Valley are documented in *SCP*; vols. 2 through 6 cover the period from the late 1760s to the mid-1770s. The provincial government also attempted to stop encroachments by the so-called Fair Play settlers on the West Branch of the Susquehanna; see *PaCR*, 10:94–95.

When the Continental army invaded in 1779, the soldiers deliberately destroyed all vestiges of the Indians' economy. Their descriptions of the destruction of Indian villages throughout the valley demonstrate the callous nature of their actions. "This evening," Lieutenant Colonel Henry Dearborn wrote in his journal in August, "the town of Owagea [Owego] was made a bone fire of to grace our meeting."[21]

The depredations on the Indians' economy had immediate and obvious effects, yet the Indians also suffered in other ways. Their decline began before Sullivan's 1779 raid and stemmed directly from their commitment to the British. After deciding to join the British war effort, many Indians moved to the crown's stronghold at Niagara, joining thousands of others forced to abandon their fields and rely on the British for provisions. Crown officials soon came to realize that these Indians were in danger of economic collapse.

John Butler, commanding the British military campaign in the backcountry, recognized signs of trouble as early as September 1778, when he toured the Indian country. "As the Young Men were already either out at War, or ready to go with me, they had nothing to subsist upon but the remains of the last Years Corn which was near expended, their hunting being neglected," he wrote to General Frederick Haldimand. "Most of them too, were very bare of Clothes, however upon my promising them Clothing this fall they were satisfied." Difficult times continued. "A Number of the Mohawks, Onandagoes and Ochquagoes are to remain here, having now no Homes to go to," Butler wrote from Niagara in February 1779. "The Ochquago Village being burnt by the Rebels, and the Villages of the Mohawks situated in them of the Enemy."[22]

By July 1779, even before Sullivan's campaign, the Indians were using up food supplies and did not have time to replenish them. "Although there was last Fall a considerable Quantity of Cattle in the Indian Country these have been chiefly consumed by the Indians themselves," Butler wrote to Haldimand. "It is well known that they never raise more Corn, Pulse and things of that Kind which com-

21. Lester Cappon, ed., *Atlas of Early American History: The Revolutionary Era, 1760–1790* (Princeton, N.J., 1976), 21; Frederick Cook, ed., *Journals of the Military Expedition of Major General John Sullivan against the Six Nations of Indians in 1779* (Auburn, N.Y., 1887), 71.

22. Butler to Haldimand, September 17, 1778, February 14, 1779, Add. Mss., 21,765, f. 34–35, 82.

pose the principal Part of their Food than will just suffice for their own Subsistence: but they were so employed on various Excursions the last Summer that they did not cultivate the usual Quantity, and great Part of what they did cultivate was destroyed by some means or other before it came to Perfection." Butler added that travelers in the region, presumably other Indians or perhaps loyalists or rangers working for the British cause, further depleted their food supplies. At towns both within the upper valley and beyond, Butler found that the Indians "have not had an Ear of Corn the whole Winter and were obliged to live such as had them upon Cattle, such as had no Cattle upon Roots. This by the Time we came into the Country made Beef exceeding scarce and dear: what there was we have made Use of, and so intirely has the Country been drained that at Shimong [Chemung] where Cattle were by far the most Plenty there is not a Creature to be got."[23]

The situation was so bleak that the rangers were sent to the Genesee Falls, where they could find enough fish to meet their nutritional needs and, Butler concluded, "neither will they have as many Indians about them to eat up their Provision, and it is impossible to avoid giving it [to] them when they are with you." Haldimand too realized the problems of providing for both the Indians and other crown soldiers; the situation had devastating implications for the British war effort. "For, after the troops have been sent into the Country," he wrote to Butler in September 1779, "to have them stand or obliged to abandon the Purpose of their Enterprise for want of Provisions, would be followed by much more fatal Consequences than if they had never undertaken it."[24]

The British struggled to supply the Indians with food. They realized, as Butler informed Lieutenant Colonel Mason Bolton, the British commanding officer at Niagara, that providing them with subsistence was essential for the Indians' continued commitment to the crown's cause. "The Indians seem in better Spirits & more determined than I have seen them since they left Chuchnut [Chugnut]," Butler wrote, "and if they get any Succour from Niagara I am in hopes I shall be able to persuade them to attack the Rebels on their March, at any Rate I shall do my Endeavour to get them to make a Stand."[25]

23. Butler to Haldimand, July 21, 1779, Add. Mss., 21,765, f. 115–116.
24. Ibid.; Haldimand to Butler, September 3, 1779, Add. Mss., 21,765, f. 136.
25. Butler to Bolton, September 8, 1779, Add. Mss., 21,760, f. 210.

British military officials realized that cattle could solve their problems, but they could not find enough to meet the Indians' needs. The price of cows soared during the war. Bolton wrote to Haldimand in September 1779 that the price had risen from eight to ten pounds per head to twenty pounds at Carleton Island; settlers near Niagara seeking profit from wartime shortages wanted to move their stocks there to receive the better price. Bolton wanted to keep the cattle near Niagara to feed the Indians and refused their request, but even these cattle proved too few to meet the Indians' needs. "The Indians have not brought in Cattle this year," he wrote, "all we have purchased was a few Cows from the distressed Families."[26]

Cattle rustling became common during military forays. As early as January 1778 soldiers had orders to bring cattle back from their raids in the upper Susquehanna Valley, presumably to feed both soldiers and Indians. "I shall collect all the Cattle of every kind I can," John McDonell wrote to Butler in July 1779 from the valley, "as I am Sensible that Provision will be an Object of the Utmost Consequence when all the Indians are Imbodied." One group of Indians and rangers at Wyalusing in September 1780 managed to take the cattle around the settlers' fort, but provisions remained scarce. Valley game populations had not recovered from the depredations of the fur trade so the party was unable to hunt. In addition, as Continental army soldiers discovered and as the Indians no doubt realized, herding cattle through the upper valley was a time-consuming and frustrating operation.[27]

The Indians' dependence on the British for food and other goods such as clothing and tools proved very expensive. None realized this more than Haldimand, who urged Butler to cut costs and to encourage the Indians to begin cultivating during the spring of 1779. Several months later, he informed Butler that the costs of the Indian Department exceeded those of every other department, including the army and navy. Although Haldimand surely exaggerated, his point was unambiguous. "I must therefore recommend to Your most Serious attention the Strictest oeconomy wherever there is a possibility of observing it," he wrote in August, "the Credit of every Person at the head of Departments being concerned, and what is Still of

26. Bolton to Haldimand, September 7, 1779, Add. Mss., 21,760, f. 208–209.

27. Butler to Haldimand, January 20, 1778, Add. Mss., 21,765, f. 9; McDonell to Butler, July 24, 1779, Add. Mss., 21,765, f. 122; William Johnston, Jr., to Guy Johnson, September 17, 1780, Add. Mss., 21,760, f. 366; Cook, ed., *Journals*, 6.

greater Import, the Public Good." But Butler believed such requests unrealistic. Providing the necessary supplies would further raise the expenses of the Indian Department. The Indians would remain firmly in the crown's interest only if the British provided them with what they needed, as even Haldimand realized by August 1779. "We are Still Strong for the King of England," David, a Mohawk, informed Haldimand, "and we will lose our Lives chearfully for him if you will Shew us he is a man of his Word, & that he will not abandon his Brother the Six Nations who always Shed their Blood for him."[28]

The condition of the British and their Indian allies worsened when Sullivan's troops destroyed the Indians' towns along the Susquehanna and its tributaries. More Indians migrated to Niagara, dependent on the British. According to Butler, they had been "driven from their Country & [had] every Thing destroyed." Still, the Indians remained firmly allied to the British. "Notwithstanding the Losses the Indians have suffered by the Destruction of their Corn & Villages," Butler wrote to Haldimand in September 1779, "I am happy to acquaint your Excellency that they seem still unshaken in their Attachment to his Majesty's Cause, and declare as soon as they have placed their Women & Children in Security they will go and take Revenge of the Enemy."[29]

Still, the situation became bleaker, leading the British to reconsider their support of the Indians. In late September, Bolton summarized the British problem. "The Indians bear this misfortune with more patience than I could possibly expect, and seemed determined to take revenge when an opportunity offers," he wrote from Niagara, "but the loss of their Corn &c and the Scarcity of provisions here to supply the number I shall have at this Post, makes it impracticable at present." Fearful that the British would have to support almost 3,700 Indians at Niagara, Bolton later wrote to Haldimand describing the situation. "I am convinced your Excellency will not be surprised if I am extremely alarmed, for to support such a Multitude I think will be absolutely impossible." Bolton prevailed upon Butler to convince as many Indians as possible to spend the winter at Montreal and urged him to "inform all the Rest who have not suf-

28. Haldimand to Butler, April 8, August 1779, Add. Mss., 21,765, f. 93, 134; Butler to Haldimand, September 20, 1779, Add. Mss., 21,765, f. 140; Message of David to Haldimand, August 22, 1779, CO 42/39, f. 247.
29. Butler to Haldimand, September 20, 1779, Add. Mss., 21,765, f. 140–141.

ferd by the Enemy, that they must return home, and take care of their corn &c." A month later Bolton was encouraged because the Continental army had not destroyed the Indians' entire crop. "Colonel Johnson informs me that the Six Nations are resolved not to leave their Country, as the Enemy might imagine they had abandoned it through fear, however they have promised (he says) to send several Families to the Villages which have not been destroyed, and Parties to bring in the Corn that the Rebels in their precipitate Retreat have left untouched."[30]

But the efforts to encourage the Indians to become self-sufficient did not succeed because the Indians could not move back to their villages. The British continued to provide corn and hoes to many Indians from the upper Susquehanna Valley and elsewhere until at least May 1781. More than fifteen hundred Indians received assistance at Niagara because their corn crop had failed.[31]

While the war years presented troubles enough for the Indians, they also faced other problems. The winter of 1779–1780 was unusually severe, with snow up to five feet deep across much of western New York. Animals died for lack of forage, making the winter hunt even less productive for Indian hunters. The end of the war brought epidemics to the Indians of the region: dysentery, measles, and smallpox devastated refugee communities. The resulting demographic decline, which, including military casualties, has been estimated at approximately 50 percent for the Iroquois from the early 1760s to late 1790s, boded poorly for economic recovery.[32]

But more than anything else it was land-hungry settlers and speculators who prevented the Indians' economic recovery in the upper Susquehanna Valley and elsewhere. Even many Oneidas and Tuscaroras who had fought for the rebels were unable to maintain their land in the Susquehanna Valley. In 1785 they sold an enormous tract, encompassing present Broome and Chenango counties. The Indians did not want to part with the territory circumscribed by the Unadilla, Chenango, and Susquehanna rivers. This region was, as

30. Bolton to Major Nairne, September 22, 1779, Add. Mss., 21,760, f. 220; Bolton to Haldimand, October 2, November 10, 1779, Add. Mss., 21,760, f. 226, 244.

31. Distribution of Corn and Hoes for the Indians of Colonel Johnson's Department, planting at Buffaloe Creek, May 13, 1781, Add. Mss., 21,769, f. 120.

32. Anthony F. C. Wallace, The Death and Rebirth of the Seneca (1970; rpt. New York, 1972), 194–196.

Petrus, an Oneida chief, declared in June 1785, "our Deer-hunting Country, and the Northern our Beaver-hunting Country." But the Indians, under relentless pressure, sold much of the land to state-appointed negotiators in New York. The sale of the land prevented the Oneidas and Tuscaroras from reestablishing communities in the upper valley.[33]

After the war some Indians tried to move back to the upper valley. Way-Way, a Nanticoke born at Chugnut, was among them. She was, she recalled later, "a little gal when the white man destroyed our crops and run us off in the war." Like other Indians she moved to Niagara and then to the Genesee, presumably remaining with the Indian women and children at these British strongholds while Indian men fought in the war. After the war she returned to the upper valley, joining other Nanticokes and some Delawares trying to reestablish themselves in the region. But economic recovery proved elusive. They found settlers living on their former lands, and though they remained in the area for two years, the Indians apparently never prospered; one settler's family, Way-Way recalled, provided them with flour "& all kinds of provisions," evidence perhaps of troubled times. Soon Way-Way left the valley, migrating with other Nanticokes to live among the Iroquois at Grand River, Ontario. Other refugees from the upper valley probably joined displaced communities in far western New York or southern Canada or, like the Delawares, migrated farther west. Many probably found themselves living in what one anthropologist has termed "slums in the wilderness."[34]

The Indians' economic decline had begun well before rebellious colonists felt compelled to sever their ties with the crown. But the long-term view minimizes the impact of the Revolution on these Indians' lives. Earlier they had rebounded from economic setbacks to

---

33. Franklin B. Hough, ed., *Proceedings of the Commissioners of Indian Affairs, Appointed by Law for the Extinguishment of Indian Titles in the State of New York*, 2 vols. (Albany, N.Y., 1861), 1:84–109; Jack Campisi, "Oneida," in William Sturtevant, ed., *Handbook of North American Indians*, vol. 15, *Northeast*, ed. Bruce Trigger (Washington, D.C., 1978), 484; Barbara Graymont, "New York State Indian Policy after the Revolution," *NY Hist.* 57 (1976), 438–474.

34. Statement of Way-Way, July 14, 1857, Draper Papers photostat, Broome County Historical Society, Binghamton, N.Y.; Wallace, *Death and Rebirth of the Seneca*, chap. 7.

establish more or less stable communities in the valley, often, as Continental army soldiers found, with a thriving agricultural economy. But the war proved too devastating, as was illustrated by the Indians' reliance on the British for food. Unable to reclaim their former territory after the war ended, these Indians once again became refugees, forced to reside far from the Susquehanna and often living in desperate economic straits.[35]

The economic misfortunes of the Indians of the upper Susquehanna Valley resembled those of many others caught in the struggle for land and power in eastern North America. In spite of its place in a long history of European colonial aggression against Indians, the revolutionary war was a stunning assault on interracial relations. Although the expansion of a commercial market weakened Indian communities before the war and helped prepare the region for colonial settlement, colonists and Indians had worked together peacefully to resolve their differences and maintain harmony in this borderland. The desire of all for peace in the valley proved a great help to local Indians in their periodic difficulties with epidemic diseases and colonial trespassers. Most Indians and colonists had demonstrated a willingness to live near each other. After the Revolution few settlers in the valley wanted Indian neighbors; they associated the Indians with the war and would never trust them again. The Indians could not reestablish stable communities in the region because their economy was in disarray. Refugee Indians could no longer find sanctuary in the upper Susquehanna Valley.

The economic decline of the valley Indians during the war years has a greater meaning as well. In the intellectual ferment of the 1780s, those involved in creating the Constitution needed more than history and ideology to establish their new system of government. What they needed, and received, was the support of people who would live with the government created by the Constitution. But when various states held ratifying conventions, few in attendance

---

35. The Six Nations of the Grand River, for example, which included refugees from the upper Susquehanna Valley like Way-Way, prospered compared to other nineteenth-century Indian communities in Canada. But by the 1830s many farming families still did not have sufficient storage facilities for their livestock and grain and as late as midcentury at least some relied on seed grants from the Indian Department to raise sufficient crops. See Sally M. Weaver, "Six Nations of the Grand River, Ontario," in Sturtevant, ed., *Handbook of North American Indians*, 15:525–529.

voiced eloquent pleas on behalf of the Indians. Even Indians who had fought for the Continental army were excluded, along with those who had been allied with the British. During the period when many declared their freedom, Indians in the valley and beyond found themselves dispossessed.

"The extreems of war"

Troops invading the valley all shared the goal of destroying the local economy. No individual or group escaped the horrors of the war. By the early 1780s surviving valley residents surveying their old farms and communities saw only ashes and fields taken over by weeds.

Soldiers spent a great deal of time and energy destroying local crops. In spite of their own food shortages, British soldiers and their Indian allies deliberately ruined the crops of settlers allied with the Continental army, presumably because they could not transport the food back to Niagara. The British soldiers and Indians under William Johnston's command destroyed one hundred bushels of rye and wheat at the fort near Chillisquaque in early September 1780. Three days later they burned two hundred bushels of the same crops at Fort Jenkins along the Susquehanna.[36]

Continental army soldiers were constantly amazed at the crop yields they found at Indian settlements in the upper valley, but this did not interfere with their destruction of these commodities. At Chemung one troop destroyed approximately a thousand bushels of corn and presumably burned extensive supplies of pumpkins, beans, squash, and potatoes as well. At Newtown, according to one soldier, another troop destroyed 150 acres of fresh produce as well as "great Quantities of Beans, Potatoes, Pumpkins, Cucumbers, Squashes & Watermellons." The company traveling with Henry Dearborn was representative of many involved in Sullivan's campaign. At Chemung they burned 40 acres of corn; at Chugnut they destroyed "plenty of cucumbers squashes turnips &c." Several miles away, at an unidentified location, the party discovered a field of "70 or 80 acres

36. Butler to Bolton, August 26, 1779, CO 42/39, f. 362.

of fine corn"; the following day it took them so long to destroy the crop that their march was delayed several hours.[37]

Many valley residents sought refuge in stockaded palisades, where there was not enough room for their livestock. Left to browse outside of the stockades, the livestock became easy victims of enemy soldiers. Both British and Continental army soldiers reported widespread destruction of all types of livestock. Butler claimed to have killed and driven off one thousand head of cattle as well as sheep and swine "in great numbers" when he attacked Wyoming. Residents of Cherry Valley who survived the attack on the settlement returned to find their livestock gone.[38] John McDonell's force of British rangers collected cattle roaming around the mountains in the valley and sent them, with a guard, to Nanticoke. He knew that cattle had great strategic value, especially because of the increased pressure put on British supplies by the Indians. McDonell realized that the valley residents could not take livestock with them when they evacuated their settlements. The settlers had "abandoned their Forts the Evening before and fled with great Precipitation," McDonell wrote to Butler from Tioga Point in early August 1779, "leaving behind a great Quantity of Goods & most of their Cattle."[39]

British, Indian, and Continental army soldiers did not limit their attacks to crops and animals; they also systematically destroyed houses, barns, and mills. Butler claimed that his soldiers burned one thousand houses and all of the mills at Wyoming. The Continental army officer Benjamin Warren lamented that in destroying Cherry Valley the invaders "burnt all the buildings." Officers in Sullivan's campaign routinely reported the burning of Indians' and loyalists' houses.[40]

The destruction of agricultural commodities and entire settlements led to large loss of human life. Valley residents were easy targets because their daily tasks made them vulnerable to quick raids. To tend their fields and livestock or to hunt animals, settlers

37. Cook, ed., Journals, 6, 27, 70–71.

38. Butler to Bolton, July 8, 1778, CO 42/38, f. 169–170; "Diary of Captain Benjamin Warren," 383.

39. McDonell to Butler, July 24, 1779, CO 5/98, f. 289; McDonell to Butler, July 24, 1779, Add. Mss., 21,765, f. 122; McDonell to Butler, August 5, 1779, CO 5/98, f. 289–290.

40. Butler to Bolton, July 8, 1778, CO 42/38, f. 169–170; "Diary of Captain Benjamin Warren," 383; see, for example, Cook, ed., Journals, 23–24, 27–28.

often traveled beyond the protection of the forts. Soldiers killed or captured at least five hundred valley residents from 1776 to 1782; most of these casualties occurred during 1778 and 1779.[41]

Most of the people killed in the valley were residents primarily interested in protecting their livelihoods, not soldiers participating directly in military campaigns. During Sullivan's campaign, soldiers provided one elderly Indian woman with goods at French Catherine's Town because she was too infirm to move, but a returning party found that she had been murdered. "Who killed her, I cannot ascertain," wrote William Barton, "but it is generally believed to be three men of ours who were sent up from Tioga express a few days before." Barton later heard of the murders of two Indians at Cayuga Lake, a young man who was "decrepid to such a degree that he could not walk" and an elderly woman "so old as not to be able to be brought off." Barton wrote that the colonel of the party in the area refused to let the soldiers hurt them and instructed his men to leave them with a house, "but some of the soldiers taking an opportunity when not observed set the house on fire, after securing and making the door fast. The troops having got in motion and marched some distance, the house was consumed together with the savages, in spite of all exertions."[42]

The Iroquois expressed shock at Continental army soldiers' atrocities. Emphasizing the "Cruelty of the Rebels" in 1779, Tioguanda, an Onondaga chief, described the sufferings of his community. "They put to death all the Women and Children, excepting some of the Young Women that they carried away for the use of their soldiers," he recalled, "and were put to death in a more shameful and Scandalous manner." The barbarity of the soldiers seemed a sharp contrast to their professed religion. "We should prevent them from Murdering us in the Night, and acting with so much cruelty and

41. Casualty estimates are based on Helen H. Russell's claim that 170 people were killed or captured on the West Branch from 1776 to 1778; the reports of the battle at Wyoming, where, according to Butler, more than 220 men were killed; and reports of various incidents throughout the valley. See Russell, "Great Runaway of 1778," 96; Butler to Bolton, July 8, 1778, CO 42/38, f. 169–170; "Diary of Captain Benjamin Warren"; and Carter, "Indian Incursions," 363–381. Estimates of Indian casualties are difficult to determine. The Indians' information-gathering network and knowledge of regional paths apparently gave them the time and ability to evacuate their towns quickly; many presumably fled to Niagara. Soldiers' diaries often noted that they entered recently abandoned Indian towns.

42. Cook, ed., *Journals*, 12–13.

inhumanity," Tioguanda continued, "& tho' they call themselves Christians, they are more cruel than the Indians who are not so."[43]

The destruction of crops, livestock, barns, houses, and mills and the violence suffered by valley residents threatened every settlement in the region. The destructive force of the war was most evident in the depopulation of entire settlements. Soldiers reported the destruction of at least twenty-five communities on the North Branch of the Susquehanna River and its tributaries. By the early 1780s Cherry Valley, Wyoming, Shawnee, Lackawanna, Quilutimack, Tunkhannock, Wyalusing, Tioga, Chemung, Newtown, French Catherine's Town, Springfield, Aleout, Unadilla, Conihunto, Oquaga, Shawhianghto, Ingaren, Otsiningo, Chugnut, Owego, Wysankin, Newtychaning, Konnawa holla, and Queen Esther's Town had few, if any, residents. Settlements along the West Branch suffered similarly and with the same results: practically no one remained in its fertile vales. Isolated farms lay deserted throughout the upper valley. Often chroniclers of the ravages arrived to find only the bleak remains of settlements. William Gray, a captain in Sullivan's campaign, drew a map of the upper valley which gave a vivid, if brief, image of the region: "Ononaughquag Burnt"; "Cunahunta Burnt"; "Unendilla Town Burnt"; "Grist & Saw Mills Burnt"; "Scotch Settlement Partly Burnt."[44]

In all, the military raids of both armies disrupted agricultural rhythms and thus forced settlers to flee their farms. In November 1777, well before the worst incidents, the Northumberland County militia colonel Samuel Hunter realized that if valley settlements were evacuated, particularly along the West Branch, the refugees would be impoverished. "The People there is in a bad way," he wrote, "as they have got in no Crops this fall, which is very hard on them being generaly Poor, & new settlers." He knew, however, that few could remain in the region because of the risk of attack. Hunter hoped that stationing the local militia in the region would convince the settlers that it was safe to return to their homes. But many valley residents refused militia duty when they found that their families had

43. Meeting of the Principal Chiefs and Warriors of the Six Nations, December 11–12, 1782, CO 42/44, f. 108–110.

44. William Gray, "Draught of Schohara, Part of the West Branch of Delaware & Part of Susquehanna Rivers," in Cook, ed., Journals.

"suffered for want of the Necessaries of life" while the men served elsewhere, and Hunter's plan could not be put into action.[45]

Even after the worst of the violence was over, Indian raids prevented many settlers from reestablishing their agrarian economy. Believing that "our Frontiers is harresed by a cruel Savage Enemy," Hunter wrote in April 1779, the settlers "cannot get any Spring crops in to induce them to stay in the County. I am afraid in a very short time we shall have no inhabitants above this place." A year later the situation looked equally bleak. The inability of the army to protect the region and the impossibility of raising the militia because of the desperate condition of the settlers meant continued depopulation of much of the area. "For if they Miss Geting spring Crops put in the Ground for the support of their Familys," Hunter concluded, the settlers "have nothing that can induce them to stay."[46]

The residents who remained crowded into the surviving towns, their families torn apart by the war. Albert and Catherine Polhemus fled Muncy for the safety of Sunbury, but they soon died, leaving seven orphans; the Orphan's Court, wishing to protect the public finances, apprenticed them out to different families. Other families fared little better. Henry Dougherty, a private in a local militia unit summoned to battle in New Jersey, returned "so badly wounded" that he was, in the words of his petition to the Orphan's Court, "incapable of labour." The court considered his plight and awarded him £21 5s., the equivalent of half of his pay for seventeen months of service. Some wounded veterans received even less compensation, although those of higher rank in the military did better. Yet even these disabled veterans fared better than the widows of soldiers killed in battle. When Robert McWilliams died while serving in the Northumberland County militia in a battle with British soldiers in Philadelphia County, he left behind his wife, Elizabeth, and three children, ranging in age from eight months to seven years. The Orphan's Court, on recommendation from the Overseers of the Poor, recognized that Elizabeth had done her best to support the children,

45. Russell, "Great Runaway of 1778," 91; Hunter to Thomas Wharton, November 1, 1777, P. Arch. 1st ser., 5:737; Hunter to Joseph Reed, December 13, 1778, ibid., 7:117; see also Charles F. Snyder, "The Militia of Northumberland County during the Revolution," in Snyder, ed., Northumberland County, 220, 226.

46. Hunter to Reed, April 27, 1779, P. Arch. 1st ser., 7:346; Hunter to Reed, ibid., 8:157; see also Snyder, "Militia of Northumberland County," 227, 232.

but by 1781, she was ill and no longer able to provide for them. The court granted her £37 10s., the equivalent of two and one-half years of her deceased husband's pay, as compensation for her loss. Sarah Campbell, whose husband, Michael, a private in the county militia, was killed by Indians in June 1778, received far less than Elizabeth McWilliams, only £7 10s., for her loss, the equivalent of six months of her husband's wages. The lessons of these decisions were painfully clear to the residents of the upper valley: those victimized by wartime hostilities would have to face the future with diminished economic prospects.[47]

Witnesses to the war also recorded its impact on the region's economy. Samuel Hunter described the plight of those who had lived along the West Branch and in the summer of 1779 were forced to take refuge in Sunbury and Northumberland. The enemy "sticking so close to this County after the Continentall troops has marched to Wyoming," Hunter wrote to Matthew Smith, a colonel in the Ninth Pennsylvania Regiment, "has intimidated the people so much that they are Realy on the Eve of deserting the County intirely as there is no Prospect of any assistance, that the People on the Frontiers Could get their Harvists put up." When Smith arrived at Sunbury early in August, he realized the accuracy of Hunter's descriptions. "The Distress of the People here is Great," he wrote in his report, "but Scarcely Can be told. The town now Composes Northumberland County. The Enemy have Burnt, Every where they have Been, houses, Barnes, Rice & Wheat, in the fields, stocks of hay, &c; is all Consumed— Such Devastation I have not yet Seen."[48]

47. Northumberland County Orphan's Court Docket 1 (1772–1785), 18–20, 27, 32, 21, NCCH; see also the cases of John Fitzsimmons and Thimothy Lennington, Docket 1, 11–12. Dougherty and Fitzsimmons apparently remained incapable of supporting themselves adequately, and each returned to the court to receive further, but still limited, compensation in 1784 and 1785. See Docket 1, 70–71, and Docket 2 (1784–1795), 17. The court also awarded a pension to Elizabeth McWilliams of £20 in 1785; see Docket 2, 17. Some were awarded more money in a lump sum, such as the £150 Martha Ross received in March 1785 in compensation for the death of her husband at Piscataway eight years earlier, but this sum represented his salary for those years during which she and her young son managed to get by on their own; see Docket 2, 20–21. On higher position and greater compensation see the case of Sergeant Adam Christ, Docket 2, 24–25.

48. Samuel Hunter to Matthew Smith, July 23, 1779, P. Arch. 1st ser., 7:574; Matthew Smith to Joseph Reed, August 3, 1779, ibid., 609–610; see also Frederic A. Godcharles, "The Battle of Fort Freeland," in Snyder, ed., Northumberland County, 134, 143.

At Wyoming the devastations of battle lingered well after the attack on the town. When John Burrowes returned to the area after the conclusion of Sullivan's campaign in October 1779, he searched for the possessions of a friend who apparently died at Wyoming. "Have been looking for his things but find very few," he wrote in his journal, "instead of finding gentlemen whom I thought would take care of them I met with robbers of the dead."[49]

The total destruction of settlements in the valley struck everyone who traveled through it. Even some involved in Sullivan's campaign expressed regret about their actions. Dr. Jabez Campfield, a surgeon from New Jersey, mourned the army's behavior. "I very heartily wish these rusticks may be reduced to reason, by the approach of this army, without their suffering the extreems of war," he wrote in his journal on August 11. "There is something so cruel, in destroying the habitations of any people, (however mean they may be, being their all) that I might say the prospect hurts my feelings." Dr. Ebenezer Elmer's journal contains perhaps the simplest yet most instructive eulogy for the region. "The devastations of war," he wrote, "are not less conspicuous here than in any place in America."[50]

Elmer understated the truth: communities in the upper Susquehanna Valley had suffered far more devastation than practically any other northern battle theater. Elsewhere in the middle Atlantic region or New England, communities survived the war with their populations largely intact. The "great runaway" in the Susquehanna Valley remains a staple of local histories because it described valley residents' particular wartime experience and forever altered their interpretation of the Revolution.

War, the Environment, and Economic Development

By the time the military efforts of the British and Continental armies shifted away from the backcountry of Pennsylvania and New York, abandoned fields and smoldering buildings dominated the landscape of the upper Susquehanna Valley. But the war years also set the stage for the next round of economic development. Burned

49. Cook, ed., *Journals*, 50.
50. Ibid., 54, 81.

fields proved a setback to those who had planted crops but remained fertile and useful for later cultivators; indeed, the cleared fields, especially around earlier Indian towns, beckoned potential settlers who benefited from the burning and the subsequent improvement of the soil. In addition, the large number of Continental army soldiers who moved through the valley spread information about it just as missionaries and travelers had done a generation earlier.

Soldiers marching through the area filled their journals with descriptions of the many grassy plains and meadows that they crossed, and some of them openly speculated about the prospects for settlement. William Barton noticed that "Queen Esther's Flats, once an Indian town, [was] now covered with wild grass of amazing length." John Burrowes praised the territory near Tioga. "As soon as our tents were pitched I amused myself with walking on the bank of the river," he wrote in his journal in August 1779, "which brought to my view a large bottom or beautiful plain, not a stump to be seen, a great burthen of wild grass, and with little industry (from the appearance of the soil) would make most excellent meadows." Some, like Dr. Jabez Campfield, realized that the fields could serve the army's immediate needs. Near Shehequanung, he saw "a beautiful plain covered with grass; very necessary for our hungry horses and cattle." Several days later his party passed through the abandoned Indian town of Cokonnuck. "This is a large fine flat of rich land," he wrote in his journal, "covered with fine grass, such as clover, spear & fowl-meadow grass, and the natural grass of the country, which here grows 8 or 10 feet high." Other former Indian settlements at Wyalusing, Tioga, and Owego offered similar resources and impressed soldiers. Dr. Ebenezer Elmer noted that the low-lying fields at Wyoming were extremely fertile. The fields at Shawnee Flats, three miles below Wyoming, similarly impressed him; they were known for "producing every kind of food in the greatest abundance."[51]

The war gave Continental army soldiers the opportunity to learn about the regional environment, such as the river's potential as a means of transportation. Army leaders planned to float supplies from Lake Otsego to Tioga, where they had set up their provisional camp. Because the water in the river was then insufficient for this

51. Ibid., 81, 5, 43, 54–55, 69–70, 82. It is unclear if Burrowes was walking along the Chemung or the Susquehanna.

transport, they constructed a temporary dam at the head of the Susquehanna, raising the level of water in the lake. When they were ready to move the provisions, they broke the dam, releasing enough water to move the goods to Tioga. Soldiers also used the river for the transportation of wounded from Newtown to Tioga and later from Tioga to Sunbury.[52]

The soldiers also discovered that water travel could be extremely dangerous. They traveled through hundreds of miles of backcountry terrain, crossing and recrossing the river and its tributaries countless times. "Our Brigade & Part of another & the artillery Baggage & Pack horses & Cattle forded the River twice this afternoon, the water was waist Deep and Very rapid," Moses Fellows wrote in his journal on June 27. "Some of our Baggage & flower [flour] and ammunition Was Lost In the ford." Near Chemung several horses were swept down the river during a crossing, and some soldiers drowned. Like the traders and missionaries who traveled through the upper valley a generation earlier, soldiers realized the necessity of gaining sound knowledge of the Susquehanna and its seasonal changes.[53]

Many fished while on the campaign, supplementing their diet with an important source of protein. A group of soldiers in Lieutenant Erkuries Beatty's party stationed at Lake Otsego caught trout in "one of the branches of the Susquehanna." Dr. Elmer and Dr. Campfield were impressed by the quantity and variety of fish near Wyoming, which included rock shad, "Sucurs," chubb, trout, and pickerel. They also ate other local foods, although some elicited less than favorable comments. "I eat part of a fryed Rattle Snake to day," Henry Dearborn wrote in his journal, "which would have tasted very well had it not been snake."[54]

Soldiers discovered that the upper valley would be an ideal place to settle, and many returned after the hostilities ended. Many of those who served in the Continental army were both young and, compared to many of their neighbors, poor. Although hope for increased economic standing would not have prompted them to enlist,

52. Ibid., 19, 27, 51; McAdams, "Sullivan Expedition," 70.
53. Cook, ed., *Journals*, 87, 44, 64.
54. Ibid., 20, 82, 53, 64.

they would naturally want to improve their condition after the war.[55] At least 300 men who served in the Continental army eventually settled in Northumberland County. Cemetery surveys indicate that at least 73 soldiers were interred at the burial ground at Warrior Run in the early nineteenth century; none of these men were casualties of the war but presumably settled in the region after its conclusion. A further 225 revolutionary war soldiers were buried in other parts of Northumberland County; only 4 of them had died during the war. Although some of these men served in the Northumberland County militia, indicating previous residence in the upper valley, an even larger number served either in the militias of other Pennsylvania counties or in the regiments of other states.[56]

War, like trade, opened the valley for settlement. Trade had encouraged many people to travel in the region, weakened the resident Indian population, and spread knowledge of a potentially rich agricultural area to a population seeking such territory. The war had a similar effect, but with a crucial difference: traders' activities weakened the valley Indians' ability to sustain their settlements in the region, but no one involved in the commercial system sought to destroy the local Indians' communities, whereas the ruin of valley settlements was the intention of those involved in the military campaigns of the late 1770s.

The war eradicated any amicable sentiments that still remained between Indians and settlers. The people who moved to the valley after the war heard about the savagery of the Indians, recounted in such tales as "The Lost Sister of Wyoming," a captivity narrative about a young girl captured by Indians at Wyoming in 1778. At least one of the four nineteenth-century versions of the story, littered

55. See Charles Royster, *A Revolutionary People at War: The Continental Army and American Character, 1775–1783* (Chapel Hill, N.C., 1979), 373–378. Royster concludes that studies indicating that economic self-interest motivated young men to enlist do not adequately assess the complex reasons why people risk their lives by volunteering to go to war. Given his important reservations, it still seems likely that however much these men were imbued with the revolutionary cause, many people living in a largely agrarian society and not able to control fully their own economic livelihoods would be attracted to an area such as the upper Susquehanna Valley when the war was over. The familiarity they gained with the region during the campaign would have prompted them to return to the region. On military service and economic standing see Shy, "Hearts and Minds in the American Revolution."

56. "Revolutionary Soldiers Buried at Warrior Run," in Snyder, ed., *Northumberland County*, 409–412; Charlotte D. Walter, comp., "Revolutionary Soldiers of Northumberland County, Pennsylvania," ibid., 413–430.

with lurid incidents depicting the brutality of the Indians toward the settlers during the revolutionary war, was intended to be pedagogic; the author hoped it would "be suitable for the child at home and at the Sabbath School and such as will be approved by Him whose approbation will one day be felt to be the only thing of any importance." In the story, Frances Slocum, captured by Delawares, grows up, marries a Delaware who later leaves her village, and later marries a Miami chief, becoming the mother of his children. When her surviving siblings locate her in a Miami village along the Missisineway River sixty years after her abduction, she refuses to return to the Susquehanna Valley with them, preferring to remain with her Indian family. Her refusal shocks her brother and sister, who cannot imagine why anyone would remain with Indians instead of returning to civilization. The story's lesson was clear: the Indians were savage because they were not Christian, and even a Christian child could become a savage if separated for too long from the gospel.[57] The story's popularity revealed a fundamental change in race relations along the Susquehanna: the worlds of the Indians and the settlers, once intertwined, had become totally distinct; never again would these peoples live in harmony in the upper valley.

57. Rev. John Todd, *The Lost Sister of Wyoming: An Authentic Narrative* (Northampton, Pa., 1842), quotation on p. 4. See also John F. Meginness, *Biography of Frances Slocum, the Lost Sister of Wyoming: A Complete Narrative of Her Captivity and Wanderings among the Indians* (Williamsport, Pa., 1891). Both of these narratives are reprinted in *The Garland Library of Narratives of North American Indian Captivities*, vol. 58 (New York, 1975).

7 Postwar Economic Development

Apart from a scattering of ruins and a few houses, especially around Sunbury, the upper Susquehanna Valley after the war appeared to many to have reverted to a previous state; it bore little resemblance to the settled landscape of the prewar period. When William Cooper toured the area in 1786, he believed it almost completely devoid of habitation, a situation he immediately helped change by establishing Cooperstown and luring settlers to his newly acquired holdings. "I am now descending into the vale of life," he wrote in 1807, "and I must acknowledge that I look back with self complacency upon what I have done, and am proud of having been an instrument in reclaiming such large and fruitful tracts from the waste of the creation."[1]

Cooper exaggerated—the valley was certainly not a primeval, untouched wilderness—yet his statement reflected the scope of the postwar economic development in the upper valley. In the 1780s and 1790s the regional economy changed in profound and permanent ways. Some of the success of the postwar years followed from the pre-Revolution phases of settlement. Indeed, postwar landlords often copied their predecessors' policies for luring settlers to the region to obtain the labor necessary for economic development.

1. William Cooper, *A Guide in the Wilderness* (1810; rpt. Freeport, N.Y., 1970), 8–9.

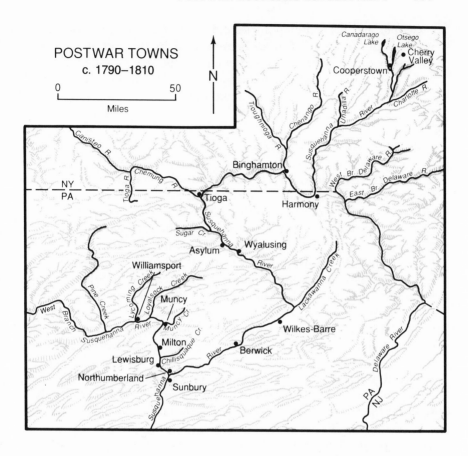

But postwar opportunities also shaped much of the emerging valley economy. Those who came to control large sums of capital during the Revolution, often through political connections, quickly obtained title to much of the depopulated region and amassed estates far more extensive than those of even the wealthiest colonists. With the assistance of state and county courts and legislatures, these landholders directed economic development after the war. Most important, they bound the local economy into the larger commercial network of the new republic. This phase of development drew strength from post-Revolution attitudes toward commercial development, which emerged in the actions of legislatures and courts legitimating state and local support of private economic development on a far more extensive scale than during the colonial period.

Cooper and his contemporaries did not rescue the area from "the waste of the creation." But, as became clear by the end of the century, they did organize the resettlement of the region, establish new export operations, and shape local attitudes toward the place of the valley in the larger Atlantic economic world.

The Postwar Real Estate Market

The valley remained largely deserted until the mid-1780s, but by the early 1790s, thousands of people had moved to the area. Some who had occupied property in the territory before the war returned to their old improvements; many others who had not lived there before soon followed, including soldiers who had fought in Sullivan's campaign. As in the prewar period, a group of wealthy landlords controlled the regional real estate market. Some of these landlords were directly involved in the financial and political institutions of the new republic; others confined their activities to the private sector. They shared basic assumptions about the valley economy and especially the need to control the local real estate market to enhance their own economic positions in the region.

The Revolution had an immediate impact on landownership in the region. States with competing claims to parts of the valley quickly resolved their differences. In two cases arbitrators awarded tracts of land along the Susquehanna or its tributaries to outsiders in compensation for their losses of land elsewhere. A group of settlers known as the "Vermont Sufferers," for example, was awarded a tract in Clinton Township along the banks of the Susquehanna in compensation for their loss of title to land in Vermont. At a conference in Hartford in 1786, New York granted an even larger tract of land, 230,400 acres in the valley just north of the Pennsylvania border, to Massachusetts in compensation for lands that New York had gained along the border of Massachusetts. To pay off war debts, the state of Massachusetts sold the tract, known as the Boston Ten Towns, or Massachusetts Ten Towns, or the Boston Purchase, to a company of sixty people interested in organizing settlement of the area.[2]

2. Ruth L. Higgins, *Expansion in New York, with Especial Reference to the Eighteenth Century* (Columbus, Ohio, 1931), 109; Robert A. Frost, *Life on the Upper Susquehanna, 1783–1860* (New York, 1951), 10; Marjorie B. Hinman, *The Creation of Broome County, New York* (Windsor, N.Y., 1981), 5–8.

Even more important, and certainly more famous, was the resolution of the dispute between Pennsylvania and Connecticut over the Wyoming territory. Representatives of the two states waged legal battles over the area from the early 1780s to the mid-1790s. In the 1782 trial at Trenton, the states submitted their grievance to a judicial body convened according to Article IX of the Articles of Confederation; the case was the only use of that article in the pre-Constitution period. The judges decided that Pennsylvania had jurisdiction over the area.[3]

Prominent political figures lauded the decision. Robert R. Livingston considered it "a singular event" and informed the marquis de Lafayette in early 1783 that "the day will come tho' when all disputes in the great republic of Europe will be tried in the same way, and America be quoted to exemplify the wisdom of the measure." Thomas Jefferson was similarly impressed. "Perhaps history cannot produce such another proof of the empire of reason and right in any part of the world as these states now exhibit," he wrote sometime after June 1784.

> Thus we see these infant states, instead of leaving their national differences to be decided by the sword, the ultima ratio regum, instead of deluging the land with human blood and covering it with human misery upon honest difference of opinion, have by wise and just arrangements submitted the causes of Nations to be weighed in the scales of justice by a tribunal so constituted as to ensure the confidence of all parties and so supported by the rest of the Union as to secure the execution of it's decisions.[4]

Despite the praise for the decision, the judges determined only Pennsylvania's jurisdiction; they did not rule on which individuals had proper claims to the land within this jurisdiction. The issue of who had legal claim to the land, more than the question of jurisdiction, had impeded but not prevented earlier settlement of the Wyoming area since midcentury; settlers with Susquehannah Company claims had waged battles with Pennsylvania soldiers in the 1770s, thereby preventing some colonists from establishing agricultural communities in the area. After the Trenton decision, the question of

3. The case is described in Robert J. Taylor, "Trial at Trenton," *WMQ* 3d ser., 26 (1969), 521–547.

4. Livingston to Lafayette, January 10, 1783, quoted in ibid., 521; Jefferson, "On the Settlement of Disputes between States by Judicial Means," in Julian P. Boyd et al., eds., *The Papers of Thomas Jefferson* (Princeton, N.J., 1952–), 6:505–506.

legal title continued to trouble investors with Pennsylvania titles and people from Connecticut who had obtained titles through the Susquehannah Company. In the mid-1780s violence again broke out over the land, and the Susquehannah Company enlisted the military support of Ethan Allen in exchange for a share in the territory.[5]

In spite of the controversy, the Wyoming region soon began to attract settlers. According to Timothy Pickering, 250 families lived in the area before the Trenton decision, most likely survivors from the prewar settlement of the area. Within four years their numbers had doubled. But not all of the people at Wyoming were content to remain there. In 1785 some migrated to Pipe Creek, a small tributary of the Susquehanna near Tioga, and established a small settlement; others moved to Owego. State courts did not finally determine the question of legal title until 1795. Then, in the decision of *Van Horne's Lessee* v. *Dorrance*, the Pennsylvania District Court ruled that a 1790 Pennsylvania statute validating the Pennsylvania claims was legal. By that time, however, many of the original claimants had sold their titles to wealthy investors who had purchased both Pennsylvania and Connecticut titles to ensure their ownership of desirable tracts. In the end, members of the Susquehannah Company received almost three hundred thousand acres in Pennsylvania, and the state compensated those who held Pennsylvania titles to these acres with land grants elsewhere.[6]

Questions over legal title to land throughout the valley led settlers to local courts. The county court at Sunbury dealt with numerous cases of forcible entry and detainer, a rare offense before the war. The cases arose because wartime migration during the "great runaway" had left much of the land apparently open to new settlers, and many with no legal claim to the tracts took possession, assuming the original owners had fled permanently. But these squatters often miscalculated. When the original owners returned, they sued the squat-

5. Taylor, "Trial at Trenton," 545–547; Ethan Allen to William Samuel Johnson, August 15, 1785, and Allen's receipt for the shares, August 19, 1785, *SCP*, 8:255–256.
6. "Extracts from Timothy Pickering's Journal," *SCP*, 8:385–386; Higgins, *Expansion in New York*, 111–112; Robert D. Arbuckle, *Pennsylvania Speculator and Patriot: The Entrepreneurial John Nicholson, 1757–1800* (University Park, Pa., 1975), 96–97; Julian Boyd, "Connecticut's Experiment in Expansion: The Susquehannah Company, 1753–1803," *Journal of Economic and Business History* 4 (1931), 69. The best summaries of the complex legislative and judicial battle over these lands are Taylor's introductory passages to volumes 8, 9, and 10 of *SCP*.

ters, seeking repossession of the land. The court sided with the origi-nal owners; those convicted had to pay a fine, from 2s. 6d. to £5, and make restitution. On the presumption that these squatters had not willfully broken the law, the court did not severely punish those con-victed of forcible entry and detainer.[7] Low fines probably encour-aged even the convicted to remain in the area, or at least did not threaten their financial stability.

But such lawsuits involved only a small amount of valley land. Much more acreage in the area, previously owned by loyalists or Indians, especially on the western side of the Fort Stanwix treaty line, remained free of such entanglements, and it beckoned wealthy financiers eager to invest large sums. When they looked to the west from their estates in Philadelphia or New York, they saw exactly what they wanted and soon found that state governments were only too willing to let them purchase it.

The states sought to sell off vast tracts in the backcountry to pay off their wartime debts. The postwar finances of the states and the new nation itself were extremely precarious. Congress's recommen-dation in March 1780 that states abolish paper money, along with the export of specie by merchants to pay prewar debts and the costs of reestablishing trade connections after the war, threatened the states' fiscal health. Like the nation, they needed to find ways to pay off their enormous debts, and the sale of western lands promised to generate substantial revenue. Even after extensive land sales, New York still owed approximately £1 million in 1790; Pennsylvania's debt amounted to over £4.5 million in 1787.[8]

The acquisitive interests of wealthy speculators and the states' will-ingness to sell valuable assets dominated the real estate market of the backcountry. In the upper Susquehanna Valley the confiscated hold-

7. Northumberland County Quarter Sessions Docket 1, 56, 107, Prothonotary's Office, NCCH; Northumberland County Quarter Sessions Docket 2, 44, 163, Pro-thonotary's Office, NCCH; Writ of Restitution against Derrick Gonsales & al, May Sessions 1790, Northumberland County Quarter Sessions, 1772–1797, Prothonotary's Office, NCCH, Box 1. On other cases in which low fines were assessed see, for exam-ple, John Robinson et al. each fined 6d. in 1788, Northumberland County Quarter Sessions Docket 2, 89, 108; and Matthew Wilson et al. also fined only 6d. each in 1793, Northumberland County Quarter Sessions Docket 2, 269.

8. Merrill Jensen, *The New Nation: A History of the United States during the Confedera-tion, 1781–1789* (New York, 1950), 302–304. The sale of the national public domain is treated in Malcolm J. Rohrbough, *The Land Office Business: The Settlement and Admin-istration of American Public Lands, 1789–1837* (New York, 1968); chap. 1 covers the period 1785–1800.

ings of prominent loyalists and the lands of many who fled and never returned flooded the regional market. The newly available tracts included vast holdings of the Penn family, confiscated in November 1779, and the estate of William Franklin near the Susquehanna's headwaters. Legislators in New York and Pennsylvania approved the sale of confiscated estates to a few wealthy investors; they also allowed some to acquire large estates by purchasing the titles to smaller parcels. Even before the end of the war, prominent investors, many of them merchants, purchased much of the confiscated and abandoned land in Tryon County. The land now available included valuable parcels west of the upper Susquehanna Valley, including much of western New York.[9]

Some who acquired large tracts had controlled lands in the valley before the war, but most were new to the valley real estate business. Any possible doubts the newcomers had were quickly overcome in the boom atmosphere of the real estate market. Although some of these investors concentrated on short-term profits, others realized that speculation in western lands was a precarious venture that required long-term commitment.

Would-be landlords plunged into the speculative boom, acquiring vast tracts in a short time. William Cooper and his partner Andrew Craig purchased a 40,000-acre tract in 1786; Cooper later acquired almost 11,000 acres farther south in the valley. At one point the prominent politician and jurist James Wilson and his partner Samuel Wallis owned over 1.2 million acres.[10] The Philadelphia merchant Henry Drinker had 70,000 acres near the Great Bend of the Susquehanna. Robert Morris, the preeminent financier of the 1780s, purchased at least 180,000 acres in the upper valley. The Asylum Company, run by Morris and John Nicholson, the comptroller gen-

9. Anne M. Ousterhout, "Pennsylvania Land Confiscations during the Revolution," *PMHB* 102 (1978), 339; Higgins, *Expansion in New York*, 101, 115–128; Catherine S. Crary, "Forfeited Loyalist Lands in the Western District of New York—Albany and Tryon Counties," *NY Hist.* 35 (1954), 242–246; Norman B. Wilkinson, "The 'Philadelphia Fever' in Northern Pennsylvania," *Pa. Hist.* 20 (1953), 42; Jensen, *New Nation*, 358–359. Wallis obtained much of his land by purchasing the titles of numerous claimants; see Wallis Papers, especially Reel 6, passim, HSP. Cooper and Craig obtained forty thousand acres of William Franklin's land in a public sale in January 1786; see Tryon County Deed Book 1 (1772–1788), 247–249, Office of the Montgomery County Historian, Fonda, N.Y. (page numbers refer to the transcription in the Office of the County Historian).

10. Tryon County Deed Book 1, 247–249; Hinman, *Creation of Broome County*, 14; Wilkinson, "'Philadelphia Fever,'" 51.

eral of Pennsylvania, claimed up to 1 million acres along Loyalsock Creek, a tributary of the Susquehanna. Nicholson actually controlled, according to his brother, 3.7 million acres or one-seventh of Pennsylvania. The Philadelphia merchant William Bingham obtained 430,000 acres between the two branches of the Susquehanna in 1792 and planned to acquire 660,000 more acres in the same region the following year. He eventually purchased 1.16 million acres, much of it located in the upper valley. He also obtained a 15,000-acre tract at the confluence of the Susquehanna and Chenango rivers, the eventual site of Binghamton.[11]

Europeans also purchased tracts in the upper valley. Phineas Bond purchased 20,000 acres around the Loyalsock for an English interest known as Robert Barclay and Company; another agent, apparently for the same company, obtained, according to Henry Drinker, 40,000 to 50,000 acres. Land in Pennsylvania especially appealed to Europeans because noncitizens were allowed to purchase tracts in the state. Fearful of religious persecution in England or fleeing France after the Revolution, some refugees sought land in the upper valley. As Morris and Nicholson discovered when they tried to sell valley tracts to Europeans in the mid-1790s, however, such transactions proved difficult and investors often did not profit as much as they hoped.[12]

Like their predecessors during the colonial period, many of the postwar landlords held public office. From 1786 to 1801 William Bingham served in the Continental Congress, the Pennsylvania Assembly, and the United States Senate. William Cooper was the first judge of Otsego County and was later twice elected to Congress. Perhaps none were as prominent as James Wilson, who attended the Continental Congress during the period of independence, served two sessions in Congress in the mid-1780s, played an active role at

11. John Lincklaen, *Travels in the Years 1791 and 1792 in Pennsylvania, New York and Vermont* (New York, 1897), 50; Barbara Chernow, "Robert Morris: Land Speculator, 1790–1801" (Ph.D. diss., Columbia University, 1974; publ. New York, 1978), 96–97; *DAB*, 2:504–505; Stevenson Fletcher, *Pennsylvania Agriculture and Country Life, 1640–1840* (1950; rpt. Harrisburg, Pa., 1971), 29–30; Wilkinson, "'Philadelphia Fever,'" 50; Margaret L. Brown, "William Bingham, Eighteenth Century Magnate," *PMHB* 61 (1937), 411–413, 432–434.

12. Drinker to Wallis, June 24, 1794, Wallis Papers, Reel 6; *Henry Wansey and His American Journal, 1794*, ed. David Jeremy (Philadelphia, 1970), 7–8, 11, 77–79; Elsie Murray, "French Refugees of 1793 in Pennsylvania," *Proceedings of the American Philosophical Society* 87 (1944), 387–393; Chernow, "Robert Morris," 109–128; Arbuckle, *Pennsylvania Speculator and Patriot*, 93–113.

the Constitutional Convention, and eventually became an associate justice on the Supreme Court.[13]

More important than their political offices, however, was the participation of some of these landlords in major financial institutions of the postwar period. Bingham, Wilson, and Morris all became associated with the Bank of North America. John Nicholson, the comptroller general of Pennsylvania from 1782 to 1796, had responsibility for settling the accounts of the state and for issuing certificates of pay and depreciation of pay to those who had served in the state's militia. Knowing about public land sales earlier than others helped him to acquire confiscated tracts in Northumberland County when the state sold them at auction. Bingham, Morris, and Nicholson all profited handsomely from wartime contracting. Indeed, Bingham raised considerable sums while running extensive mercantile operations from Martinique, where the Continental Congress had sent him to procure French arms for the American war effort in the early 1780s. While there he organized shipments of other goods, including molasses, rum, coffee, linen, and salt, to the new country. He returned one of the wealthiest people in America, and the firm of Morris and Nicholson profited hugely from his activities. This wartime profiteering aroused resentment and suspicion, leading to an investigation by the board of treasury, which found that Morris owed the United States considerable sums, although he avoided payment for many years.[14]

Like some of the colonial landlords, these postwar landlords often worked together, occasionally pooling their resources and providing services for one another. Wallis performed various tasks for Wilson: organizing surveys, attending to business in the Pennsylvania Land Office in Philadelphia when Wilson was in New York, arranging for

13. For Bingham see *DAB*, 2:278–279, and Brown, "Bingham, Eighteenth Century Magnate," 391–393; for Wilson see *DAB*, 20:326–330; for Cooper see *DAB*, 4:417–418; Ousterhout, "Pennsylvania Land Confiscations," 341. Other major landholders also played prominent roles in the revolutionary struggle: Benjamin Rush signed the Declaration of Independence and Robert Lettis Hooper was an officer in the Continental army. On Rush's speculation see, for example, Northumberland County Deed Book G, 107–108, describing land he sold to Joseph Priestley; on Hooper's career see Charles Henry Hart, "Colonel Robert Lettis Hooper: Deputy Quarter Master General in the Continental Army," *PMHB* 36 (1912), 60–91.

14. For Morris see *DAB*, 13:222–223; for Nicholson see *DAB* 13:504–505; Bingham to Morris, August 7, 1781, E. James Ferguson et al., eds., *The Papers of Robert Morris, 1781–1784* (Pittsburgh, Pa., 1973–), 2:31–32; Morris to Fernand Grand, December 3, 1781, ibid., 3:322; Margaret L. Brown, "William Bingham, Agent of the Continental Congress in Martinique," *PMHB* 61 (1937), 62–64; Jensen, *New Nation*, 380–381.

the sale of tracts of Wilson's land, protecting the lands from others who wanted to claim them. Wilson and Wallis used their contacts with state surveyors to determine the best lands and acquire them before others had an opportunity. At times, Wallis sold lands that he and Wilson owned to other wealthy landholders, including a sale of one hundred thousand acres to Henry Drinker and others in February 1797; he also bought land for Wilson. Wallis received a commission from Wilson for many of these transactions. Wallis also dealt with other landholders, including Robert Lettis Hooper and Robert Morris; he worked with Henry Drinker, beginning as early as 1766, and their association continued, often to Drinker's chagrin, through the 1790s. Cooper managed tracts in four patents he did not own, at one point receiving a commission from Drinker to sell eight thousand acres near Tunckhannock Creek in 1789. Landholders also cooperated in mercantile transactions: Wallis arranged with Wilson to ship grain from Middletown to Muncy and once purchased a boat, with Wilson's money, to haul his supplies up the Susquehanna to Muncy; Drinker shipped goods from Philadelphia to both Cooper and Wallis. Nicholson and Morris together owned a glassworks, and their real estate interests extended as far as the new Federal City, where they owned seven thousand town lots; in the mid-1790s they organized six land companies together.[15]

Although these investors acquired title to thousands of acres of

15. On Wallis and Wilson see receipt between Wallis and Baldwin, February 22, 1793, Account of Wilson and Wallis with Brodhead, n.d., and receipt, June 7, 1795, between Wilson and Wallis, Wallis Papers, Reel 6; Wallis to Wilson, April 3, 17, 19, 20, June 14, 29, July 15, August 7, 1793, Wilson Papers, Land Correspondence, 5:59–67, and account of Wilson with Wallis, ibid., 9:100, HSP. On Wilson and Hooper see receipts of Hooper to Wilson, January 22, May 6, 1785, ibid., 89, and Hinman, *Creation of Broome County*, 14–16; Fletcher, *Pennsylvania Agriculture*, 29–30; *DAB*, 4:417. On Cooper and Drinker see Drinker Papers, Land Correspondence, Cooper file, HSP; Henry Drinker Journal, 1776–1791, entry for October 30, 1790 (pp. 438–439), HSP; and David W. Maxey, "Of Castles in Stockport and Other Strictures: Samuel Preston's Contentious Agency for Henry Drinker," *PMHB* 110 (1986), 426. For Wallis's relations with Drinker see, for example, a 1788 account between them, Wallis Papers, Reel 5, and Drinker to Wallis, June 24, 1794, ibid., Reel 6; Henry Drinker Journal, 1776–1791, entry for June 24, 1789 (p. 309); and four folders of correspondence in Drinker Papers, Land Correspondence, HSP. On Morris and Wallis see JK (?) Stone to Wallis (?), December 28, 1785, and receipt between George Munro and Wallis, April 25, 1792, Wallis Papers, Reel 6. For Wallis's relations with Hooper see, for example, Samuel Harris, Jornel and field Notes . . . don for Robt Lettis Hooper and Compy, ibid. Norman B. Wilkinson has traced connections between some of these landholders as well; see his "Land Policy and Speculation in Pennsylvania 1779–1800: A Test of the New Democracy" (Ph.D. diss., University of Pennsylvania, 1958; publ. New York, 1979), 143–158, and "'Philadelphia Fever,'" 41–56, esp. 53–54, for the connections between Morris and Nicholson.

backcountry lands, some of them could not maintain possession of their tracts. Like George Croghan a generation earlier, Morris, Nicholson, and Wilson all found themselves caught in financial crises in the 1790s that forced them to give up their claims in the valley. Extensive speculation in lands and overextending their capital caused Morris and Nicholson to lose their lands in the upper Susquehanna Valley and elsewhere. These onetime partners engaged in patently unsound credit schemes, even endorsing each other's notes. Failure to lure sufficient settlers to their estates, combined with poor returns on other investments, ended their speculative dreams when their notes fell due beginning in 1797. Both eventually found themselves in debtors' prison. Wilson escaped their fate, but when he died in 1798 he was heavily in debt, including £98,000 owed to Samuel Wallis, a sum that remained unpaid and led Wallis's executors to sell off parcels of Wallis's lands to pay off his own debts.[16]

But the financial ruin of some speculators did not lead to a wide redistribution of the land in the valley. Other wealthy investors bought up the properties when they became available. Thus, when Morris lost his land in the valley, William Cooper acquired almost eleven thousand acres through foreclosure; John Watts purchased a tract of approximately fourteen thousand acres; and Henry Nichols bought another with over six thousand acres. On the advice of Henry Drinker, Wallis's executors sold off large parcels of his holdings. But when Wallis's lands became available, the purchasers were also wealthy: one bought a prime parcel of a thousand acres at the confluence of the Susquehanna and Loyalsock Creek for over £5 per acre; another offered the best price for a number of tracts sold off in 1803; a third purchaser bought at least fifty-five hundred acres from the estate.[17]

16. Arbuckle, *Pennsylvania Speculator and Patriot*, 185–195; see the 1818 report of Thomas Hays describing the decisions of the Lycoming County Orphan's Court regarding Samuel Wallis's holdings, listed as "Phineas Bond, Samuel Wallis Estate," Cadwallader Collection, HSP. Wallis had had financial troubles earlier as well; see his appeals for funds in his letters to Henry Drinker of January 3, 1789, July 19, September 5, 1796, February 28, and March 5, 1797, all in Drinker Papers, Land Correspondence, HSP.

17. Hinman, *Creation of Broome County*, 14–16; Henry Drinker to Daniel Smith and John Wallis, May 25, 1803, Wallis Papers, Reel 6; "Phineas Bond, Samuel Wallis Estate," 7, 10; "Description of Property sold by John Smith Marshal as late the Estate of Samuel Wallis deceased to Pierce Butler, Esquire," Family Deeds: Wallis Papers, LCHS. Drinker remained interested, or perhaps entangled, in Wallis's real estate affairs after Wallis's death; see his notes on his account with Wallis's estate from 1803 to

The Valley Economy in the Postwar Period

In the 1780s and 1790s the valley population grew rapidly, easily surpassing prewar levels. Farmers and their families returned to their old improvements. Soldiers who had fought in the area also came back, this time to settle. Landlords established vast estates and lured tenants to work their lands. Settlers who had purchased tracts from wealthy investors or state land offices migrated to the region for the first time. So did nonagricultural workers seeking work in the developing towns. These individuals and their dependents greatly increased the available labor pool in the valley and thus stimulated economic development.[18]

The vast majority of these postwar settlers were farmers. Their interests were local: they wanted to provide for themselves and their families. But even isolated farmers found themselves increasingly drawn, willy-nilly, into participation in the larger exchange cycles of the Atlantic market.

Economic development took time, and valley residents suffered hardships before they reaped genuine rewards from their labor. Like those who sought to establish farms before the Revolution, these settlers endured periods when they were unsure of their survival. During the late 1780s settlers near the Susquehanna's headwaters planned to purchase food in Albany before their own crops came in. But a staggering rise of grain prices in Albany after the winter of 1788–1789 threatened the residents of Cooperstown with famine. To stay alive, they ate wild roots, supplemented for the fortunate ones by milk and for those less fortunate by a drink of maple sugar and water. One man perished from eating a poisonous plant he thought was an edible leek. The situation appeared increasingly bleak. "A singular event seemed sent by good Providence to our relief," Cooper recalled. "It was reported to me that unusual shoals of fish were seen moving in the clear waters of the Susquehanna. I went, and was surprised to find that they were herrings. We made

1807 in the last folder of their correspondence in Drinker Papers, Land Correspondence, HSP. Some of Wallis's lands were auctioned in sheriff's sales, and Henry Drinker purchased some through such a sale on October 17, 1805; see Northumberland County Deed Book Q, 78.

18. Higgins, *Expansion in New York,* 100–101, 112; Frost, *Life on the Upper Susquehanna,* 8; Crary, "Forfeited Loyalist Lands," 247; Lincklaen, *Travels,* 39, 39n, 55–56; Hinman, *Creation of Broome County,* 8; "Journal of Timothy Pickering's Visit to Wyoming," *SCP,* 8:39.

something like a small net, by the interweaving of twigs, and by this rude and simple contrivance we were able to take them in thousands. In less than ten days each family had an ample supply with plenty of salt." Legislators in New York also provided assistance, giving valley settlers seventeen hundred bushels of corn to ease the crisis.[19]

Not all valley settlers were patient enough to wait for government assistance. Like their counterparts during the war years who protested higher grain prices, settlers along the Susquehanna still held traditional ideas about the moral economy. Faced with the prospect of too little food in the weeks before the rye harvest, they sought to purchase flour from backcountry developers and storekeepers. But when sellers of flour charged too much, the settlers believed they had the right to seize the grain they needed. "When people have not had cash to buy with," Samuel Wallis informed Henry Drinker in July 1789 about a dispute at Tioga, "they have gone in arm'd body's & taken it from those who had carry'd [it] there for sale. This has been so frequently done that the Adventurers have declined carrying any thing more for sale." Wallis told Drinker that one of his neighbors had twenty barrels of flour stolen from him by armed residents. But the settlers were not lawless bandits. "The people," Wallis wrote, "as I before observed collected about him in arms & told him they would not starve that they had not money to pay him but must have flour & would pay him when they were able." Such promises did not convince Wallis, who chose to avoid taking provisions into the region at the time. Never one to shy away from a chance to profit, Wallis merely bided his time, and when the fall harvest still did not provide valley residents around Tioga with sufficient food, he shipped one ton of flour upriver hoping, as he informed Drinker in September 1789, that "it may be sold to Advantage."[20]

The occasional lack of food was but one problem new settlers encountered. The initial absence of mills and stores hampered the new communities; colonial roads proved insufficient for the postwar settlers' needs. During the 1780s some valley residents lived in poverty. When Timothy Pickering toured the Wyoming area in August 1786,

19. Cooper, *Guide*, 11; Jessica Foy, *A Vision of Cooper's Town: A History of the Founding of Cooperstown and the Settlement of Otsego County, New York* (Cooperstown, N.Y., 1986), 8.

20. Samuel Wallis to Henry Drinker, July 12, September 12, 1789, Drinker Papers, Land Correspondence, HSP.

he thought the residents' agriculture "slovenly" and "the hovels they dwell in . . . wretched beyond description." Houses did not have chimneys, and the children were "often very ragged and the whole family very dirty." He did not feel that the dispute between Pennsylvania and Connecticut over the area could account for the settlers' inattention to necessary tasks. "Indeed," Pickering wrote in his journal, "I did not imagine such general apparent wretchedness could be found in the United States."[21]

Despite these occasional times of dearth, most postwar valley residents fared reasonably well; conflicts such as the confrontation over the price of flour at Tioga in 1789 were remarkable because they represented a dramatic departure from daily life. Many of the new settlers grew wheat and rye and supplemented these grains with corn, various legumes, and fruit. Some tapped maple trees to obtain sugar. Many also grew flax. When Pickering visited Exeter in January 1787, he saw a family dressed mostly in linen clothing, performing all the tasks except weaving, a service "well executed in the settlement." The family had turned to flax cultivation after the loss of their sheep. Levi Beardsley later recalled that most families around Richfield made their own cloth from both flax and wool.[22]

Within a few years the domestic economy had stabilized. Rural families throughout the valley tended to be large, often with more than six children. The population was also overwhelmingly young; census enumerators noted in 1800 that over half of the residents were under age sixteen. Few slaves lived in the valley, and the sex ratio among the residents was almost balanced, further proof that the family remained the basic unit of production in the region. Indeed, in 1790 Northumberland County had the largest households in Pennsylvania. Even travelers noted this unusual demographic characteristic. "The number of children is, in proportion to the habitations," Duke de la Rochefoucault Liancourt wrote at the end of the century, "very great indeed."[23]

Many of the children in the valley were born there, but migrants

21. Levi Beardsley, *Reminiscences; Personal and Other Incidents; Early Settlement of Otsego County; Notices and Anecdotes of Public Men; Judicial, Legal and Legislative Matters; Field Sports; Dissertations and Discussions* (New York, 1852), 19–34; "Extracts from Timothy Pickering's Journal," *SCP*, 8:384.

22. "Journal of Timothy Pickering's Visit to Wyoming," *SCP*, 9:39; Beardsley, *Reminiscences*, 36–37, 25–26, 31.

23. Estimates of family size are based on *ABV*, passim; Northumberland County Orphan's Court, Books 1 and 2, Office of the County Recorder and Register of Deeds, NCCH; and "The Records of the Probate Court of Westmoreland in the

continued to move into the region from New England and from more densely settled portions of Pennsylvania during the decades following the war. When these settlers set to work creating farms, they altered the landscape, clearing fields and cultivating those abandoned during the war, which were beginning to revert to forests, and thinning wooded areas for fuel, fences, and building supplies. Farmhouses and their outbuildings dotted the landscape; towns, some laid out on grids, appeared at the junctures of important travel routes.

Within the valley variations in soil quality and terrain limited settlers' economic choices. In Harpersfield, for example, John Lincklaen, surveying areas for a land company, found that local farmers enjoyed wheat harvests of approximately thirty bushels per acre. Wheat seemed particularly suited to the "mountainous country, stony in some places, but free from rocks," he wrote, adding that the hills were "arable to their tops." But the farmers in Harpersfield found that they could not successfully cultivate corn. "In its place," Lincklaen wrote when he toured the area in 1792, "they raise another kind of grain called Millet, which is said to be excellent for fattening pigs." Others nearby were more successful with corn cultivation. "It was nearly the first of June that we planted," Levi Beardsley recalled, "but the corn was soon up, grew rapidly, and with but little more than one slight dressing with the hoe, we had fifty bushels of good corn to the acre, with any quantity of large yellow pumpkins." Along Loyalsock Creek the traveler Henry Wansey found "very rich black mould, several feet deep," but the land was not good for every crop. "*It is too rich for wheat*, but is excellent for Indian corn, or for grazing."[24]

Throughout the valley farmers planted diverse crops, although most planted grains. "The variety on the Farms & in the River is

---

County of Litchfield, in the Colony of Connecticut. Liber A. From January 6, 1777, to June 16, 1783," *Proceedings and Collections of the Wyoming Historical and Geological Society* 18 (1923), 139–242. In 1790 the average household in Northumberland County had 8.15 members; see *Heads of Families First Census of the United States: 1790, State of Pennsylvania* (Washington, D.C., 1908), 10. For 1800 see *Return of the Whole Number of Persons within the Several Districts of the United States (Second Census)* (Washington, D.C., 1808); Duke de la Rochefoucault Liancourt, *Travels through the United States of North America, the Country of the Iroquois, and Upper Canada, in the Years 1795, 1796, and 1797,* 4 vols. (London, 1800), 1:147. See Table 1 in the Appendix.

24. Lincklaen, *Travels*, 120; Beardsley, *Reminiscences*, 37; *Henry Wansey and His American Journal*, 119.

delightful," the Devonshire traveler William Davy wrote in 1794, "the former in Orchards, Meadow, Pasturage & Tillage, the Wheat in which is now very strong." Probate inventories from the Wyoming region indicate that residents grew flax in addition to corn and grains. Many settlers also kept livestock. Indeed, for those who could not afford land or chose not to purchase it, their livestock, generally a cow but sometimes horses, pigs, or sheep, were their most important investment. In Turbut Township, where landownership was more widespread than in townships such as Muncy, where one landholder controlled so much of the available land, tax records reveal that ownership of livestock, at least one cow, was virtually universal among those owning land. From the early 1790s to the early 1810s three-fourths of the taxables who owned land also possessed at least one horse. One-third to one-half of those who owned no land possessed at least one cow. In addition, one-half of those owning town lots had cows and a sizable number (one-fifth by 1802 and almost one-third by 1812) owned horses. In a region where land often sold for as little as 10s. an acre and the price of a cow could go as high as £7 10s. and an inexpensive horse cost £9, ownership of livestock apparently represented a sensible economic choice for settlers, an understandable sentiment in a region where prevailing free-range practices allowed those who owned no land to maintain their livestock.[25]

Free-ranging livestock feasted on the valley's natural resources. "The Woods here are so full of Walnuts, Chestnut, Hickory & Hazle Nuts & Acorns," Davy wrote, "that great quantities of Hogs are made fat by feeding on them alone." He also believed that cows fended for themselves. In Northumberland Town, Davy observed, "every House has a Cow which stays in the Woods all day but returns every Morning & Evening of herself to the Door of her Owner who has no other Trouble but that of keeping a Bell about her Neck & milking her."[26]

Farming spread throughout the upper valley in the decades following the war, and even some who had questionable legal title to lands were busy changing forests to fields. Thus some members of

25. Norman B. Wilkinson, ed., "Mr. Davy's Diary, 1794," *Pa. Hist.* 20 (1953), 261; "Records of the Probate Court of Westmoreland," passim. Livestock estimates for Turbut Township are based on tax records for 1792, 1802, and 1812, Northumberland County Pennsylvania Board of County Commissioners Tax Records, LR 91.7 and LR 91.8, PHMC. See Table 7 in the Appendix.
26. Wilkinson, ed., "Mr. Davy's Diary," 265, 270.

the Susquehannah Company pressed their claims in the late 1780s, resisting for a time the wealthy landholders' economic order. Some remained so determined in their pursuit that in 1788 they captured Timothy Pickering, then a county official and landholder, and held him hostage for several weeks. These settlers, like others scattered in the hinterland, created sufficient solidarity among themselves to delay the spread of the new land system into their locales. Pickering discovered that his captors were trained husbandmen who knew how to make their sows grow to desirable weights, how to use oxen-powered plows in ways that minimized damage to corn crops, and how to produce good yields of flax and wheat.[27] But their agrarian skills notwithstanding, their resistance withered in the early nineteenth century; more prominent members of their alliance redefined their position in response to a shift in the political climate, ending any sustained protest against the emerging economic system and its proponents.[28]

The agricultural sector of the regional economy boomed by the mid-1790s, and valley residents shipped surplus produce down the river to external markets. By 1795 boats descended the Susquehanna carrying 500 to 1,400 bushels of wheat. Boats loaded with up to 250 barrels of flour arrived at the port of Havre de Grace at the mouth of the river, testifying to the growing production of the valley mills. In 1790 the Society for the Improvement of Roads and Internal Navigation in Pennsylvania estimated that 150,000 bushels of grain traveled via the Susquehanna to Middletown and thence to market in Philadelphia. Much of this yield came from the upper reaches of the river and its tributaries; grain from areas farther south generally went to markets in Maryland. By 1795 perhaps 180,000 bushels of grain were transported down the river to Middletown each year; the volume continued to grow throughout the next thirty years, surpassing 800,000 bushels by 1824. Valley residents also exported clover seed, whiskey, pork, and cattle.[29]

27. "Journal Kept by Timothy Pickering during His Captivity," *SCP*, 9:406–409.
28. Alan Taylor, "The Backcountry Conclusion to the American Revolution: Agrarian Unrest in the Northeast, 1750–1820," in Alfred F. Young, ed., *The American Revolution: Further Explorations in the History of American Radicalism* (DeKalb, Ill., forthcoming).
29. David Bard, *A Description of the River Susquehanna, with Observations on the Present State of Its Trade and Navigation, and Their Practicable and Probable Improvement* (Philadelphia, 1796), 41–43, 46; Lincklaen, *Travels*, 74; Fletcher, *Pennsylvania Agriculture*, 286–287; see also Thomas Cooper, *Some Information Respecting America* (London, 1794).

Nowhere was the swift development of the grain industry more apparent than in Northumberland County. In 1788, according to David Bard, county residents imported "large quantities" of wheat and flour; by 1790 the county had become an exporter of grain, sending 30,000 bushels of wheat down the river to market. An assessment of the county's resources the following year enumerated over one hundred mills. But the grain industry was in its nascent stage, or so Bard thought: "The grain at present floated down the Susquehanna is but trifling when compared with the quantities which the future cultivation of those territories will produce."[30] Bard's commentary, which appeared in a pamphlet written to encourage the Pennsylvania legislature to spend money to improve transportation in the state, exaggerated the potential of the region. But his views on the rapid development of the upper valley corresponded with those of other observers.

Small-scale industries soon developed throughout the upper valley. Some settlers, as John Lincklaen discovered, established coal mines and forges, taking advantage of the region's prehistoric legacy. Others established pot and pearl ash works, turning the ash from burned trees into a marketable commodity; the ash, which sold for fifty to sixty pounds per ton in New York, was used in the production of soap and gunpowder. Moss Kent set up a store and pearl ash works two miles northeast of Lake Otsego; his business was soon thriving. "He has 6 kittles mounted, & near 50 large leach tubs," his brother James wrote in September 1792. "It is a most excellent country for the business. My brother only began to leech in June, & he will make 120 barrels of pearl-ash this season." Kent, apparently believing the forests were so heavily timbered that he need not fear deforestation, hoped his pearl ash works would, in his brother's words, develop into the "first manufactory of the kind in the State." His business benefited when William Cooper built a road along the eastern side of Lake Otsego from Cooperstown to Kent's store so settlers could transport their ashes to him more easily.[31]

In addition to selling the ash from their burned fields, many valley settlers used their grain to produce whiskey, either for their own use or to supplement their income. By 1791 there were sixty-three dis-

30. Bard, *Description of the River Susquehanna*, 41–43, 46; Table of Assessments for the Year 1791, Northumberland County, County Commissioners Minutes, vol. 1 (1786–1808), LR 12.1, PHMC.

31. Lincklaen, *Travels*, 36, 39, 71, 76; [James Kent], "Judge Kent's 'Jaunt' to Cooperstown, 1792," ed. Edward P. Alexander, *NY Hist.* 32 (1941), 453–455.

tilleries in Northumberland County, many of them small-scale operations. Valley residents shipped surplus whiskey down the Susquehanna, and much of it was eventually sold in Philadelphia and Baltimore. Jonathan Holleback, a resident of Wyoming, was only one of the many valley residents who took advantage of local grain surpluses to establish a distillery. "He used to sell one gallon of whiskey for 2 bushels of rye," reported Timothy Pickering, "which two bushels would make at least 4 gallons." Holleback's operating costs were low. According to Pickering, "his wood cost him nothing but the cutting and halling: for every body cuts wood where he pleases on the un-inclosed grounds; and none are inclosed but the *flats*." Pickering was so impressed with Holleback's profitable operation that he wrote the recipe for whiskey in the journal of his trip. He also remembered Holleback's opinions on the types of grain suitable for a distillery. "Rye whiskey (he says) is preferred, because more fiery than whiskey made of wheat, which is soft and mild," Pickering wrote, "tho' rye produces rather the most liquor." Valley settlers also used the by-products of whiskey production for their livestock. "The wash," Henry Wansey wrote, "is good for the hogs."[32]

While settlers turned forests into fields and began to establish industries using valley resources, artisans and merchants moved to the developing towns. Some blacksmiths and gunsmiths had lived in the valley earlier, serving the Indians and colonists who had inhabited the region, but their numbers remained small. In the postwar period many more nonagricultural workers, lured by the possibility of providing services to an expanding agricultural population, migrated to the area.

When these artisans set up shop in valley towns, they extended the range of services available. Cooperstown became the most important of the new towns in the area around the headwaters of the Susquehanna and, through the guidance of William Cooper, it was soon peopled with artisans who attracted clients from the surrounding agricultural settlements. By 1803 there were three hatters, two shoemakers, three blacksmiths, two tanners, four carpenters, two tailors, two potters, two joiners, and two masons, as well as a brickmaker,

32. Table of Assessments for the Year 1791, Northumberland County Commissioners' Minutes vol. 1 (1786–1808), LR 12.1, PHMC; Fletcher, *Pennsylvania Agriculture*, 291; "Journal of Timothy Pickering's Visit to Wyoming," *SCP*, 9:31; *Henry Wansey and His American Journal*, 120.

baker, watchmaker, silversmith, cooper, miller, and assorted other artisans and laborers in Cooperstown. Residents could shop at four stores, consult with three doctors and apothecaries, and visit four inns as well.[33]

Other towns also attracted artisans, millers, and merchants, including new towns that grew up at Mifflinburg, New Berlin, and Binghamton; some previous settlements, such as Wilkes-Barre and Muncy, became popular trading centers. By the mid-1790s Northumberland had a tannery, two potteries, a potash factory, and a watch- and clockmaker. A weaver lived nearby, who, according to William Davy, wove "Bed Quilts of new patterns & something like Carpeting at 2 Dollars each Quilt. The Family dye & spin the Wool & deliver the Yarn to him." Within a decade of its founding in 1785, Derr's Town (now Lewisburg), became the focal point for economic development along one stretch of the West Branch. In 1785 Ludwig Derr set up the first store in the town; by November 1788, when William Gray surveyed the town, there were several mills, two tanyards, two ferries, a cabinetmaker, and a tailor. In 1790 Josiah Haines and John Thornburg set up another store in the town, transporting their wares up the river from Sunbury.[34] Settlers moved to Mill-town (now Milton) along the West Branch in the early 1790s; by 1796 it had fifty to sixty houses and was apparently prospering. In 1794 Sunbury and Northumberland Town each had between 100 and 150 houses, and the value of some lots had increased by as much as 500 percent in just two years. Valley inhabitants opened taverns and inns in towns and along travel routes, thereby encouraging traffic in people and goods between settlements. Two of Wallis's tenants opened an inn near Muncy Creek, paying him one-third of their agricultural produce for rent.[35]

These commercial entrepôts, primitive compared to such urban

33. I[saac] Cooper, An Abstract taken from the Population of Cooperstown, March 1, 1803, CM 42.39L, NYSHA.

34. *ABV*, 237, 242, 238, 254–255, 264, 277, 279; Wilkinson, ed., "Mr. Davy's Diary," 259–260, 270–271; *Journal of Samuel Maclay, While Surveying the West Branch of the Susquehanna, the Sinnemahoning and the Allegheny Rivers, in 1790*, ed. John F. Meginness (Williamsport, Pa., 1887), 13.

35. Cooper, *Some Information Respecting America*, 111, 113; Frost, *Life on the Upper Susquehanna*, 27; Lincklaen, *Travels*, 57, 121; Bard, *Description of the River Susquehanna*, 17; *Henry Wansey and His American Journal*, 119; Beardsley, *Reminiscences*, 27–28; *ABV*, 206, 232; Higgins, *Expansion in New York*, 100. For the proportion of town dwellers in one township see Table 3 in the Appendix.

centers as Philadelphia and New York, represented a profound development in the valley's history. The towns attracted growing numbers of wage laborers who owned no land. Although some of these people had skills that would make them especially desirable in the region, such as carpentry or masonry, many by the end of the century made a living by doing any available labor. A 1799 tax assessment for Shamokin provides some insight into the precise composition of this group of valley residents. At that time there were twenty-nine single freemen enumerated on the tax list. Some had skills that made them valuable to farming families concentrating on cereal production: two carpenters, two blacksmiths, two distillers, one mason, one weaver, and two storekeepers. One was listed as a "farmer" and thus represented a true anomaly in this region: a single man running a farm. In addition to these eleven men who possessed identifiable skills, there were eighteen others listed simply as "laborers." On the eve of a new century the presence of these men, apparently unable or unwilling to become farmers, indicated a shift in the rural economy.[36]

By the end of the century the valley supported a population far larger than it had for at least a century. In 1770 the population of Indians and colonists was approximately five thousand. In 1790, only a decade after the war had wiped out most valley settlements, the region had perhaps thirty-five thousand residents; by 1800 the population exceeded seventy-five thousand.[37] In many ways the landscape resembled that of longer-settled areas closer to the Atlantic: cleared fields replaced densely timbered forests; a network of towns and stores provided necessary commodities for the farming population.

All valley residents, those with leases or freeholds, farmers or villagers, sought security for themselves and their families in the local commercial system. In some ways the emerging economy resembled that of New England, where production for external markets was generally subsidiary to family subsistence. In New England, slaves and indentured servants were rare; the family performed the neces-

36. Shamokin tax assessment for 1799, Northumberland County Board of County Commissioners Tax Records, vol. 3, LR 91.6, PHMC.

37. See the maps estimating population in Lester Cappon, ed., *Atlas of Early American History: The Revolutionary Era, 1760–1790* (Princeton, N.J., 1976), 23, 65; Frost, *Life on the Upper Susquehanna*, 13; *Heads of Families First Census of the United States*, 10; *Second Census*, 32 (New York), n.p. (Pennsylvania).

sary labor. Stability of the family economy necessitated certain choices, such as diversified production, which minimized risk; such security measures limited the potential profits that families could make from more specialized production for market.[38]

In the upper Susquehanna Valley farming families rarely isolated themselves from the local market. While possession of livestock was widespread, at least among those owning land, most local residents could not acquire enough land to produce everything they needed. Many had only one cow, presumably to supply them with milk, but this would not provide them with any meat. More crucial for any attempt at isolation from the market was access to land to grow grain, especially wheat, rye, and corn. Besides land for tillage to produce the foods they needed to eat, the family would require pasturage, although free-ranging practices, at least during the early decades of settlement, reduced the need to own pasture land. Household gardens, fruit trees, sheep or flax or both for clothing materials, and equipment such as spinning wheels, plows, and cider presses would also be needed. Finally, even if the farming household was able to produce most of the goods it needed, money had to be earned from the sale of surpluses to pay for the services of smiths, physicians, ministers, carpenters, masons, and millers, to name but the most obvious people whose skills the vast majority of rural families would have required at some time.[39]

These various demands required possession, if not actual ownership, of a sizable tract of land. In southeastern Pennsylvania, a family of five could produce most of what it needed on a carefully managed 125-acre farm. Since farming households in the upper Susquehanna Valley had, on average, six to eight members, most families could manage equally well on a 150- to 200-acre tract. But in the upper

38. James A. Henretta, "Families and Farms: *Mentalité* in Pre-Industrial America," *WMQ* 3d ser., 35 (1978), esp. 15–32.

39. On the needs of a family farm see James Lemon, *The Best Poor Man's Country: A Geographical Study of Early Southeastern Pennsylvania* (1972; rpt. New York, 1976), 152–155, and Bettye Hobbs Pruitt, "Self-Sufficiency and the Agricultural Economy of Eighteenth-Century Massachusetts," *WMQ* 3d ser., 41 (1984), 333–364. In southeastern Pennsylvania, as Lemon points out, families used 40 percent of the income from their yields to acquire what they did not produce themselves; see *Best Poor Man's Country*, 180–181. The notion that self-sufficiency was a genuine goal of farming families has been challenged most recently in Daniel Vickers, "Competency and Competition: Economic Culture in Early America," *WMQ* 3d ser., 47 (1990), 3–29, esp. 7, and Christopher Clark, *The Roots of Rural Capitalism: Western Massachusetts, 1780–1860* (Ithaca, N.Y., 1990), 12.

Susquehanna Valley, the number of households controlling such tracts remained small into the nineteenth century. In the early 1790s, 61 out of 135, or 45.2 percent, of the taxables in Shamokin Township possessed at least 150 acres; by 1802 the number had increased to 94 (13 of them tenants), but the percentage of the population had decreased to 29.6 percent.

Similar developments occurred elsewhere. In Turbut Township, 87 out of 243 (35.8 percent) of the households had at least 150 acres in 1792; a decade later that number had grown to 104 out of a total of 454 (22.9 percent). The trend continued into the early 1810s. In 1812, 112 taxables in Turbut Township owned over 150 acres, out of a total of 482 rural residents (23.2 percent); including the 93 residents with town lots, who chose to avoid even the effort to become self-sufficient in basic goods, the proportion of taxables with at least 150 acres dropped to 19.5 percent. Muncy Township, home of the wealthy landholder Samuel Wallis, also possessed a low number of married taxables who had at least 150 acres: 26 out of a total of 111 (23.4 percent) listed in the tax records. In Muncy Creek Township, which broke off from Muncy Township, at least one-third of the residents were tenants in 1798, although some leased more than 150 acres from their landlords. In all, no more than 45 percent, and usually less, of the taxables during these years could even consider the possibility of becoming more or less self-sufficient, if that had been their goal. Indeed, the chances for success were becoming statistically more difficult, especially for younger children whose parents did not own sufficient land to set them up on their own farms. In this economy, participation in the market became a necessity for at least two-thirds of the population.[40]

Even those with the ability to be self-sufficient participated in local and long-distance trade. Rochefoucault Liancourt described the home of Abraham Miller, "a farmer," who kept a shop and ran an inn on Fishing Creek. Miller owned three hundred acres, seventy of them cleared. But he found that transforming forests into fields was difficult. "He clears annually about twelve or fifteen acres more," Rochefoucault Liancourt wrote, "but not without considerable trou-

40. See Tables 2, 3, and 4 in the Appendix. On Muncy Creek Township see United States Direct Tax of 1798: Tax Lists for the State of Pennsylvania, Lycoming County, Microcopy Number 372, National Archives and Records Service. Unfortunately, data for Turbut, Shamokin, and Muncy townships are not as complete in the surviving records of the 1798 direct tax.

ble, as labourers are very scarce." Miller, like other settlers, had to pay high costs for the most demanding work: clearing fields and harvesting crops. Still, he apparently fared well, selling maple sugar and other commodities, imported from Philadelphia overland to Catawissa and then up the Susquehanna, as well as taking in visitors. Miller thus was in no way self-sufficient. He imported goods from Philadelphia to sell at his store and hired laborers to tend his fields; taking in travelers was a further way of accumulating cash, which he could then use to purchase more goods or to pay his workers. The success of this farmer hardly insulated him from the workings of the local market.[41]

Although self-sufficiency eluded most households in the valley, if it had been their goal, communities possessed the necessary resources to remain isolated from the larger Atlantic market if they so chose. Individual settlers could acquire most of what they needed locally: they could purchase grains, seed, tools, livestock, and salted meat and other foodstuffs at local stores; obtain wood for fuel, fences, and buildings from local forests; wear homespun clothing and consume maple sugar and cider produced locally; use local potash for fertilizer; and employ local artisans to provide them with necessary services. In some sense, the region remained a valley of opportunity, still possessing both the resources needed for community survival and the residents with the necessary skills for transforming those resources into usable commodities. Valley inhabitants also exchanged their labor with each other, just as settlers elsewhere in eastern North America had done.[42]

Yet though settlers, tenants, and freeholders alike had the resources to create self-sufficient communities, they chose, no doubt through the enticements of the wealthy landholders, to participate in the larger market. In this sense, the farmer and innkeeper Miller

41. Rochefoucault Liancourt, *Travels through the United States,* 1:145–146.
42. Labor exchanges worked on different levels: residents exchanged labor with each other and some also worked for wealthy landholders. On exchange not apparently involving wealthy landholders see the farm account book of Thomas Ransom, covering the years 1785–1788 and 1790–1796, NYSHA. On working for wealthy landholders see Day Book of Muncy Farm, Wallis Papers, Reel 6. Two important essays that describe the workings of local exchange in other communities are, for the Connecticut Valley, Christopher Clark, "The Household Economy, Market Exchange and the Rise of Capitalism in the Connecticut Valley, 1800–1860," *Journal of Social History* 13 (1979), 169–189; and for the Hudson Valley, Michael Merrell, "Cash Is Good to Eat: Self-Sufficiency and Exchange in the Rural Economy of the United States," *Radical History Review* (1977), 42–71, esp. 54–61.

was no exception. Although little evidence exists to suggest that valley residents engaged in long-distance trade on their own, their behavior at local stores indicated their desire to participate in the larger market. No rustic provincials, valley inhabitants purchased a variety of imported goods at local stores: tea and silks from India, Irish linen, cotton, and calico. Local merchants and landholders, sensing an opportunity for profit by reselling valley produce outside the region, presumably in urban markets to the east, advertised the sale of liquor from all over the Atlantic world: rum from Antigua, gin from Holland, brandy from France, wine from Lisbon. Settlers had not initiated these long-distance exchanges and may have been unaware of how these commodities came to the valley from exotic locales, yet they, like the Indians who traded peltry for kettles and rum, became participants in a system of economic exchange that stretched over thousands of miles. The desire to purchase more than was needed to survive linked valley residents to an economic world with potentially boundless horizons.[43]

Those economic horizons appealed to freeholders and tenants alike. Samuel Wallis's account book reveals that he had ongoing commercial relations with scores of local residents. His records fail to indicate how much of their yield families brought to exchange, but they demonstrate that most valley residents took advantage of trading terms to acquire a wide range of goods they could not provide for themselves. Thus William McCauseland, who apparently owned land, frequently visited Wallis's store, stopping there seventeen times from May to September 1792. Eight times he brought grain to Muncy Farm, either as rent for land he might have leased from Wallis or because Wallis's store was the most convenient outlet or offered the best price for his wares. On five occasions McCauseland purchased corn, tea, cloth, or handkerchiefs, and on four visits Wallis paid McCauseland for threshing rye and cradling buckwheat.[44]

Yet such transactions were not limited to freeholders. Moses Rush,

43. On alcohol see ad for Rensellaer Williams, Jr.'s, store in Cooperstown, *Otsego Herald*, September 4, 1795; on the range of goods available see Day Book of Muncy Farm.

44. See entries for May 24, June 1, 9, 16, 21, 26, 28, July 2, 17, August 11, 20, September 11, 13, 22, 25, 1792, Day Book of Muncy Farm. McCauseland's name does not appear in the index for the Deed Books for Northumberland County, but a William McCaslin is listed in the Muncy Township tax list for 1790 and is assessed for acres; see Northumberland County Pennsylvania Board of County Commissioners Tax Records, LR 91.5, PHMC.

apparently one of Wallis's tenants, visited the store at Muncy Farm twenty-four times from May to December 1792. On most of those occasions grain was exchanged, presumably as rent payments. Yet besides the commodities a tenant would need to survive, such as a sickle purchased in July and a bay mare and pork a month later, Rush at times bought goods that reveal that he had wider tastes: cotton handkerchiefs, Irish linen, blue silk India pullicate, calico. Like McCauseland, he received cash, or more likely book credit, for doing spinning for Wallis.[45]

Such face-to-face transactions did not represent a new development in the upper valley. Rather, they echoed earlier exchanges between Indians and traders. In each instance, valley residents traded local resources for goods brought in from the outside world. Each transaction also involved the labor of valley residents channeled to serve a larger market, although Wallis's payments to McCauseland and Rush for their labor also had benefits for the wealthy landholder in the local market when he sold the cloth they had produced and the grain they had harvested.

Together, these exchanges constituted vital stages in the spread of the Atlantic market into the hinterland. But as the Indians had discovered during the early part of the century, the desire to purchase imported goods made residents ever more dependent on those who controlled the movement of commodities into and out of the valley. In the process, these tenants and freeholders enhanced the wealth and prestige of the developers.

"An excellent Patriarchal Establishment"

Wealthy investors who gained title to large tracts in the valley organized most of the region's postwar economic development. Like their colonial predecessors they lured settlers to the region by offering advantageous leasing or selling terms. They established commercial operations—mills, pot and pearl ash works, maple sugar refineries, distilleries—and often employed their tenants to manage them. Soon the landlords, at least the successful ones, began to ex-

45. See entries for May 24, 26, 29, June 4 (two entries), 9, 12, 16, 18, July 2, 10, 23, August 4, 9, 10, 11, September 8, 27, October 10, November 10, December 1, 5, 17, 31, 1792, Day Book of Muncy Farm.

port valley commodities to markets in Philadelphia, Baltimore, and elsewhere. By the end of the century they had integrated the regional economy into the larger market-oriented Atlantic commercial network.

To manage their properties, most landlords hired agents. John Jhones supervised John Nicholson's holdings at Thornbottom; John Hilborn managed Henry Drinker's Harmony settlement along the Susquehanna. Some landholders employed agents to find settlers for their lands. Joshua Whitney organized the settlement of William Bingham's valley holdings, promising "by every exertion in his power" to "increase the Settlements in [Binghamton], by encouraging mechanics, manufacturers & other artisans to remove there." Whitney, who received a 5-acre town lot and purchased a 215-acre farm for well under the market value, quickly began to sell parcels of Bingham's lands at $10 to $15 per acre, a sizable profit because Bingham had acquired the land for about twenty cents per acre. Nicholson sent agents to France, Holland, Germany, and England to sell shares in the Asylum Company.[46]

Agents managed the day-to-day affairs of the landholders in the backcountry and were especially important for landholders who did not reside in the upper valley. Bingham and Drinker stayed in Philadelphia and Banyar lived in Albany; all had agents overseeing their hinterland estates. Joshua Messereau (or Mersereau), a backcountry settler and an agent for Robert Lettis Hooper's lands at the confluence of the Susquehanna and Chenango rivers, offered his services to Banyar in January 1790. "I am going to settle on the Unidilla near Your lands," he wrote, "& am now on my return from building a Mill, and Shall Joyn my Children in Setling and promoting the Settlements there." Messereau wondered if Banyar would "see Cause to imploy me, to dispose of your lands by sale, or lease," and he offered to "readily attend to the business." "You must know the necessaty," Messereau concluded, "of having a person on the spot, in order to Settle Lands to advantage; and as I shall be on the Spot, and attend to the business, [I] have to hope I shall merit your attention." It is

46. Lincklaen, *Travels*, 43, 48–49, 51–52; J. B. Wilkinson, *The Annals of Binghamton, and the Country Connected with It, from the Earliest Settlement* (Binghamton, N.Y., 1840), 12–13; TJC (?) to Wallis, June 23, 1795, Wallis Papers, Reel 5; William Ellis to Wallis, August 1, 1790, ibid., Reel 6; William F. Seward, ed., *Binghamton and Broome County, New York: A History*, 3 vols. (New York, 1924), 1:28–29; Arbuckle, *Pennsylvania Speculator and Patriot*, 99–100.

unclear whether Banyar accepted Messereau's offer, but Messereau did move to the area and acted as a go-between for Banyar and his tenants.[47]

Distance also prevented Henry Drinker from adequately supervising affairs on his lands in northeast Pennsylvania. He hired John Hilborn to be the agent for his settlement at Harmony. Hilborn was fifty-one years old when he became Drinker's agent. When he moved to Harmony, Hilborn might not have realized the extent of the commitment he was making to Drinker. But when, in early July 1809, he looked back on his almost two decades of service, he was pleased that he had chosen this career, even though it meant separation from his old friends and coreligionists. His personal sacrifice benefited Drinker. During the early years of his agency, Hilborn had established Drinker's sugar-making industry in Harmony; he made the necessary collecting trays and hauled goods to the settlement on his back when the sleds his party was using became useless because there was not enough snow. He even endured personal suffering: his feet froze on his journey to Harmony in February 1790, temporarily preventing him from walking. But Hilborn proved a very able manager. From the early 1790s into the first decade of the nineteenth century, he organized sugar production, cleared and leveled roads, tended oxen, ordered supplies for Drinker's workers, forced squatters off Drinker's lands and brought ejectment suits against those who refused to move, and arranged for settlers to purchase or lease Drinker's lands.[48]

Most important for economic development, the landlords knew, was to get settlers on their lands as quickly as possible. Thus, like earlier landlords, they offered generous leasing terms. In some areas the landlords actually allowed squatters to remain on their tracts, though by the early 1790s they began to press these settlers for one-third of their yields as rent. The tenants on Wallis's lands were apparently so satisfied with their arrangement that they refused to move when another landlord made them a competitive offer. Timothy Pickering, developing his lands at Wilkes-Barre in the Wyoming

47. Messereau to Banyar, January 9, 1790, and David Baits to Banyar, September 4, 1794, Banyar Papers, Wallace and Misc. Patents, NYSL.

48. Hilborn to Drinker, May 9, 31, 1789, January 25, February 2, 15, March 5, 1790, March 3, May 9, 1801, January 2, March 30, October 14, 1802, March 11, 1803, July 4, 1809, Drinker Papers, Land Correspondence, Hilborn file, HSP; Drinker to Cooper, March 16, 1791, Henry Drinker Letter Book A, 1790–1793, 158, HSP.

region, was willing to go deeper into debt to support the "families of some poor labourers" whom he employed; he knew he needed their labor to establish his estate. Those who failed to attract enough settlers, such as Morris and Nicholson, made no profits from their holdings and could not satisfy their creditors.[49]

William Davy, the Devonshire traveler, described the squatters he found on Wallis's lands. "They came from no Body enquires where, or how," he wrote, "but generally with Families, fix on any Spot in the Wood that pleases them." The squatters would quickly build a rudimentary house and "clear away the underweed & girdle (girdling is cutting a ring of the Bark off, which kills the Tree when they are either left to rot down or are burnt down in the Winter)." They then planted potatoes and corn and continued to work "without ever enquiring whose the Land is, until the Proprietor himself disturbs & drives them off with Difficulty." Wallis chose not to force the squatters off his lands, even though more than one hundred were settled there. His generosity paid off: many of the squatters eventually became "good Tenants or Purchasers."[50]

Landlords often rented portions of their estates and sold others. Goldsbrow Banyar used this tactic successfully, enabling him to profit from an extremely valuable tract along the upper reaches of the Susquehanna River until well into the nineteenth century. The tract, originally patented to Alexander and Hugh Wallace, came under Banyar's control during the colonial period. Banyar remained neutral during the Revolution and in the 1780s was well equipped to profit from the settlement of the region. His papers relating to the patent reveal how wealthy landlords dealt with people moving onto their lands.

From the late 1780s and into the early nineteenth century Banyar arranged for many people to lease his lands. Leases were generally for three lives or thirty-one years. Most tenants did not pay any rent for the first three or four years, a familiar practice in the colonial period, so they could begin developing their farms. By the early nineteenth century, however, Banyar's tenants had to pay half their annual rent during the first four years. Rents varied depending on

49. Lincklaen, *Travels*, 55; Copy of Tenants Letter, June 20, 1795, included in TJC (?) to Wallis, June 23, 1795, Wallis Papers, Reel 5; Pickering to Samuel Hodgdon, May 18, 1788, *SCP*, 9:373–375; Arbuckle, *Pennsylvania Speculator and Patriot*, 112–113.
50. Wilkinson, ed., "Mr. Davy's Diary," 261–262.

the acreage and location and were higher if the tract had previously been improved by clearing fields or putting up buildings. Most settlers paid rent in cash, although some, like David and John Ogden and Uriah White, who together leased a 390-acre tract in February 1798, arranged to pay with crops, usually wheat or rye. Some tenants did not stay for the duration of their leases, and Banyar took careful note of each change in possession, renegotiating the tract's worth with the new tenants.[51]

Settlers who had sufficient cash purchased land, bargaining with the landholders for the best terms. For example, Silas Bennet wrote to Banyar in November 1796 about a tract along the Susquehanna. The lot attracted Bennet, but he was concerned about the erosion occurring each year when the river covered much of the land. He informed Banyar that some individual or group had cut timber on the land, thereby reducing its value. Still, Bennet wrote, he was willing to take the land if the price was low and he could move to the area immediately so that he could try to prevent more erosion. Bennet eventually purchased an adjacent tract from Banyar; he also leased other lands from the landholder and, in the early nineteenth century, purchased the title to some of this land from Banyar's family.[52] John Winn, representing a group of German settlers, wrote to Banyar in October 1785 trying to negotiate a price for two lots totaling four thousand acres. The Germans already owned and inhabited land in Montgomery County but wanted to move to the Susquehanna. They could not afford to pay for the land immediately because they would not at that time receive sufficient money from the sale of their other tracts: "To expose their Own Estates to immediate Sale for Ready Money the Lands wou'd not sell for half their Value." But the prospective purchasers wanted more than a postponement of payment. They expected Banyar to offer them the "same number of years" previously allowed others before they had to pay. They asked for this, according to Winn, because "the Settle-

51. See, for example, Timothy Birdsall's rent in Memorandum of Wallaces Patent, notation for July 21, 1800, and Rent Roll of Wallaces Patent, Leases & Lives, Banyar Papers, Wallace and Misc. Patents, NYSL.

52. Bennet to Banyar, November 7, 1796, March 15, 1805, receipt for Bennet's deed for lot no. 46, August 19, 1807, and Bennet to Miss Banyar, July 4, 1808, Banyar Papers, Wallace and Misc. Patents, NYSL.

ment in a New Country" was "attended with great Labour & Expence without any Profit for a Number of Years."[53]

Land prices varied depending on a variety of factors: proximity to reliable sources of water, soil quality, timber stocks, access to roads, previous use, and the landholders' plans for the area. John Lincklaen, traveling through the region scouting lands for a settlement company, found varying prices for land in the early 1790s. He had "no doubt" that James Wilson would sell his lands at four dollars per acre but offered no similar judgments for Samuel Wallis and Levi Hollingsworth, who were offering their lands at Tunkhannock at 10 1/2s. per acre for an area with good land but located on a creek that could be traversed only by canoe. Robert Lettis Hooper, Lincklaen wrote, had sold some of his land for as little as one dollar per acre, attracting a group of Connecticut settlers who took up a seven-hundred-acre tract. John Lindley, who purchased a tract of approximately twenty-three thousand acres from Phelps and Gorham, offered to sell half of his holdings for only one-third of a dollar per acre, but he made one important stipulation: he would sell, according to Lincklaen, only "on condition that the buyers build & cultivate," thereby raising the value of nearby tracts which Lindley presumably hoped to sell later at a higher cost.[54]

Perhaps no one entered the local real estate market more zealously, or with more success, than William Cooper. The founder of Cooperstown was both a shrewd manager of his holdings and an able propagandist. His posthumously published A Guide in the Wilderness documents the ideology of landlords in the postwar period. The pamphlet, taken together with Cooper's financial papers and travelers' accounts of Cooperstown, allows rare insight into the relationship between wealthy investors and the migrants purchasing their lands.

Cooper knew he had to sacrifice short-term profits to gain long-term economic stability. He valued the improvement of his lands more than holding unimproved tracts; even if tenants were unable to pay their rent for several years, he wrote, the landlord benefited from their labor. Cooper felt that such an approach was profitable

53. John Winn to Banyar, October 21, 1785, Banyar Papers, Wallace and Misc. Patents, NYSL. Winn did not specify whether the Germans lived in Montgomery County, New York, or Montgomery County, Pennsylvania.

54. Lincklaen, Travels, 55, 41, 48, 60. On the factors influencing land prices see Cooper, Some Information Respecting America, 107–108, 116.

because settlers on his lands would serve as a magnet drawing others to the area, further increasing its value. Cooper based his ideas, in part, on the failure of the Burlington Company to settle its tract near Lake Otsego before the Revolution; he particularly criticized the company members' allocation of lands. Cooper believed he succeeded because he had "made no partial gifts, but sold the whole at a moderate price with easy payments, having for myself a handsome profit; and people were readily induced to come when they saw a number of cooperators, and the benefits of association." Lincklaen noted that Cooper offered his tracts at reasonable rates, including an initial ten-year period when no payments were due. By the early 1790s, Cooper was selling between ninety and one hundred thousand acres of his lands for prices ranging from one dollar to twenty shillings per acre.[55]

Cooper succeeded in drawing thousands of people to his holdings. By 1791 he claimed that thirty families were living at Cooperstown and a total of 3,800 people on all of his lands. Cooperstown's population continued to grow steadily, reaching 339 in 1803 and 826 in 1816. By that time 8,000 people were living on lands he once owned. At the time of his death in 1809, Cooper had 137 tenants, who, with their families, continued to farm his lands. Cooper made a very substantial profit from settling his lands. He and Andrew Craig had purchased their 40,000-acre tract in January 1786 for £2,700 New York currency. Six months later, they sold four tracts within their purchase, totaling 5,702 acres, for £2,281 12s. New York currency, thus earning back almost all of the principal expenditure by selling only one-sixth of the land.[56]

Cooper organized Cooperstown to meet the needs of new settlers but made sure that he profited at every stage of the town's development. Critical of traditional divisions of land that gave settlers separate town, meadow, and back lots, Cooper sold or leased either farm lots or town lots but would not let any prospective settlers acquire both. To prosper, he wrote, it was "essential to the progress of a trading town, that it be settled quickly and compactly"; town resi-

55. Cooper, *Guide*, 12–14; Lincklaen, *Travels*, 73–74.

56. Lincklaen, *Travels*, 73; Cooper, *Guide*, iii, 11–12; I[saac] Cooper, Abstract taken from the Population of Cooperstown, March 1, 1803, and Population of Cooperstown, taken the first day of January 1816, NYSHA; Copy of Cooper's will, Cooper Papers, NYSHA; Tryon County Deed Book 1, 247–249, 280–283.

dents, free of the burdens of tending a farm, would spend their time working at their trades.[57]

Like other landlords, Cooper understood the importance of extending credit to settlers. He opened the first store in the region at a time when the settlers were desperate for the grain that he stocked during the winter. He then established sugar and potash production, borrowing kettles from Henry Drinker. "By this means I established a potash works among the settlers, and made them debtor for their bread and laboring utensils," he wrote in his *Guide*. "I also gave them credit for their maple sugar and potash, at a price that would bear transportation, and the first year after the adoption of this plan I collected in one mass forty-three hogsheads of sugar, and three hundred barrels of pot and pearl ash, worth about nine thousand dollars." But profit alone, Cooper claimed, did not encourage him to make the settlers indebted to him. His extension of credit and advancing of necessary commodities had "kept the people together and at home, and the country soon assumed a new face." Only twenty years after he had first encouraged settlement on his tract, Cooperstown had become, in his words, "a market town. It annually yields to commerce large droves of fine oxen, great quantities of wheat and other grain, abundance of pork, potash in barrels, and other provisions; merchants with large capitals, and all kinds of useful mechanics reside upon it; the waters are stocked with fish, the air is salubrious, and the country thriving and happy."[58]

Cooper's *Guide* was not an objective portrayal of life in the upper valley. He published it first in Dublin to encourage migration to America and to the northern backcountry, where he held title to thousands of acres of unpeopled land. It was not the only tract that land promoters circulated in Europe. In the mid-1790s the scientist Thomas Cooper, no relation to William Cooper, published *Some Information Respecting America*; an English version was printed in London in 1794, and a French version, published in Paris, appeared the next year. Thomas Cooper, an intimate of Thomas Jefferson, hoped to stimulate migration to the upper Susquehanna Valley where he and Joseph Priestley, perhaps the most famous scientist in eighteenth-century America, had land to sell. Like William Cooper's *Guide*, Thomas Cooper's tract extolled the virtues of the backcountry

57. Cooper, *Guide*, 17.
58. Ibid., 10–11.

and presented success stories of settlers in the area. Other promotional literature, such as Crèvecoeur's *Letters from an American Farmer*, first published in 1782, provided similar information. The lesson of each of these works was clear: if migrants crossed the Atlantic and settled in the backcountry they would soon establish profitable farms and live in greater comfort and security than they could in Europe.[59]

Although these promotional tracts exaggerated the likelihood of profit, William Cooper's success was very real. From the 1780s into the early 1800s he lured many tenants to his holdings. Cooper demanded rents in four marketable commodities: wheat, corn, butter, or pork. Tenants could also pay their rent in cash, but this value was not included in the lease; those paying in cash had to pay the equivalent of the market value of one of the four commodities enumerated in their lease. Such a strategy allowed Cooper to acquire a constant supply of grain, butter, and pork and thus served as a hedge against inflation. Tenants were responsible for producing and transporting these goods to Cooperstown, where Cooper could sell them locally or ship them downriver to other markets. Leases had no expiration date; their terms passed to future generations, allowing Cooper and his heirs to retain control over the marketing of backcountry goods.[60]

Cooper charged low rents for his lands. For example, on November 1, 1800, Cooper leased a 57.25-acre lot to Ebenezer Hubbard. In return for undisputed right to farm the land, Hubbard owed Cooper 21.3 bushels of wheat, or 36.5 bushels of corn, or 128 pounds of butter, or 320 pounds of pork. On the same day Seth Shippy rented a nearby tract of 60 acres. His annual rent was 22.75 bushels of wheat, or 36.5 bushels of corn, or 136.5 pounds of butter, or 343 pounds of pork. Since land in the region generally yielded 10 to 15

---

59. Promotional literature had been important to the peopling of British North America since the seventeenth century, and following the Revolution there was a burst of such efforts. J. P. Brissot de Warville's *Nouveau voyage dans les Etats-Unis de l'Amerique septrentionale, fait en 1788* appeared in two editions in Paris in 1791, and English translations began to appear the next year, first in London and later in pirated editions in Dublin and New York and several years later in Boston; corrected editions appeared in English in 1794. There were also five German editions of the work, as well as Dutch (Amsterdam, 1794) and Swedish (Stockholm, 1797) published before the end of the century. See Durand Echeverria, ed., *New Travels in the United States of America, 1788 by J. P. Brissot de Warville* (Cambridge, Mass., 1964), xxvi–xxvii. On the circulation of promotional literature in France see Durand Echeverria, *Mirage in the West: A History of the French Image of American Society to 1815* (Princeton, N.J., 1957), 133–136, 209–210.

60. Cooper's leases can be found in the Cooper Papers, NYSHA.

bushels of wheat per acre, with yields up to 20 bushels possible during early years of cultivation, Cooper's tenants should have had no
difficulty making their payments. In addition, the rents became easier to pay over time because tenants cleared more acreage the longer
they remained on their farms. Thus, with rents remaining constant
and the tenants' overall yields rising, tenants could use their surplus
crops to purchase goods at local stores, which generally accepted
"country produce" in lieu of cash.[61]

Cooper's leases contained a clause that allowed tenants to purchase their farms, but the precise value of the tracts was not given in
the lease. Indeed, the purchase price was not determined until the
tenants sought to buy the land, at which time they had to pay an
amount approximately fourteen times greater than their annual
rent. These "redemption leases," to use the term employed by Cooper in his will, appealed to cash-poor migrants who wanted to own
land but needed time to raise sufficient capital.[62]

Some prospective settlers wanted to own land immediately instead
of taking out redemption leases. If they were unable to pay for the
land, they took out mortgages with Cooper. In April 1795, Samuel
Ingles wanted to purchase a hundred-acre tract in the Ballstown
purchase near Lake Otsego. Cooper valued the tract at £67 6s. 3d.
Ingles agreed to pay the purchase price within three years, at which
time he would own the land. If he failed, he would owe Cooper
double the value of the tract, and Cooper would retain possession of

61. Both leases dated November 1, 1800, Cooper Papers; see, for example, the ad
for Van Alstine's store, *Otsego Herald*, September 4, 1795. On yields see Cooper, *Some
Information Respecting America*, 113, 125; and Percy Bidwell and John Falconer, *History
of Agriculture in the Northern United States, 1620–1860* (New York, 1941), 101. Cooper's
rents averaged 0.363 bushels of wheat per acre; this estimate is derived from analysis
of twenty-one leases, covering the period 1800 to 1808, in the Cooper Papers. These
leases were selected because they were complete; they provided the name of the tenant, the amount of produce demanded in rent, the location of the tract, and the date
the lease was signed. The terms of the leases were perpetual, passing down to Cooper's heirs, on one side, and the heirs of the tenant, on the other. Cooper's rents were
slightly higher than rents elsewhere in New York, where tenants had to pay, on the
average, 0.1 to 0.2 bushels of wheat per acre; see David M. Ellis, *Landlords and Farmers
in the Hudson-Mohawk Region, 1790–1850* (1946; rpt. New York, 1976), 228.

62. Cooper's leases contained a clause that allowed the tenant, after the payment of
rent, further to pay "as much current Money of the United States of America, as that
the annual interest thereof, at the time of such payment, will readily purchase the
quantity of Merchantable Wheat, or Corn, or Butter, or Pork, as is herein stipulated
at Cooperstown aforesaid." After making this payment, the tenant could obtain a
deed for the tract.

the land. The length of mortgages varied, but, as John Lincklaen learned when he traveled through Cooperstown in the early 1790s, anyone who took out a mortgage had to sign a bond promising payment as well as pay fourteen shillings for the deed.[63]

Purchase of land through mortgages was common in the upper valley, even though settlers had to pay a higher price for the land because of the interest payments. "We were told that cleared land near the river," Thomas Cooper wrote in the mid-1790s, "and adjoining to the Loyalsock was worth 6l. and if sold in gales, 7l. 10s an acre." Cooper defined gales as "periodical payments or installments." He explained to his readers why settlers chose to gain land in this way. "This is the common mode of purchasing," he wrote. "But although the purchaser, who pays by gales, pays interest at 6 per cent. on the purchase money not immediately paid down, land sells much higher in this way, from the facility of making much better interest, by employing ready money in fresh purchases and improvements."[64]

Once they had attracted settlers to their lands, the landholders needed to know how to capitalize on the natural resources of their holdings. In many parts of the valley, especially the lowlands near the Susquehanna and its tributaries, agriculture was profitable. But landholders had to know how to gain income from uplands as well. Thus they encouraged their tenants or nearby settlers to establish sugar refineries, pot and pearl ash works, mills, and lumbering operations. By exploiting a wider range of resources, the landlords maximized their gains.

Sugar production, which was cost- and labor-efficient, became widespread in the upper valley. Many landholders actively pursued the business, anticipating profits from the sale of maple sugar in the country and abroad. John Nicholson provided Jhones, his agent at Thornbottom, with the tools necessary for sugar production. Because the kettles arrived too late in the year, Jhones was unable to produce much sugar in 1791, but he planned, according to Lincklaen, "to tap 2000 trees next spring, having 12 workmen among whom there are some young lads." Nicholson also had residents pro-

63. Lincklaen, *Travels*, 124; Cooper's deed and agreement with Ingles both dated April 23, 1795, Cooper Papers. For an example of Wallis's mortgage practices see his arrangement with William Donaldson, August 27, 1793, Northumberland County Deed Book I, 308–309, NCCH.

64. Cooper, *Some Information Respecting America*, 115; see also Wilkinson, ed., "Mr. Davy's Diary," 271.

ducing sugar at Wilkes-Barre and planned to have his European settlers at Asylum, when they arrived, active in the business. The potential for making sugar from Nicholson's holdings was enormous.
Of his twelve thousand acres, three thousand had an average of
thirty maple trees each, a total of ninety thousand trees. The trees,
mostly fifteen to twenty inches in diameter, were expected to produce twenty-five gallons of sap each, which, after it was processed,
would yield five pounds of sugar. Lincklaen wrote that the great
quantities Nicholson could produce induced him "to establish a distillery."[65]

Other landlords also profited from the sugar industry and encouraged their tenants to become actively involved in the business. Henry
Ellisson, a tenant of Wallis and Hollingsworth, tapped 150 trees on
the three-hundred-acre tract he settled between the north and east
branches of the Tunckhannock; he made 200 pounds of sugar and
had begun selling it in the area, at a price of one shilling per pound,
within a year of the time he first settled. Ulrich Swingel also produced 200 pounds of sugar on Hooper's lands during the spring of
1791. John Hilborn, Henry Drinker's agent at Harmony, made 120
pounds of sugar during the same season. William Cooper and other
landlords estimated that, in all, over 150,000 pounds of sugar were
produced in the Otsego region in 1793 and, at 9d. per pound, the
potential profit seemed great indeed.[66]

David Bard suggested that sugar production was an ideal pursuit
for settlers along the Susquehanna. "This article though as yet, only
made by farmers in small quantities and generally for domestic use,
offers a great and certain profit to those, who shall carry on the
manufacturing of it to any extensive degree," he wrote. "As the liquor begins to run towards the close of the winter, and ceases early
in the spring, its collection cannot interfere with the other occupa-
tions of the farmer."[67]

Attracted by the profits from the sugar business, a group of investors, including Henry Drinker and John Nicholson, promised to
purchase 15,800 pounds of valley sugar, presumably collected at

65. Lincklaen, *Travels*, 42–44; Arbuckle, *Pennsylvania Speculator and Patriot*, 103–
104.

66. Lincklaen, *Travels*, 44, 47, 52; Tench Coxe, *A View of the United States of America,
in a Series of Papers Written at Various Times, in the Years between 1787 and 1794* (1794;
rpt. New York, 1965), 80.

67. Bard, *Description of the River Susquehanna*, 13.

Cooperstown, for three years beginning in 1789. According to their subscription list, they were "desirous to promote & encourage the manufacture & consumption of Maple Sugar in the United States," and their efforts no doubt greatly encouraged production. Drinker, hoping to sell sugar in Philadelphia and elsewhere, supplied Cooper with kettles for sugar boiling and kept the backcountry landholder abreast of fluctuations in the sugar market. Drinker remained optimistic in spite of initial problems, including two successive bad crops, failure to raise the promised subscription, inability to sell the product in an oversupplied market in Philadelphia, and the inferior quality of Cooper's sugar caused by poor boiling. Indeed, even after Drinker had to assume responsibility for the entire subscription in the late 1780s, indicating the problems of maple sugar sales in the domestic market, he arranged to ship two or three hogsheads to London, where he believed it would find a market among the abolitionist English who did not want to purchase slave-produced West Indian sugar.[68]

Benjamin Rush, who also was involved in land speculation in the upper valley, became the most vigorous proponent of the maple sugar industry. In August 1793 he delivered an address to the American Philosophical Society on the benefits of maple sugar; the lecture was published in that year's *Transactions* of the society, perhaps the most illustrious American journal in the decades following the Revolution. Rush described the workings of the industry, the medical benefits of maple sugar, and the potential it held for enhancing the new nation's economic standing. Like Drinker, Rush believed that the most important benefit of maple sugar production would be the competition it would present to the slave-based economy of the West Indies. "I cannot help contemplating a sugar tree with a species of affection and even veneration," he wrote, "for I have persuaded myself to behold in it the happy means of rendering the commerce and slavery of our African brethren in the sugar Islands as unnessary, as it has always been inhuman and unjust." Yet even Rush's enthusiasm could not make the industry successful. By

68. Agreement dated September 3, 1789, Cooper Papers, NYSHA; Drinker to Cooper, January 15, February 7, March 16, 1791, March 29, 1792, Henry Drinker Letter Book A, 1790–1793, 129, 138, 158, 164, 279, Drinker Papers, HSP; Henry Drinker Journal, 1776–1791, 346, 439, HSP; see Thomas M. Doerflinger, *A Vigorous Spirit of Enterprise: Merchants and Economic Development in Revolutionary Philadelphia* (Chapel Hill, N.C., 1986), 323.

the time he delivered his address, others were abandoning hope for the industry; those who had invested in it, including Morris, Nicholson, Wilson, and even Rush himself, never received the profits they thought maple sugar would bring them. In 1795 they dissolved the company they had created to promote the industry.[69]

Notwithstanding the demise of the industry in the mid-1790s, the developers' interest in maple sugar revealed their desire to transform the resources of the upper valley into commodities that could be sold in eastern cities and, they hoped, overseas. Yet their desire to develop the industry provides insight into the ways the landholders looked at the resources of the upper valley. Like traders who sought to transform beavers into profits, these developers wanted to convert natural resources into gains in their ledgers. The energy Drinker, Rush, Cooper, and others put into the maple sugar industry reveals a continuity of thought among entrepreneurs; nature's bounty could bring great profits, they believed, especially if those in control of resources were sensitive to the range of resources that could be harvested.

Although landholders had hoped sugar production would generate substantial profits in external markets, other business operations allowed them to enhance their economic position in the valley. Milling is perhaps the best example. Rural settlers always wanted mills built as close as possible to their farms. Local sawmills were a great boon to settlers building houses and outbuildings. Gristmills were perhaps even more important for the landholders because they encouraged local settlers to concentrate on grain production both for their own use and as a cash crop. The mills also allowed landholders who accepted rents in grain to transform payments into marketable commodities. Specialized production made the settlers dependent on local stores to provide them with goods, including food, which they chose not to produce for themselves. Given the advantages, it was no

---

69. Benjamin Rush, "An Account of the Sugar Maple-tree of the United States, and of the methods of obtaining Sugar from it, together with observations upon the advantages both public and private of this sugar," *Transactions of the American Philosophical Society* 3 (1793), 64–81 (quotation on p. 78). On the failure of the industry see Drinker to Cooper, June 13, 1793, Drinker Letter Book, 1793–1798, 23–24; George Corner, ed., *The Autobiography of Benjamin Rush* (Princeton, N.J., 1948), 177; and an agreement to sell off the property of the Society for Promoting the Manufacture of Sugar from Sugar maple trees, November 9, 1795, Society Misc. Colls., Box 7-B, HSP.

surprise that those with large real estate holdings became involved in milling, often reserving important mill sites for their own use.[70]

The landholders exerted control over many aspects of valley milling operations. When Andrew Culbertson wanted to erect a gristmill he sought help from Wallis, particularly in transporting iron, nails, and clapboard. In exchange for these commodities Culbertson promised not only "full Satisfaction" but also that he would "Make a Point of Endeavouring to oblidge you on any occasion." Wallis apparently provided the assistance that Culbertson required and became accustomed to dealing with his mill. William Cooper believed that landlords should encourage some settler to run the local mill. "Sell the mill place to a man that can build upon it," he wrote in his *Guide*, "or if you should sell it to one who has not the means, furnish them to him, and make him debtor to you for the advances. He will work better and cheaper for himself than for you; you will not be cheated, and you will have a good profit in the convenience and advantage which your settlement will derive from it."[71]

Using their control of mills and forested lands to their advantage, the landlords also organized the developing lumber industry of the valley. Philip Antes, probably one of Wallis's tenants, ran a sawmill on Wallis's lands. Despite an illness that hampered his activities, he was able to prepare two thousand feet of white pine boards during the summer of 1795. Antes and other valley sawyers supplied Wallis's lumber trade. At the time of his death, Wallis had seven thousand oak shingles and an unspecified number of white pine shingles, as well as twenty thousand feet of pine boards; like many of the other goods enumerated in the inventory of his estate, the lumber and lumber products were apparently intended for sale. Lumber from the upper valley also reached downstream millers, Thomas Cooper wrote; these sawyers purchased lumber from "people who live up the country" and sent it down the Susquehanna in rafts fifty to one hundred logs across. The downstream sawyer would cut the logs and sell the lumber locally.[72]

70. See, for example, Lincklaen, *Travels*, 49, 56, 57.

71. Andrew Culbertson to Wallis, January 20, 1784, Stephen Hollingsworth to "Brother," January 9, 1797, Wallis Papers, Reel 6; Cooper, *Guide*, 38.

72. TJC (?) to Wallis, June 23, 1795, Wallis Papers, Reel 5; An Inventory and Appraisement of the Personal Estate of Samuel Wallis, November 16–17, 1798, ibid., Reel 6; Cooper, *Some Information Respecting America*, 132–133.

By the end of the century such operations had blossomed in the region. "Large quantities of lumber have been brought down the Susquehanna from the distance of three hundred miles above its mouth during the freshes of the spring," David Bard wrote in 1796 in a pamphlet aimed at encouraging the Pennsylvania legislature to finance efforts to improve navigation on the river, "and rafts of boards, masts, and all kinds of timber have been floated from the state of New-York, and the head waters of the Susquehanna, as well as down the Tioga, and Juniata branches for several hundred miles in their different windings." He especially noted the fine quality of the pine masts, including white pine, then used on frigates being built at Philadelphia and Baltimore.[73]

In spite of occasional references to deforestation in travelers' journals, the upper valley provided the landholders with an abundant supply of timber and an excellent source of revenue from lumbering and potash production. Thomas Cooper reported that on his journey to the upper valley, the "*trees* fell much short of my expectations: I recollect none from Philadelphia to Sunbury, of any kind, that would measure 18 inches diameter. Indeed they grow so close and so tall, that there is no reason to expect much dimension of breadth, but they certainly appear slender and feeble to an Englishman, who has visited the park and forest scenery of his own country." Once in the upper valley, however, Cooper found better timber stocks. "About half a dozen miles from Northumberland, the trees began to assume a more luxuriant appearance, and to become of respectable size." Although he still had not seen the best trees, he had heard of "much larger timber on the rich lands at the heads of the creeks, such as Lycoming, Loyalsock, Muncy, &c." When surveyors sent their reports to the landholders, they proved the truth of what Cooper had heard. When William Ellis surveyed a fifty-thousand-acre tract north of the West Branch in 1793, for example, he was impressed with the forest of the area, particularly the quantity of maple, poplar, and beech; at one point he traveled through "as level deep heavy timbered genuine Beech land as I know."[74]

John Nicholson and William Cooper both hoped that potash production would reap great profits. Nicholson planned to use valley potash to supply his glassworks on the Schuylkill, four miles from

73. Bard, *Description of the River Susquehanna*, 41.

74. Cooper, *Some Information Respecting America*, 104, 112; William Ellis to Wallis, August 2, 1793, Wallis Papers, Reel 6.

Philadelphia. Employing recent technology, Nicholson built potash works at Asylum and Wilkes-Barre. He then provided potash kettles to local residents. When the potash business proved unprofitable, he switched to pearl ash production but still found profits elusive. Indeed, so many people produced pot and pearl ash that the market had become saturated, driving prices down. Cooper was more fortunate. He quickly found a market for valley potash and contracted to send it to the Albany merchant Leonard Gansevoort, although poor roads occasionally delayed deliveries.[75]

The landholders' export operations were only one part of their mercantile enterprises; they also profited from importing goods and selling them at their stores. At Wallis's store settlers could purchase an extensive assortment of wares, including domestic cloth, Irish linen, blue silk India pullicate, a variety of handkerchiefs and metal buttons, and all sorts of foodstuffs, including grains, salt, bacon, lard, maple sugar, and salted shad. He also sold seeds, tools, and livestock. Nonresident landholders also set up accounts at valley stores to provide settlers associated with them with ready access to necessary supplies.[76]

Valley landholders solidified their economic position by hiring local settlers to perform labor for specific projects. Wallis paid valley residents to spin yarn and weave cloth; he hired others to clear fields, thresh rye, and cradle buckwheat. Landholders also hired residents to perform jobs such as carpentry, road clearing, or hauling on a temporary basis; Wallis also hired local inhabitants for longer periods of time, either for specific services, such as shoemaking, or for less specialized tasks. By the end of the century, wage labor had become an accepted part of the valley economic culture, just as it had become common elsewhere in Pennsylvania.[77]

By the end of the century the wealthy landlords had precisely de-

75. Arbuckle, *Pennsylvania Speculator and Patriot*, 102–103; Memorandum of an agreement between Cooper and Leonard Gansevoort, July 21, 1790, Cooper Papers, NYSHA.

76. Day Book of Muncy Farm, Wallis Papers, Reel 6, passim; Mathias Hollenback Accounts, Account Book, 1788–1789, Sequestered John Nicholson Papers, Roll 4 (1787–1800), PHMC.

77. Day Book of Muncy Farm, Wallis Papers, Reel 6, passim; Article of agreement between Cooper and Cyrenus Clark, November 1, 1803, typescript in Cooper Papers, NYSHA; *Otsego Herald*, March 24, 1796. On wage labor elsewhere see Paul G. E. Clemens and Lucy Simler, "Rural Labor and the Farm Household in Chester County, Pennsylvania, 1750–1820," in Stephen Innes, ed., *Work and Labor in Early America* (Chapel Hill, N.C., 1988), 106–143.

fined their role in the valley economy. They were not wholly responsible for the repopulation of the region, although they certainly lured many into the area through attractive leasing and purchasing terms. They did not exercise complete control over the many agricultural settlements throughout the valley; decisions over matters such as crop mix or how much livestock farmers should keep often remained beyond the landlords' dominion. But by controlling access to land, the import and export of goods, and the extension of credit, the landholders exerted an enormous influence over the entire regional population. They became the link between the valley residents and the Atlantic economy. Thus, though families remained the basic economic unit, they found themselves increasingly bound into an elaborate system of debt, mortgages, or tenancy. Economic security in this rural hinterland, all valley residents knew, meant living in the landholders' commercial world.

That commercial world was, according to tax records, one of contrasts. Nowhere was the disparity between a landlord and his neighbors as clear as in Muncy. In 1790 there were 42 married taxables and 11 single freemen, who possessed no land in the township. Forty-three others owned 150 acres or less. Another 24 had between 151 and 500 acres. At the top end of the scale sat only two township residents: Philip Francis (who owned 1,400 acres, five horses, and four cows) and Samuel Wallis. Wallis, assessed for 2,450 acres, ten horses, twenty-four cows, and an unspecified number of mills and servants, was far and away the richest man in the township. His acreage surpassed that of the bottom 69 (out of 111) married taxables combined. That is, his holdings exceeded those of the lowest 62 percent of the township's family households. Looked at from a different perspective, Wallis owned 16 percent, or almost one-sixth, of the land claimed by residents of the township.[78]

Startling as these contrasts appear in such quantifiable measures, the discrepancies between the worlds of the wealthy and their tenants were just as obvious to contemporary observers. Indeed, the valley's prosperous landholders lived in splendor compared to their tenants. William Davy recognized the disparity when he traveled to Wallis's homestead, which extended "in a direct Line without an in-

<hr />

78. Muncy Township tax assessment for 1774, in Northumberland County Pennsylvania Board of County Commissioners Tax Records, LR 91.2, PHMC; see also Table 2 in the Appendix.

tervening Acre of another Person's Six Miles on each side of the Susquehanna River." Wallis's "Mansion House, a solid Stone Building on the Margin of the River," greatly impressed the Devonshire traveler. The household had thirty-five residents in the mid-1790s, twenty of them servants, "almost all of them Germans," whose contracts Wallis had purchased in Philadelphia. Wallis's plantation had, to Davy, "the appearance of an excellent Patriarchal Establishment in which Order, System & Economy reign." The estate's self-sufficiency especially impressed Davy. "Every Necessary is provided in the Family," he wrote. "They last Year Kill'd 8000 lbs of Beef, Pork, & Mutton, 500 Fowls, a great Quantity of Game, 3 Hogsheads of Shad (a Fish Salted & Pickled like Salmon), made 1000 Yards of Linnen, work'd up their own Wool, made their own Sope & Candles & a good supply of Maple Sugar." Wallis's seven thousand acres on the estate had "an abundance of Wood, Lime Stone, & Streams of water for watering Meadows of which there is great Plenty." Given the advantages of Muncy Farm, it was no wonder that Davy, comparing it to the manors of England, believed that Wallis's holdings were superior to those of "any lord in yon Lordly Countries."[79]

Most settlers, Davy discovered, lived much more modestly. Even those who owned land were never entirely secure. Indeed, Davy and his associate, the scientist Joseph Priestley, purchased a 204-acre farm from a settler named Mackensy, a onetime British soldier captured during the Revolution, who chose to remain after the end of the war. The land had "plenty of Springs" and good soil, as well as abundant timber stocks which could be easily transported to the river to be carried downstream. Rather than moving to new lands, Mackensy remained on the tract as a tenant. "By this he & his Wife are render'd Comfortable & happy." The land's new owners gave Mackensy directions on the long-term plans for the tract, including instructions to protect some of the trees and thus prevent the excessive forest thinning which Davy believed characterized American farms. But though Mackensy's farm promised economic security, the family house paled in comparison to Wallis's stone mansion. "Their Habitation," Davy wrote, "is a mere open Log House without Door, Window or Chimney but a very neat Room with 3 beds in it." So equipped, Mackensy and his family, like the tenants and families of tenants on other landholders' estates, produced goods for eastern

79. Wilkinson, ed., "Mr. Davy's Diary," 262–264.

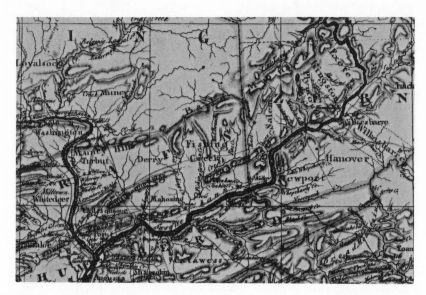

Detail, "Pennsylvania," Daniel Friedrich Sotzmann (Hamburg, 1797). Courtesy, Map Collection, Harvard College Library

markets, further enriching their landlords and reinforcing the economic gap between the residents of the upper valley.[80]

Transportation Networks

Following the Revolution, landholders, government officials, and the courts together promoted the developing valley economy. State and local legislators and courts sanctioned and funded efforts to improve transportation routes connecting the valley with important markets; they allocated public funds to finance the construction and maintenance of roads and the attempts to improve navigation of the Susquehanna and its tributaries. The projects to facilitate transport eclipsed any similar efforts before the Revolution. Tench Coxe, for example, estimated that more money was spent on improving river and road travel in Pennsylvania from 1790 to 1793 than had been spent for these tasks during the previous century.[81]

80. Ibid., 269–271.
81. Fletcher, *Pennsylvania Agriculture*, 251.

The need for improved transportation routes grew along with the volume of trade descending the Susquehanna. George Fry, a miller in Middletown, realized that poor roads, especially from the valley to Philadelphia, threatened the grain trade. "The consequences are of Importance to the Public in General and to this, neighbouring Places & the Settlements up the Susquehanna & Juniata Rivers in particular," he wrote in 1793, "because the large Quantities of Wheat & other Produce which are brought to this Town by Water, and the Flour &c. manufactured about here, and which are to be forwarded by Land [to Philadelphia], remain on Hand for want of Teams which are terrified by the bad and dangerous Roads over Connowago & other Hills." Fry feared that the flour would remain in Middletown "and be Subject to Suffer during the Warm Season by laying in crowded Storehouses, not to mention that by such Delay the Credit of many People may be hurt for want of Cash which they expect to draw from their Property as soon as they could get it delivered at the Place of its Destination."[82]

In the 1780s and 1790s local courts dealt with a number of cases involving the ability of valley settlers to move through the region along its public highways, both on roads and in certain waterways. As early as September 1778, in the midst of the Revolution, the Tryon County court had ordered the overseers of the highways to "direct the Inhabitants of their respective Districts, Wards or Beats to go upon the Roads and cause the same to be sufficiently repaired within twenty days after notice." From August 1781 until November 1794 the Northumberland County Quarter Sessions Court heard six cases involving people who had erected fences across public roads impeding foot, horse, and carriage travel; one resident even planted wheat and other grains on the road, making it completely impassable. In all cases the court found the fence builders at fault and ordered them to remove the obstructions.[83]

82. Quoted in James W. Livingood, *The Philadelphia-Baltimore Trade Rivalry, 1780–1860* (Harrisburg, Pa., 1947), 40.

83. For Tryon County see September 1778 Sessions, County of Tryon, Court of General Sessions Minutes, 1, 1772–1808, NYSL. For Northumberland County see Respublica v. Robert Martin, August Sessions 1781, Resp. v. William Biles, August sessions 1781, and Commonwealth v. Mathew Smith and Samuel Jones, August sessions 1788, Pennsylvania v. Nicholas Miller and Daniel Farmer, April Sessions 1792; Pennsylvania v. Francis Fisher, April Sessions 1792; and Resp. v. Peter Wiser, Robert Woodride, Christian Gettig and George Harrison, November Sessions 1794, all in Quarter Sessions, 1772–1797, NCCH.

County courts punished overseers of the roads who failed to perform their jobs conscientiously. In October 1780 and October 1786
the Tryon County court ordered the overseers to fulfill their duties
and repair the roads quickly. In November 1794 the county court in
Sunbury brought charges against some of the overseers for neglect-
ing their duty. Henry Baugher and Daniel Whitmore, two of the
overseers for Augusta Township, were accused of failing to organize
the labor necessary for maintaining the roads in the area. Their neg-
ligence had led to serious deterioration of the roads from the township to Shamokin and Catawissa townships. The court believed that
the rights of valley residents to travel in the region had been violated. The roads, the court wrote in its decision, "became so decayed
& still so decay for want of repairing" that local residents "cannot
with their Horses Carts & Carriages go safely go pass & travel as of
Right they ought." The wording of these decisions unambiguously
reflected the rhetoric of the Revolution: valley residents, in the
court's opinion, had a right to travel without hindrance, and public
institutions had to protect that right even when it meant convicting
county officials.[84]

Without proper roads valley inhabitants could not transport goods
within the valley and to external markets; residents remained, like
their predecessors before the war, isolated from neighbors, churches,
and nearby settlements. In 1790 Levi Beardsley's family had to leave
their wagons and furniture several miles from their home because
the roads were "broken up and almost impassable." The landholders, however, worked to remedy the situation. The agents of
John Nicholson and Henry Drinker organized road-clearing efforts
during the late 1780s and early 1790s. William Cooper organized
local settlers to cut roads in the region, suggesting that such labor
could be obtained by offering alcohol to the laborers. At Oquaga the
settlers had begun to cut a road from the Susquehanna to Cook-
house on the Delaware. "It will be 14 miles long," Lincklaen wrote in
his journal, "& will serve to transport their commodities to the Philadelphia market." Valley landholders and settlers wanted to avoid the
plight of John Schaffer, a farmer who had established a homestead

84. See entries for October 1780 and October 1786 sessions, County of Tryon,
Court of General Sessions, Minute Book 1; Pennsylvania v. Daniel Whitmore and
Henry Baugher, November 1794 Sessions, Quarter Sessions, 1772–1797, NCCH; Res.
v. David Shannon and Thos. Stratton, November 1794 Sessions, Quarter Sessions,
1772–1797, NCCH; Res. v. John Fuselman and Nicholas Miller, November 1794 Sessions, Quarter Sessions, 1772–1797, NCCH.

near Tunkhannock in 1785; he had cultivated enough land to support his large family but, according to Lincklaen, "the lack of communication prevents all the inhabitants of this country getting anything to market."[85]

Valley residents, especially the wealthy landholders, believed that state and local governments should provide funds for road construction. Their attitudes emerged clearly in the writings of the Pennsylvania Landholders Association, an organization of landlords who took up a subscription to finance three roads through northern Pennsylvania. Several valley landlords, including Drinker, Wilson, Nicholson, Wallis, and Reuben Haines contributed to the fund. But the Pennsylvania Landholders did not intend to finance the roads themselves. They petitioned the state legislature to fund the project, dismissing any possible protest over the use of state funds by noting that the roads would open an enormous territory for new settlements and that the state would earn more from the sale of the tracts and the associated warrants and patents than the road would cost.[86]

The association argued that the state should use public funds because the roads would have innumerable economic benefits for its residents. The roads would lure much of the commerce of New York into Pennsylvania, especially down the Susquehanna and Delaware. Further, the great pasture land in northern Pennsylvania was ideal for cattle, capable of supporting a booming beef business and thereby making the state less reliant on European cattle. "At present," the association wrote in a broadside, "we are tributary to foreign countries for barrelled beef, which is imported from Ireland by a voyage of three thousand miles." The state would also benefit from the export of potash produced in the area, an industry they valued at $200,000 annually in New York. A road to Tioga would bring revenue from the Indian trade at Lake Ontario into Pennsylvania. The roads would also be useful in suppressing any insurrections among Susquehannah Company members in the Wyoming region.[87]

The association argued that the greatest benefit for the state would be from the opening of new lands for settlement. "A great

85. Beardsley, *Reminiscences*, 20–21; Lincklaen, *Travels*, 43, 53, 47; John Hilborn to Drinker, May 31, 1789, Drinker Papers, Land Correspondence, Hilborn file, HSP; Arbuckle, *Pennsylvania Speculator and Patriot*, 100; Cooper, *Guide*, 10, 37–38.

86. Minutes of a meeting of the Pennsylvania Landholders, February 27, 1788, *SCP*, 9:327–329; Subscription List for Road for the Pennsylvania Landholders, February 28, 1788, ibid., 329–330; "Observations by the Committee of the Pennsylvania Landholders," March 5, 1788, ibid., 330–331.

87. "Observations by the Committee," 331–333.

part of New York, New Jersey and Massachusetts, and nearly the whole of Connecticut and Rhode Island, lie due east of the Lands thro' which these roads are proposed to pass," the broadside maintained, "so that all the emigrants from those parts, now known to be too full of inhabitants, will be induced by good roads to take this country in their way westward, which will give Pennsylvania a great opportunity of acquiring settlers, citizens, and taxables." Given the desire of these migrants to find lands quickly, the landholders urged "that time should not be lost, for by getting the start of a season we may turn the tide of emigration into this channel." Given the advantages involved, the landholders felt justified in soliciting state funds: "How grand an object then does this appear to the manufactures, internal and foreign commerce, agriculture and general resources and powers of the state."[88]

Although the landholders' rhetoric was self-serving, public officials in New York and Pennsylvania agreed that governments should allocate funds for road building. In 1785, for example, the commissioners for Tryon County organized the surveying and building of a road from the lower end of Cherry Valley to the Susquehanna. By 1792 the state of New York had financed a ninety-mile road from Kaatskill to the Susquehanna. By the end of the first decade of the nineteenth century several roads ran between settlements in the uppermost reaches of the valley, including roads from Unadilla to Cayuga Lake and from Lake Otsego to the Pennsylvania border. In the early 1790s the state of Pennsylvania authorized a series of roads for the upper Susquehanna Valley, including improvements and completion of a road from Philadelphia to Sunbury and others from Northampton to the mouth of the Tioga, from Wilkes-Barre to Wyalusing, and from Bald Eagle's Nest to Erie. Legislators in New York and Pennsylvania continued to finance roads to the Susquehanna Valley into the early nineteenth century.[89]

Local authorities also paid for the construction of bridges which allowed for quicker and more direct overland travel. In 1794 the Northumberland County Quarter Sessions Court paid £50 to construct a bridge over Buffalo Creek at its mouth. County commissioners financed the construction of bridges over other creeks, con-

88. Ibid., 332.

89. Tryon County Deed Book 1, 227–228; Lincklaen, *Travels*, 121; Frost, *Life on the Upper Susquehanna*, 28; Bard, *Description of the River Susquehanna*, 53–55; Livingood, *Philadelphia-Baltimore Trade Rivalry*, 46–47.

necting important roads and thereby allowing easier travel to towns and mills.[90]

In spite of the efforts to cut roads and build bridges, valley residents realized that overland travel was often much more expensive than water travel. Apart from the costs of cutting the trees and clearing the stumps, roads required constant maintenance to keep them cleared of fallen trees and their surfaces sufficiently level for wagons. Wagon travel was difficult during much of the year when snow, ice, and rain made the roads slippery or muddy; the unpaved paths became deeply rutted. Valley residents knew that poor roads hampered the movement of goods. "The Horrid Situation of the road renders the United Strength of wood and iron insufficient to withstand the Surges of a Moderate Load," William Cooper wrote to Leonard Gansevoort in November 1790, "the way being new and full of roots together with the softness of the soil by nature, and made more so by the wet weather this fall, all which reasons Causes me to inform you that after Repeted attemts I was Obligd to Abandon Any further thoughts of bringing my Pot and Perl Ash to Albany before Haying."[91]

Because hauling along roads took longer than water travel, it meant lower profits. "For, laying aside the expense of carrying a good road through an extensive country, over every variety of ground," Bard wrote in 1796, "land carriage if extended to any considerable distance, must, from the length of time, and the quantity of labour consumed, eat up the price of the articles conveyed." Bard's impression was accurate. As late as 1816 the cost of transporting wheat to Philadelphia from a distance of only fifty miles amounted to one-fourth of the already high price that it commanded on the market.[92]

The limitations of road travel spurred those involved with developing the commercial network of the upper valley to investigate use of the Susquehanna and its tributaries to solve their transportation needs. Cooper realized that residents of the upper valley were ide-

90. Northumberland County Commissioners Minutes vol. 1, bridge expenses noted in entries for February 27, June 2, June 20, August 15, October 4, December 1, 1796, September 22, November 1, 1797, February 10 (?), 1798; *ABV*, 283. The December 1 contract to John Adams and Elija Davis was for a bridge over Chillisquaque "near Boyd and Wilsons Mills."

91. Cooper to Gansevoort, November 23, 1790, Cooper Papers, NYSHA.

92. Bard, *Description of the River Susquehanna*, 6–7; Henretta, "Families and Farms," 17.

ally situated for transporting their goods to market if they took advantage of the waterways in the region; residents in Tioga, Otsego, Broome, Chenango, Steuben, and Allegany counties could use the Susquehanna and its tributaries to transport lumber and grain to Baltimore. William Cooper's son Isaac echoed his father's opinion. "The Roads were very poor," he wrote in 1790, "the chief of all produce came and went by water to and from the head of [Otsego] Lake. All communications between Albany and the Village passed over the Ice in the Winter—and by Water in the Summer."[93]

Valley residents soon learned how to construct boats that drew little water, that could be made quickly, and that could transport grain to market towns along the Susquehanna, including Harrisburg, Middletown, Columbia, and Baltimore. These boats, often referred to as arks, were wide and flat-bottomed, a necessary shape for navigating the often shallow waters of the Susquehanna. They could transport large quantities of grain downriver but were not designed to make the difficult journey upstream; they were broken up and sold for lumber at the end of each trip.[94]

The legislatures of New York and Pennsylvania recognized the importance of water travel in the valley and worked to protect and improve these channels. They passed laws to keep the river and its major tributaries free of human-made impediments such as milldams and fishing weirs, and they allocated funds to improve navigation in shallow areas where rocks blocked boat travel. By the early 1790s the Pennsylvania legislature had authorized funds for the improvement of the Susquehanna and its tributaries and had sent out a team to survey the West Branch to determine how it could be improved for inland navigation. These surveyors hoped to find a suitable location for a road to connect the Susquehanna with the Allegheny, thereby facilitating portage between these two rivers.[95]

In addition to funding improvements in watercourses, state legislators made efforts to ensure that people and goods could travel along the Susquehanna and its tributaries without difficulty. In 1788 state legislators in New York passed a law prohibiting the construction of fishing weirs in the Susquehanna because such devices impeded navigation and diverted "the free course of the fish" up the

93. Cooper, *Guide*, 15; I[saac] Cooper, Population of Cooperstown in the Year 1790, NYSHA.

94. Cooper, *Guide*, 15–16; Isaac Cooper, Population of Cooperstown in the Year 1803, NYSHA; Fletcher, *Pennsylvania Agriculture*, 239–241.

95. Bard, *Description of the River Susquehanna*, 51; *Journal of Samuel Maclay*, 5, 15–16.

river. A decade later legislators declared the Susquehanna and its principal tributaries in New York to be public highways; the act levied a fine of $25 on anyone who erected a milldam or fishing weir in these waterways or cut wood and left it to obstruct travel. The act did not prevent use of the water to drive mills, but it required those who built milldams to provide a canal to allow travel.[96]

Legislators in Pennsylvania were more vigorous in their efforts to protect and improve water travel in the Susquehanna drainage basin. There was some colonial precedent for this legislative activity; a 1771 Pennsylvania statute prohibited the construction of fishing weirs on the Susquehanna and its major tributaries because they impeded trade in the region.[97] In September 1789 state legislators allocated £2,500 for "clearing and making navigable" the Susquehanna above its confluence with the Juniata and appointed commissioners to study the region and determine the best places for locks and canals to allow travel around waterfalls and natural obstructions; two and one-half years later the state legislature provided funds for this project. Pennsylvania legislators also extended the scope of the 1771 statute, declaring Penn's Creek below the mouth of Sinking Creek a public highway.[98]

Increased use of the river for transport led to conflicts over riparian rights. The development of milling operations and the use of the river for transport pitted two groups of entrepreneurs against each other. Millers required water to operate their mills; milldams provided a constant supply of water, a valuable improvement in a drainage system that was widely known for its dramatic seasonal shifts. But dams impeded or prevented the transportation of people and commodities along the waterways. During the early 1790s the court in Sunbury found that two dams on the Susquehanna and one on Penn's Creek, ranging from one and one-half to three and one-half feet tall, were illegal because they impeded boat travel and so had to be removed.[99]

These local conflicts anticipated later struggles over the use of

96. *Laws of New York*, 2:646, 4:296–297.

97. *Pennsylvania Statutes at Large*, 8:36–44.

98. Ibid., 13:354–356, 14:301, 231–232.

99. Resp. v. Simon Snyder, November 1792 Sessions, Quarter Sessions, 1772–1797, NCCH; see also Resp. v. Adam Kastator, Resp. v. John Kastator, and Pennsylvania v. Frederick Tarr et al., all in November 1791 Sessions, Quarter Sessions, 1772–1797, 168, NCCH. Subsequent court decisions reinforced this policy; see, for example, the case against John Hougher, Northumberland County Quarter Sessions Docket 2, 203, 281, 287, 301.

rivers in other developing regions. Elsewhere milldams flooded farmers' fields, pushing the conflict between agriculture and industrialism into the courts; the dams also impeded fish runs, thereby depriving backcountry settlers of what they believed was their customary right to fish. During the late eighteenth century and early decades of the nineteenth century many courts ruled in favor of the millers over the farmers, thereby establishing a vital legal concept: the public good was best served by development, even when such operations impeded or even eliminated traditional agricultural pursuits.[100]

Lawmakers with jurisdiction over the Susquehanna Valley shared this enthusiasm for economic development and sought to find a compromise between the interests of millers and those of shippers. In April 1793, Pennsylvania legislators found just such a compromise. They allowed millers along Penn's Creek, who had previously been forced by the county court to remove their milldam, to erect a new dam on the condition that it be equipped with an opening to allow rafts through and that they "erect, or cause to be erected and kept in good repair, a complete lock of twelve feet wide, through which boats and canoes may at all times safely and conveniently pass." If the millers failed to provide adequate channels for boats, they would be liable to a fine of up to £50. During the next few years state legislators allowed millers to build dams on other tributaries of the Susquehanna; all dam builders had to make provisions to allow boats to pass their improvements.[101]

Because their mercantile operations were at stake, wealthy landholders were most desirous of improving shipping in the region. To facilitate the transport of goods into and out of the valley the landholders organized canal companies to connect important water routes. Perhaps the most important of these was the Schuylkill and Susquehanna Navigation Company, a project of Robert Morris, organized in the 1790s to establish water routes connecting the Delaware at Philadelphia with the Ohio at Fort Pitt and the Great Lakes at Presque Isle. The joint stock company raised its money through private subscriptions, particularly from people who owned extensive

---

100. See Morton Horwitz, *The Transformation of American Law, 1780–1860* (Cambridge, Mass., 1977), chap. 2; and Gary Kulik, "Dams, Fish, and Farmers: Defense of Public Rights in Eighteenth-Century Rhode Island," in Steven Hahn and Jonathan Prude, eds., *The Countryside in the Age of Capitalist Transformation* (Chapel Hill, N.C., 1985), 25–50.

101. *Pennsylvania Statutes at Large*, 14:404–405, 15:283–284, 398–399.

real estate in rural Pennsylvania. The company received help from the state legislature: in April 1794 legislators made sure that prospective millers wanting to build a milldam on Swatara Creek did not interfere with their canal; in 1795 and 1797 legislators passed acts to allow the company to raise additional funds through a new subscription, lottery, and tolls. The project, finished in 1828, connected the Susquehanna, via the Union Canal, to Reading and from there, along the Schuylkill Navigation Canal, to Philadelphia. Canal building reached booming proportions in the first half of the nineteenth century, especially after the success of the Erie Canal. By midcentury canals traversed Pennsylvania and New York, greatly improving shipping in the Susquehanna drainage basin and elsewhere.[102]

When state and local legislators provided funds to improve transportation through the backcountry or passed laws that encouraged economic development, they believed they were helping the entire hinterland population. Even acts that benefited specific groups, such as the statutes involving the Schuylkill and Susquehanna Navigation Company, had a universal purpose: to enhance the general welfare. Nevertheless, such legislative acts reinforced economic inequality. Laws intended to keep the Susquehanna and its tributaries open for navigation helped settlers transport their wares to local markets, but these statutes were even more helpful for wealthy landholders, who used the waterways to send valley goods to external markets and thus profit from their real estate holdings. These acts proved vital to developers in the nineteenth century who controlled valuable parcels in the valley and used the river and canals to transport lumber and coal out of the backcountry.

The use of public institutions to support economic development was the last step the landholders needed to consolidate their control over the valley economy. The stage was finally set for the spread of the industrial revolution into the upper Susquehanna Valley. Nineteenth-century developers did not wait for a second invitation.

A Vision of the Future

Near the end of the century Tench Coxe, one of the premier economic essayists in America, an assistant to Alexander Hamilton in

102. Ibid., 15:30–31, 216–217, 331–333; Schuylkill and Susquehanna Navigation Company, Minutes No. 1, HSP; Wilkinson, ed., "Mr. Davy's Diary," 140n; George Rogers Taylor, *The Transportation Revolution, 1815–1860* (New York, 1951), 41–45.

the Treasury Department, and an active land speculator who had subscribed to the Pennsylvania Landholders Association, mused about the nation's future economic development. He did more than dream, however. Coxe's views were highly regarded in the new republic, and the plan he wrote for the development of the interior provides insight into the entrepreneurial mind at free play and thus allows us novel access into the economic culture of the developers.

His essays, compiled in *A View of the United States of America* and published in Philadelphia in 1794, provide a thorough overview of the nation's economy at the end of the eighteenth century. Coxe stressed the need for America to develop its own economy and not be reliant on European goods. One essay extolled the importance of clearing forests for fields but retaining sufficient timber for lumbering. Another described a theme popular among valley landholders: the ways in which maple sugar production could bring profit with limited expenditure of labor. He provided tables showing imports and exports of selected commodities. His essays were both descriptive and pedagogic; he not only celebrated postwar commercial expansion but also indicated the most profitable areas for future development.

Coxe understood the relationship between American economic growth and the larger Atlantic commercial world. In commenting on the French Revolution, his concerns were not about the plight of people caught up in the violence in that country or the causes of those cataclysmic events but in the economics involved, particularly the threat that any expansion of the war would have on transatlantic commerce. He worried that the French crisis and the international conflicts it spawned would interrupt the shipping of goods across the ocean and that American farmers would have to pay much more for the manufactured goods they needed. But the situation was not hopeless. The solution lay in the development of new market towns in the United States. To illustrate his ideas, he devised a plan for a commercial center along the Susquehanna.

Coxe's Susquehanna town would cost $500,000, a large sum considering the finances of the states in the early 1790s. He believed, however, that the necessary funds could be raised either through a joint stock company selling shares of $100 each, a lottery, or even the use of treasury money from the state of Pennsylvania. The source of the money was not important, however, because Coxe optimistically believed that the town would quickly prosper and investors would reap profits of approximately 100 percent.

Coxe's vision for the town remains an artifact of the post-Revolution commercial imagination. He believed the town should have a variety of industries. It needed mills for hemp, flax, paper, and other goods, as well as distilleries, coopers, bakers, smiths, and boat builders. It should also have four lumberyards and four slaughterhouses, as well as a steel furnace, kilns, and potteries. Coxe then proposed building a number of other commercial operations, many intended for marketing the supplies of these industries. There should be, he wrote, one hundred houses for "tradesmen's and manufacturer's shops, stables, &c. as occasion may require." The town would also need a "large scale house to weigh loaded waggons, to be erected on the market square." Finally, in addition to schools, churches, printers, taverns, and stables, Coxe believed the town needed a library "to be composed of books relative to the useful arts and manufactures."[103]

Coxe expected the new town along the Susquehanna to become an "*auxiliary* to Philadelphia, as Manchester, Leeds, Birmingham, and Sheffield, &c. are to the sea-ports of Great Britain." Thus roads would be needed to connect it to turnpikes and to other developing cities. Once the roads were cut, Coxe argued, the town would prosper. "Thus circumstanced," he wrote, "and with the supplies of wood-fuel, coal, bark, grain, cattle, hemp, flax, wool, timber, iron, stone, lime, forage, &c. which those roads, and the Susquehannah and its branches, would certainly and permanently afford, this place could not fail to become of very great profit to the subscribers or prize holders, or the state, and to the landed interest, both tenants and owners."[104]

Coxe castigated attempts at earlier settlement for their failure to determine the future needs of the communities. "It cannot but be perceived," he wrote, "that most of the American inland towns have been commenced without due attention to the powers of water, the advantages of interior navigation, and a copious and certain supply of other fuel, when wood shall become scarce and dear." Growing communities, he recognized, led to scarcity of fuel supplies. Perhaps the greatest asset of the town along the Susquehanna was its location: the river would be a perpetual source of waterpower to drive mills and would provide the town's merchants and factories with access to an extensive transportation network. The town should be lo-

103. Coxe, *View of the United States of America*, 380–393.
104. Ibid., 394.

cated at some place along the river "where the river can be so drawn out of its natural bed, as to create those mill-seats and falls."[105]

Coxe envisioned a new world along the banks of the Susquehanna that would evolve naturally from the existing regional economy. Earlier traders had realized the value of the river for transportation, as had colonists who inhabited the region before the war. Postwar settlers, especially landlords, busily developed their local industries and integrated them into the growing market economy of the nation. The next step, as Coxe realized, was to establish factories and processing centers in the region, taking advantage of local energy supplies for manufacturing and thereby protecting the republic's economy from external threats. The transition from farming to factory life involved a shift in the way people thought about the world around them; the regimens of the clock-oriented factories differed in fundamental ways from the seasonal labor of farmers. But for those in control of economic opportunity, the transition required a far less difficult mental leap. Indeed, Coxe's writings reveal that such development fit perfectly into the economy of the new nation.

Here, then, was the future as it was envisioned by one of the developers. Coxe believed that the future should be like the recent past, characterized by the discovery of resources to be harvested and the creation of the economic infrastructure for bringing these resources to those who demanded them. There was no sense of finite resources in this vision, a startling notion given the decline of the first export economy of the valley when the local supply of furbearing animals dwindled. Coxe, like other developers, believed the natural world was intended to serve its inhabitants and that it was their duty to take advantage of the available resources. He ignored the potential social, economic, or environmental costs of his proposed venture.

The world Coxe imagined belonged to the developers. The developers who migrated to the upper valley in the nineteenth century seeking coal and lumber agreed. They inherited an economic culture that supported development regardless of potential environmental problems and saw no need to share the resulting riches equally among valley residents. So circumstanced, the new developers eagerly began to transform the valley into a supplier of raw materials for an industrializing nation.

105. Ibid., 401, 396.

Conclusion:
The Economic Culture
of the Revolutionary
Backcountry

In 1823, James Fenimore Cooper published *The Pioneers, or the Sources of the Susquehanna*. He thus joined a long line of prominent people who had written about the Susquehanna Valley, beginning when William Penn first considered the region in the late seventeenth century. John Bartram, Benjamin Franklin, Sir William Johnson, George Washington, Thomas Jefferson, Thomas Cooper, Joseph Priestley, and Tench Coxe all wrote about this river valley, inscribing it in American lore well before the appearance of *The Pioneers*. Their accounts, combined with other documents, attest to the importance of the region's transformation through the spread of the Atlantic market into the backcountry, the impact of a series of conquests in the area, and the furor of the Revolution. By the end of the century, the valley landscape was dramatically different than it had been in 1700. Yet the lure of the area remained strong in spite of, or perhaps because of, these changes in the environment. At the end of the eighteenth and well into the nineteenth century, this valley of opportunity continued to draw migrants. The allure of the upper valley reached across the Atlantic to England, where a young Samuel Taylor Coleridge thought it an ideal place to establish what he termed a "pantisocracy" where everyone would have equal rights. The valley appealed to the poetic ear of Coleridge who wanted to go there, among other reasons, because he liked the mellifluous sound of the river's name: "Susquehanna."[1]

Unlike these many others, James Fenimore Cooper grew up in the valley, and his childhood there colored his view of it. Where outsiders had seen virtually unlimited promise, the son of William Cooper realized that nature's resources were limited. He came to believe, as he made clear in *The Pioneers*, that local settlers, if left to their own devices, would squander the valley's resources. The yeomanry would never rescue the region from the "waste of the creation," to borrow a phrase from his father, but would denude the forest of its trees, even its precious sugar maples; they would deplete local supplies of fish and kill off or drive away other animals. To prevent such a catastrophe, the pioneers needed to be restrained, and in the novel Cooper employed Judge Temple to restrain them. Although Temple was not always successful or noble, he represented the law and order necessary to keep settlers from despoiling the region.

James Fenimore Cooper's fears reflected his belief that new settlements needed to be directed by someone familiar with the area and able to organize a functioning economy in the region. In *The Pioneers* the younger Cooper elevated the entrepreneurial land speculator to a paterfamilias without whom civilized society could not exist in the hinterland. The conclusion of the novel reinforces its social message; Natty Bumppo, the leatherstocking, leaves the valley while Judge Temple remains. The future, as the novelist knew all too well, belonged not to the woodsmen or Indians but to those with economic power: landlords and entrepreneurs.

Touching on both the valley environment and its economy, *The Pioneers* encourages us to look back over the history of the valley in the eighteenth century. How had the world Cooper knew come into existence? What motivated people to live there? The answers to these questions bring us to a surer understanding of the valley's economic culture and the lessons that the upper valley's history can teach us about the forces shaping the world we inhabit.

The Valley Environment in 1800 and Beyond

Cooper began *The Pioneers* with a description of the valley environment in the late 1780s. He set an idyllic scene, with references to

1. Walter Jackson Bate, *Coleridge* (New York, 1968), 16.

"beautiful and thriving villages," mountains "arable to the tops," and vales "narrow, rich, and cultivated" with "a stream uniformly winding through each." Cooper continually reminded his readers of the valley's abundant natural resources. For him, the upper valley in the late eighteenth century, on the eve of postwar settlement, remained essentially pristine or, to use his word, a "wilderness."

Cooper got the story wrong, just as his father had in *A Guide in the Wilderness*. The landscape of the upper valley after the Revolution bore the marks of profound change. Searching to create their economies, each group of residents had learned how to extract valuable resources from the environment. But in the process they had transformed the valley: they had cleared densely forested areas, substantially altered the regional stocks of flora and fauna, and, by the end of the century, begun to change the river itself. In different ways, fur traders and farmers each left a legacy of ecological instability in the upper valley.

In the beginning of the century forests dominated the valley. But every group that moved into the region threatened the forests. When the Iroquois extended their suzerainty to the upper valley and peopled the river basin and its tributaries with dependent tribes, they destroyed selected parts of the forests, mostly for fuel and to clear fields for agriculture. Colonists cleared even more of the region's forests for similar purposes. After the Revolution the further expansion of agriculture, joined with the development of the lumber industry, made more dramatic inroads into the native stocks of timber in the area.

Fires, one method employed by valley residents to clear forests, had a variety of effects on the environment. Fires altered the physical and chemical properties of the burned area; eliminated dry matter, such as cones and needles from the conifers, which had accumulated on the ground; influenced the population of various plant species in the area; and changed the habitat of the indigenous mammals, insects, parasites, and fungi that were integral elements of the forest. Fires also had varying effects on the trees in the forests. Areas dominated by northern hardwoods were only gradually replenished with these same species because these trees, especially maple and beech, grew less successfully than others after a fire. Fires favored the growth of white pines by providing more suitable seedbeds and limiting succession to species such as the sugar maple, which are more tolerant of shade. Oaks, which were more successful than the northern hardwoods after fires, began to decline in the Northeast when there were fewer fires.[2]

The Indians' practice of setting fires to clear fields improved the land for agriculture. Burning removed the trees so that more light could reach the ground. The soil in newly cleared regions was probably three to five degrees centigrade higher in temperature than in comparable nonburned areas. This increase in temperature, caused largely by the blackening of the land's surface and the new presence of charcoal, inhibited the development of new forests. Unless the fires were very severe and burned off the soil, the land in cleared tracts could soon support a variety of crops. Thus early European settlers in the northeastern colonies also used fire to clear land; they knew that only grass would grow in the area immediately following a fire.[3]

Yet during the eighteenth century fires were used to a limited extent in the upper Susquehanna Valley. The Delawares used fire only in spring and autumn, when seasonal weather conditions prevented the uncontrolled spread of their fires.[4] Many steep hills in the valley which could not support agriculture also escaped deliberate burning. Indeed, though the Indian population of the upper valley grew during the first half of the century, the food needs of the resident tribes could be met using only the more level lands in the region. The fields surrounding local towns were occasionally extensive, but the Indian populations migrated to new sites rather than attempt to cultivate steeper lands or lands located far from the village. Geographical and cultural patterns thus prevented widespread use of fires to clear land.

Still, people traveling through the region saw signs of the use of fire. Crèvecoeur noted that the evidence of the Indians' fires around Wyoming survived into the mid-1770s. "These ridges of timbered lands have been much injured by repeated fires kindled by the Indians in order to frighten and to inclose their game," he wrote. "These fires have greatly exhausted the surface of these grounds and prevented the growth of the young shoots and small timber." The tree species noted by Timothy Pickering in 1787 in the valley

2. Stephen H. Spurr and Burton Barnes, *Forest Ecology*, 3d ed. (New York, 1980), 275; Silas Little, "Effect of Fire in Temperate Forests: Northeastern United States," in T. T. Kozlowski and C. E. Ahlgren, eds., *Fire and Ecosystems* (New York, 1974), 231–234.

3. Spurr and Barnes, *Forest Ecology*, 292; Little, "Effect of Fire," 227.

4. Little, "Effect of Fire," 226–227.

swamps, including white pine, hemlock, beech, maple, birch, and wild cherry, were all suited for burned-over areas.[5] Further, the use of fire to keep hunting territories in proper shape was a technique that various Indian groups used throughout the Northeast. This practice encouraged a wider range of desirable animals to live in the area than might otherwise have been there because burning created a greater diversity of habitats. Some species, including the heath hen, passenger pigeon, and wild turkey, preferred such cleared areas. When colonists and post-Revolution settlers moved to the valley they too used fires to clear fields and then transported the ash to a pearl or potash works.[6]

Indians, colonists, and postwar settlers cleared much of the forested area in the valley by cutting instead of burning. Although the ecological shifts involved with this method of clearing land differed from those associated with fire, extensive deforestation resulted. Cutting practices, often notoriously wasteful in New England,[7] had begun to worry some valley residents by the end of the century. William Cooper feared that local forests would be depleted by settlers cutting trees for fences and fuel. "Our winters require large supplies of fuel," he wrote in his *Guide*, "and we have neither peat nor coal to resort to, when constant consumption in fuel and fencing will have rendered that most necessary article scarce. Nor have we other mountainous lands to resort to for wood, nor stony ground for the construction of stone fences. The soil being all fit for culture, will all be cultivated, and the wood of course wasted." Cooper's fears were somewhat justified. Before the development of coal mining in Pennsylvania, much of the timber in the northeastern part of the state was cut to provide fuel; native stocks of some hardwoods, including hemlock and beech, were unable to recover from the joint pressures of this cutting and the periodic fires in the area.[8]

5. H. L. Bourdin and S. T. Williams, eds., "Crèvecoeur on the Susquehanna, 1774–1776," *Yale Review* 14 (1925), 568–569; "Journal of Timothy Pickering's Visit to Wyoming," *SCP*, 8:30; Little, "Effect of Fire," 230–234.

6. See Little, "Effect of Fire," 226; E. L. Jones, "Creative Disruptions in American Agriculture," *Agricultural History* 48 (1974), 516; Levi Beardsley, *Reminiscences: Personal and Other Incidents; Early Settlement of Otsego County; Notices and Anecdotes of Public Men; Judicial, Legal and Legislative Matters; Field Sports; Dissertations and Discussions* (New York, 1852), 36.

7. William Cronon, *Changes in the Land: Indians, Colonists, and the Ecology of New England* (New York, 1983), 120–121.

8. William Cooper, *A Guide in the Wilderness* (1810; rpt. Freeport, N.Y., 1970), 28; Spurr and Barnes, *Forest Ecology*, 570.

Following the Revolution, when developers built sawmills throughout the upper valley, forest clearing became far more selective. Those involved in lumbering, either for local building purposes or for export to the lumber and shipbuilding market, were selective in the species of trees they cut. Such concern was clear both to landlords who exerted control over large areas of the valley and to settlers who were concerned with the trees in their immediate vicinity. Philip Antes, who may have been one of Samuel Wallis's tenants, cut trees selectively, waiting until seasonal conditions allowed him to obtain a load of yellow pine trees, presumably recognizing the value of this particular species.[9] Such selective or partial cutting encouraged the growth of trees already well established in the area. Unlike the later clear-cutting practices of loggers, which opened whole tracts for new species, the habits of those involved in lumbering in the upper valley in the eighteenth century probably limited the diversity of tree species in particular areas. This practice increased the risk that desirable species, such as hardwoods or white pines, would be substantially reduced.[10]

When not seeking forest products, eighteenth-century valley residents cleared extensive tracts because they believed that forests impeded agriculture and travel. But in the process of removing the forests these inhabitants initiated changes in the regional ecology that they could not understand and generally failed to recognize. The densely wooded tracts throughout the upper valley were essential in maintaining the level of water in the region; when residents cleared stands of trees, the land was less able to retain water. Extensive clearing thus increased the possibility of floods because tree roots and the forest's litter no longer held the moisture in the land; spring runoff occurred earlier and more violently when snows melted more quickly in the unshaded areas. Years of clearing in the Wyoming region made the area especially susceptible to flooding; severe floods in the area in May 1784 and October 1786 in particular caused much damage. Water draining through floods rather than more controlled runoff deprived many regions of important sources of water and, in the process, caused many small streams to dry up.[11]

9. "TJC" (?) to Wallis, June 23, 1795, Wallis Papers, Reel 5, HSP.
10. See Spurr and Barnes, *Forest Ecology*, 441–443.
11. Cronon, *Changes in the Land*, 123–124; "Journal of Timothy Pickering's Visit to Wyoming," *SCP*, 8:49. At least one twentieth-century flood proved as devastating as

When another James Fenimore Cooper, a descendant of William Cooper, wrote an introduction to an 1897 edition of *A Guide in the Wilderness*, he realized that deforestation had had a direct bearing on the settlers on his ancestor's lands. "One element in the speculative value of land, which investors apparently overlooked, was the effect which the clearing of the forests would have on the streams," he wrote. "Large tracts of land, then deemed valuable because they were located on the banks of some stream, navigable for scows and small boats, soon lost the advantage of such a location by the shrinking of the streams, due to the cutting away of the woods."[12]

Erosion also became a major problem after deforestation, especially when valley residents removed bushes and trees near the river. The ecological effects of clearing were perhaps most evident in Wyoming, a long-settled agricultural area. "The bank along the bend is in a ruinous condition, tumbling in & washing away at every thaw after frost, & at every fresh," Timothy Pickering wrote in 1787. "The earth is extremely tender, & without any gravel or stones for perhaps 10 or 12 feet in depth. Many acres have already washed away since the N. England people settled here." Pickering believed that the bank could be saved if it were "formed into a gentle slope, & seeded with some deep-rooting & strong swarded grass," but given the cost and labor involved for such a task he did not expect such action to be taken "for many years." Farther down the Susquehanna he noticed fewer problems of erosion, although he did not associate this with the trees and bushes he saw along the river's banks.[13]

The spread of agriculture and the deforestation that preceded it had devastating consequences for the indigenous fauna of the upper valley. The few references to the fur trade after the 1760s indicated that this economic activity, so important for the establishment of commercial relationships in the region, had become largely extinct because of the furbearers' inability to replace their former numbers. After the Revolution the loss of forested habitat, not the fur trade, prevented the reestablishment of these animals. Deforestation forced the furbearers either to leave the region or to restrict their movements within it. Certain animals were particularly at risk. Among these were the martens, fishers, and wolverines that required exten-

---

its eighteenth-century counterparts; see Paul Warnagiris and John Rygiel, *The Great Flood of 1972* (Wyoming, Pa., 1973).

12. Cooper, *Guide*, ii.

13. "Journal of Timothy Pickering's Visit to Wyoming," *SCP*, 8:45.

sive forested tracts to survive and presumably migrated north and west out of the valley to less settled areas. In addition, species inhabiting the banks of streams and lakes, such as beavers, muskrats, mink, and otters, migrated when deforestation dried up their watercourses.[14]

Still, colonists and postwar settlers associated the shift from forest to field with ecological changes that they believed to be very beneficial. Abandoned Indian settlements and fields provided them with encouraging evidence about environmental changes that followed deforestation. In many places colonial settlers were drawn to these sites because the neglected fields produced ideal forage, at least initially, for their livestock. Crèvecoeur learned that the Connecticut settlers of the Wyoming region had found it "covered with a sort of wild grass peculiar to these low lands, commonly called *Blue Bent*, so extremely high that its tops reach'd a man's shoulders on horseback," he wrote. "When this grass is cut early it makes an excellent fodder, but maturity gives it too great a degree of coarseness." At Wyalusing, another former Indian town only recently sold to a colonist, Crèvecoeur found that "the soil has a greater mixture of clay than any other spot, therefore richer pastures." He apparently attributed the excellent condition of the local livestock to this food source. "I have seen nowhere larger cows and oxen." In August 1786 Timothy Pickering thought that the area around Shawnee was "the most beautiful tract of land my eyes ever beheld! The soil appeared to be inexhaustibly fertile, and tho' under very slovenly husbandry, the crops were luxuriant, and the Indian corn and grass of the richest green." Such lands proved ideal for the colonists and postwar settlers, who employed free-ranging techniques for their livestock so they could devote their energies to their agricultural work.[15]

But former Indian sites did not always have the best soil. Indeed, by the early 1770s the soil around Sunbury and Northumberland Town, perhaps the site with the longest tradition of Indian settlement in the upper valley, seemed exhausted. Crèvecoeur found that

14. See Eric Duffey, *The Forest World: The Ecology of the Temperate Woodlands* (London, 1980), 97.

15. Bourdin and Williams, eds., "Crèvecoeur on the Susquehanna," 566–567, 583, 561, 575; "Extracts from Timothy Pickering's Journal," *SCP*, 8:383; Robert Albion and Leonidas Dodson, eds., *Philip Vickers Fithian: Journal, 1775–1776, Written on the Virginia-Pennsylvania Frontier and in the Army around New York* (Princeton, N.J., 1934), 51, 57.

the land both in the town and in the surrounding area was covered with "nothing but pine" and consisted of "extremely poor and sandy" soil.[16] But he failed to associate the poor land and abundance of pines with the processes of soil exhaustion and the probable use of fire to clear the area in the period before colonial settlement.

Further, the settlers' agricultural activity provided ideal habitats for a wide range of unfavorable species. Crows and passenger pigeons, longtime valley residents, found ample food supplies in the region; they occasionally devastated fields and at times ate so many nuts that some settlers' hogs were threatened with starvation. Levi Beardsley noted that local residents killed and ate many of the wild pigeons that flocked to the area. He also recalled that foxes arrived after the establishment of settlements, presumably lured by the inhabitants' livestock. Squirrels became troublesome throughout Pennsylvania; their periodic migrations through settlers' fields prompted the state to establish bounties for them in 1749 and later. Many particularly liked the corn crops in the upper valley. "The black and grey squirrel, it is known, hardly ever precede civilization but follow it," Beardsley wrote. "We had been there several years before any were seen." European agriculture and the techniques used by colonists and postwar settlers to pursue it also led to problems associated with weeds, crop diseases, and insects. Although many of these pests were not a serious plague, they probably caused some problems. Such pests were a direct result of settlers' clearing forests and planting fields. Certain species, once living in modest numbers within a restricted niche in the earlier climax forest, found the fields ideal feeding and breeding grounds, and their numbers grew.[17]

Agriculture also initiated further ecological changes. The increased commitment to livestock prompted county authorities to eliminate predators in the upper valley. Local officials realized that the wolf population was a threat to livestock, especially free-ranging cattle or hogs. Thus county authorities posted bounties throughout the valley and surrounding areas to encourage the destruction of wolves, and in the early 1780s residents of Montgomery County were bringing in hides to collect payment.[18] Other valley fauna also

16. Bourdin and Williams, eds., "Crèvecoeur on the Susquehanna," 576.
17. Jones, "Creative Disruptions," 518–523, 513; Beardsley, *Reminiscences*, 37, 57.
18. Bourdin and Williams, eds., "Crèvecoeur on the Susquehanna," 574; Minutes of the Board of Supervisors of Montgomery County, 1784–1810, 3–4, Montgomery County Office of the County Historian, Fonda, N.Y.

threatened livestock. Bears favored hogs, cougars and panthers attacked cattle, and foxes were fond of chickens.

The valley's stock of fish, like that of wolves, was increasingly threatened by the growing population. People living and traveling through the region had long relied on the fish, shellfish, and eels of the river, its tributaries, and local ponds and lakes for important dietary supplements. Indians in the valley ate freshwater mussels, a variety of fish, snapping turtles, and green frogs. Colonial settlers around Wyoming regularly caught large supplies of shad and trout. During the war Continental soldiers found that local supplies of fish amply met their needs. The herring of Lake Otsego proved an invaluable source of food in 1786 when a famine was imminent.[19]

These fishing activities were, by their nature, limited; the fish were consumed only by the local population. But even before the war the situation began to change. In response to lower yields of fish the Pennsylvania legislature passed two laws, one in 1761 and the other in 1771, forbidding the use of seines and nets on the Susquehanna and other important fishing waters.[20] After the war commercial fishing developed in parts of the valley. Only three years after the settlers around Lake Otsego relied on herring to stave off starvation, some residents began to seine for Otsego bass. This method of catching fish, along with the netting that was introduced in the 1850s, eventually threatened the indigenous bass population and was finally prohibited in 1915.[21] The real threat to local species occurred in the nineteenth and twentieth centuries, when Lake Otsego became a center for both commercial and sport fishing, but this later development stemmed from the eighteenth-century belief that any natural products of the region, from fish to beaver pelts to white pines, were suitable for the market and that commercial networks based on those commodities should be established.

19. William A. Ritchie, *The Chance Horizon: An Early Stage of Mohawk Iroquois Cultural Development*, New York State Museum Circular 29 (Albany, N.Y., 1952); Thomas E. Harr et al., "Limnology of Canadarago Lake," in Jay Bloomfield, ed., *Lakes of New York State*, 3 vols. (New York, 1978–1980), vol. 3, *Ecology of the Lakes of East-Central New York*, 133; Bourdin and Williams, eds., "Crèvecoeur on the Susquehanna," 570; Frederick Cook, ed., *Journals of the Military Expedition of Major General John Sullivan against the Six Nations of Indians in 1779* (Auburn, N.Y., 1887), 20, 82, 53; Cooper, *Guide*, 9.

20. *Pennsylvania Statutes at Large*, 6:86–91, 8:36–44.

21. Willard N. Harman and Leonard P. Sohacki, "The Limnology of Otsego Lake (Glimmerglass)," in Bloomfield, ed., *Lakes of New York State*, 3:3. For one mid–nineteenth-century analysis of the situation see *Report of Col. James Worrall, in Relation to the Passage of Fish in the Susquehanna River* (Harrisburg, Pa., 1869).

After 1800 even more far-reaching changes occurred in the valley environment, stemming from the expansion of lumbering and coal mining. By the 1830s Williamsport became the center of a logging boom, and as a result the forests dwindled far more than ever before. Coal mining eventually surpassed lumbering and became the dominant economic pursuit in much of the valley. In the nineteenth century technological developments increased the capabilities of developers to harness nature's bounty, and those in control of capital proved eager to supply eastern markets, with no thought of how their efforts affected the environment of the upper valley.

Perhaps the clearest indicator of ecological transformation was evident in place names, which, even by the end of the eighteenth century, no longer possessed the environmental characteristics that had made them relevant. When Levi Beardsley wrote his *Reminiscences* during the early nineteenth century, he remarked that Oaks Creek, which ran from Canadarago Lake to the Susquehanna, had lost the timber that had once given the area its identity. "Since the early settlement," he wrote, "this area has been lumbered and there are few trees remaining that provide remembrance of the origin of the name of the creek." By the end of the century, the Great Swamp no longer dominated maps of the region. In 1792, when Reading Howell made his map of Pennsylvania, the term *Great Swamp* had apparently fallen into disuse. In its place on Howell's map was a term reflecting the new valley economy: "Country abounding in the Sugar Tree."[22] The perceptions about the dangers of the swamp had receded during the creation of the valley economy, replaced with new sensibilities stressing the economic potential of the region.

The Economic Culture of the Backcountry

James Fenimore Cooper erred in believing that the valley had not undergone a profound ecological transformation in the decades preceding his father's migration to the headwaters of the Susquehanna. Yet his views on the society that emerged in the upper valley after the Revolution have proven more accurate. Cooper's fictional characters represent the history of the valley developed so far in this

22. Quoted in Harr, "Limnology of Canadarago Lake," 142; "Journal of Timothy Pickering's Visit to Wyoming," *SCP*, 8:30; Reading Howell, "A Map of the State of Pennsylvania" (1792). Copies of Howell's map can be found in the Map Library of Harvard College Library and at HSP.

study. The documentary evidence that survives from the eighteenth century—mortgages and leases, travelers' accounts and tax lists, account books and landholders' propaganda pieces, the records of criminal and orphans' courts—points to the same conclusion as his novel. These documents too emphasize the links between the wealthy landholders and the valley population, although with perhaps quite different implications than the younger Cooper intended.

Over the course of the eighteenth century, valley residents created an export-oriented local economy and bound it to the larger Atlantic commercial world. To valley inhabitants, furs, grain, potash, maple sugar, whiskey, and lumber shared one important characteristic: all could be transported to markets where there was demand for them. During the century, fur traders and wealthy landholders, sensing available opportunities, organized the trade in these commodities. They offered other valley residents—Indians, poor settlers, or recent migrants—incentives to work in these trades. Even the valley farmer who possessed a freehold contributed labor to these mercantile operations. Every time the farmers purchased goods at local stores or sold their wares in trade centers, they were supporting the commercial economy of the region.

Throughout the eighteenth century, valley residents had felt the impact of the demographic forces that were reshaping the Atlantic world. By the beginning of the nineteenth century few, if any, Indians lived in the upper valley. Some remained in upstate New York, largely on reservations farther west, and they had hardly any contact with the commercial world of the valley. Many of the descendants of valley Indians had migrated to Canada, and others went farther west to Indian reserves. By the beginning of the nineteenth century, practically the entire valley population was of European descent. But the migrations did not end in 1800. By the mid-nineteenth century, when a coal mining boom had reshaped the economy of the Wyoming region, thousands of people from England, Wales, Ireland, and Germany moved to the upper valley. Like the eighteenth-century migrants to the region, they came looking for economic opportunity.[23]

During the eighteenth century daily life had become increasingly comfortable for those who managed to find a secure home and work

23. On coal mining and immigration see Anthony F. C. Wallace, *St. Clair: A Nineteenth-Century Coal Town's Experience with a Disaster-prone Industry* (New York, 1987), chap. 2.

in the valley. By the nineteenth century valley residents no longer feared drowning in ice-swollen streams or losing their way in dense forests where all was dark and forbidding. Indians, colonists, and postrevolutionary settlers had thoroughly altered the natural landscape. Only the river and the mountains seemed resistant to the myriad changes of the environment, although in some areas dams, canals, and mines changed even these. And because they no longer had to worry about surviving the journey, nineteenth-century travelers to the valley appreciated its beauty. Artists painted idyllic scenes of valley farms, and tourists visited to refresh their senses from the ever more heavily populated and urbanized cities of the East.[24]

Its beauty did not prevent the valley from becoming part of a larger economic world. The wealthy landholders, supported by legislatures and courts, lived in comfort and directed the economic maturation of the region. They believed that they had created economic order out of chaos.

Yet the landholders could not have succeeded on their own. Every successful landholder knew, just as fur traders had before them, that the valley's profits went to those who managed to harness the one commodity that nature had not created in the region: labor. Had it not been for the Indians who hunted pelts and the efforts of their communities to provide support for these ventures, fur traders would never have made any money in the area. Indian expertise and labor, enhanced no doubt by trade goods, were necessary for the traders' success.

Similarly, landholders relied on the labor of thousands of valley residents to produce marketable commodities and make the hinterland more appealing to prospective settlers. Robert Morris and John Nicholson failed because they could not attract sufficient laborers to make their investments profitable quickly enough; William Cooper and Samuel Wallis succeeded because they managed to lure people to their lands who then improved the region, creating marketable commodities and making their investments profitable.

The ties that bound laborers to developers reflected profound shifts in the economic culture of eastern North America and Eu-

24. James Fenimore Cooper, "The Chronicles of Cooperstown," in S. M. Shaw, ed., *A Centennial Offering, Being a Brief History of Cooperstown* (Cooperstown, N.Y., 1886), 56–57; Roger B. Stein, *Susquehanna: Images of the Settled Landscape* (Binghamton, N.Y., 1981).

rope. Everywhere between the Atlantic and the Appalachians during the eighteenth century natives and newcomers transformed the American economy. These changes forced people to redefine their relationships to one another and to their communities.

What was at stake in the upper Susquehanna Valley and elsewhere was not whether the countryside would have a capitalist economy. Once the Fort Stanwix treaty in 1768 enabled colonists to take control of vast tracts in the area, there was no doubt that capitalism, with its emphasis on market relations, would become the dominant economic system in the upper valley, just as it was elsewhere. To be sure, remnants of earlier economic ideas still survived in the region, such as local Indians' beliefs in the connections between daily life and the spirit world and the occasional reminders of the moral economy of the crowd. But these attitudes were disappearing. After the Indians left the valley, no group revived their spiritual beliefs. Manifestations of the moral economy also faded. Colonists and postwar settlers had accepted committee control of vital resources and the seizure of food only in times of crisis during the early stages of economic development; each group hoped to create a market economy in the region. This should come as no surprise since colonists, inheriting their economic ideas from England, staunchly supported a market-oriented ethos long before Adam Smith and later commentators endowed this economic orientation with its moral underpinnings.[25] Participation in the market economy of the Atlantic came indirectly for most valley residents, who spent their energies modifying the local environment to suit their needs and provide themselves with goods valued for local exchange. What was at stake in the upper valley was not whether to create a market economy but how to make a profit.

The process of profiting from nature demanded constant attention to local circumstances and a willingness to adapt dreams to quotidian realities. Yet profit-seekers' efforts to enhance their futures had unsettling consequences for the region's other inhabitants. In this sense, the history of the upper valley brings to mind Edward Spicer's monumental book on the Southwest, *Cycles of Conquest.* Spicer realized, as have other historians, that Europeans did not simply march across North America leaving yeoman farmers in their

25. See Cronon, *Changes in the Land*; and Joyce O. Appleby, *Economic Thought and Ideology in Seventeenth-Century England* (Princeton, N.J., 1978).

wake. Instead, colonizing could occur only through a series of conquests.[26]

The history of the upper Susquehanna Valley in the eighteenth century demonstrates that one did not have to live in the trans-Mississippi West in the nineteenth or twentieth century to suffer from what Patricia Nelson Limerick has aptly termed the "legacy of conquest." Different historical actors played their parts in the upper valley than in the West, but the history of this eastern region also reveals a series of conquests: struggle between the Susquehannocks and the Iroquois and the rise of the Iroquois-allied refugee groups in the valley in the early decades of the century; the emergence of a trade system that systematically undermined these Indians and paved the way for colonial settlers; the destructions of the war and the rise to prominence of a new group of settlers. And the cycles of conquest did not end in 1800. In parts of the valley where coal deposits had lain virtually undisturbed for aeons, a new group became the next conquerors. Like the developers who had preceded them, those who controlled the mines quickly set about harnessing labor to obtain coal. The pattern remained largely intact: a new resource to be harvested, the rise of a new group to profit from the industry, the growth of a group of laborers with little prospect of great economic success yet caught up for their own reasons in the new developers' schemes.[27]

The rise of the mine owners, some of them with direct connections to the post-Revolution settlement of the region,[28] would not have surprised Tench Coxe. Although he did not foresee the rapid development of the valley's coal industry, he would, no doubt, have been pleased by this new economic activity. Aside from missing this detail, Coxe's vision had become, with minor modifications, a reality in nineteenth-century Wilkes-Barre, Williamsport, Scranton, and Binghamton. These towns, like his planned town along the Susquehanna, became processing centers, supplying the markets of New York City, Philadelphia, and Baltimore with goods just as the industrial cities of Britain supplied London. Smaller communities, popu-

26. Edward Spicer, *Cycles of Conquest: The Impact of Spain, Mexico, and the United States on the Indians of the Southwest, 1533–1960* (Tucson, Ariz., 1962).

27. Patricia Nelson Limerick, *The Legacy of Conquest* (New York, 1987); Wallace, *St. Clair*.

28. Edward J. Davies II, *The Anthracite Aristocracy: Leadership and Social Change in the Hard Coal Regions of Northeastern Pennsylvania, 1800–1930* (DeKalb, Ill., 1985), 42–44.

lated by farming families, served these larger population islands; in return, farmers and their families could purchase imported and manufactured goods in valley cities.

Yet the cycles of conquest in the upper valley were not inevitable; the history of the region proved anything but predictable during the eighteenth century. The economy that emerged there was the product of a specific set of sensibilities shared by those in control of vital resources who sought to profit in a region containing desirable resources. Those sensibilities were not immune to events reshaping the Atlantic world in the eighteenth century.

No single event was more important than the American Revolution. The shot heard 'round the world awakened the aspirations of Americans who struggled to create a society in which all would have the freedom to pursue happiness or economic gain on equal terms. The American rebels of the late eighteenth century demanded that political institutions serve the needs of the people; they fought for freedom from what they termed "slavery" even though they kept slaves themselves. But just as the revolutionary generation failed to free the slaves, failed to offer full political equality to women, and failed to offer citizenship to Indians, so it failed to create an economic world in which all could compete on equal terms.

Yet the dramatic divergence between ideals and realities did not mean that the Revolution had a limited effect on the peoples of the upper valley. Most obviously, the Revolution was the final event in the decline of the refugee Indians' world. Never again would a substantial number of Indians inhabit the region, nor would the post-Revolution settlers who migrated to the area have any tolerance for Indians. The legacy of the Revolution was bitter: animosity replaced amity in the relations between the races.

The Revolution also ushered in a new age of government support for private economic development. From the Fort Stanwix treaty of 1768 to the Revolution, local courts and colonial legislators had provided funds for internal improvements and punished anyone who threatened the emerging economy. After the war, courts and state legislators went much further. They allocated more money for internal improvements, especially roads and canals. Officials more vigorously punished those who threatened the economy. Such efforts to support economic development extended beyond the confines of the upper valley, but everywhere these actions reflected a new sensibility: public institutions, as creations of the people, should support economic development that benefited as many people as possible. The language of the court documents shifted to reflect the changed premise. No longer living under the crown's jurisdiction, these citizens of the commonwealth punished delinquent overseers of the roads because their failure to keep roads clear threatened the ability of citizens to travel "as of right they ought." Valley residents employed the language of the Revolution to express fundamental aspects of their economic culture. Government of, by, and for the people, in their view, had to protect and enhance economic development.[29]

Other events, perhaps less dramatic than the Revolution but important nonetheless, also shaped the economic culture of the valley. The landholders succeeded in the 1790s, in large measure, because of the great expansion in European demand for American grain. This demand led to a new age of prosperity for Americans, especially those in the fertile grain-producing regions from New York to the Chesapeake. This prosperity had an enormous impact on the economic attitudes of the people of the new republic. Middling farmers, riding the crest of this new demand for their goods, experienced real growth in their economic prospects and thus gained the comforts they had long desired but had been unable to obtain earlier because of the limited market for their wares. The rising price of farm products also pushed up wages in cities as employers strove to keep their labor supply in place. This economic buoyancy had political ramifications as well: it created a vision of a new society in which all could succeed and thus helped solidify the Jeffersonian political consensus that emerged by the end of the century.[30]

The new economic sensibilities urging farmers to embrace the market more directly had a direct impact on the policies of the federal government. Struggling to maintain sufficient land for an ever-expanding population, the Jeffersonians realized that they would need an expanding supply of land as well. This perceived need for "an expansion across space," to borrow a phrase from Drew McCoy, influenced vital matters of national policy, ranging from access to

29. See, for example, Pennsylvania v. Henry Baugher and Daniel Whitmore, November 1791 session of the Quarter Sessions Court of Northumberland County, NCCH.

30. See Joyce Appleby, "Commercial Farming and the 'Agrarian Myth' in the Early Republic," *JAH* 68 (1982), 833–849; Appleby, *Capitalism and a New Social Order: The Republican Vision of the 1790s* (New York, 1984), esp. chap. 2.

European markets to the maintenance of shipping routes along the Mississippi.[31]

This economic orientation had political meaning as well. Jefferson believed there was a direct connection between an agrarian economy and a viable republic. Farmers, he realized at least by the 1780s and wrote in his *Notes on the State of Virginia,* were "the chosen people of God, if ever he had a chosen people, whose breasts he has made his peculiar deposit for substantial and genuine virtue." Believing that "corruption of morals in the mass of cultivators" was a "phenomenon of which no age nor nation has furnished an example," Jefferson placed a heavy burden on the yeomanry. They alone had the moral integrity to sustain a republic. They possessed such virtue because, unlike those involved in manufacturing, they were economically independent. "Dependance begets subservience and venality," Jefferson declared, "suffocates the germ of virtue, and prepares fit tools for the designs of ambition." For a republic to succeed, Jefferson believed, its citizens had to work the land, and land had to be available to all who wanted to cultivate it. Touring prerevolutionary France in the 1780s, Jefferson had seen what happened when a small group controlled most of the land: the mass of the population had become servile, and many were reduced to absolute poverty. Given his experiences, it was not surprising that he praised the "small landholders" and termed them "the most precious part of a state."[32]

But Jefferson, "conscious that an equal division of property is impracticable," as he wrote to James Madison in October 1785, did not advocate seizing land from wealthy landholders. Instead, he believed that access to land, not outright ownership, was necessary. "The earth is given as a common stock for man to labour and live on," he informed Madison. "If, for the encouragement of industry we allow it to be appropriated, we must take care that other employment be furnished to those excluded from the appropriation. If we do not the fundamental right to labour the earth returns to the unemployed." It was too early, Jefferson continued, "to say that every man who cannot find employment but who can find uncultivated land,

31. Drew McCoy, *The Elusive Republic: Political Economy in Jeffersonian America* (Chapel Hill, N.C., 1980), esp. 9–10, 84, 122–123, 196–199, 237–238.

32. Thomas Jefferson, *Notes on the State of Virginia* (1787; rpt. Chapel Hill, N.C., 1955), 164–165; Jefferson to James Madison, October 28, 1785, in Julian P. Boyd et al., eds., *The Papers of Thomas Jefferson* (Princeton, N.J., 1950–), 8:682.

shall be at liberty to cultivate it, paying a moderate rent. But it is not too soon to provide by every possible means that as few as possible shall be without a little portion of land."[33]

Seeking a "little portion of land" for those who wanted it, coupled with a growing population, meant a commitment to expanding the nation. That is, it meant a commitment to further conquest over the peoples who inhabited needed territory and continued "improvement" of the environment. When the demand for grain grew in the 1790s, and visions of economic prosperity became a reality for thousands who had not yet shared the rewards of the market, the emerging political consensus included the notion of continued expansion, regardless of the potential costs. The vision of the developers of the upper valley meshed perfectly with this view of economic growth. After all, it was the wide distribution of access to land, not landownership, that had fueled the rise of the landholders after the Revolution.

But the new political climate that nourished the wealthy landholders, evident in the support they received from state and local governments, had a high social cost for thousands of others. By providing credit to new settlers, these landholders lured laborers to their tracts. The settlers, who understood the market, moved to the region because the incentives seemed attractive. Given the limited finances of most valley residents in the postwar period, the promise of a secure lease, or a mortgage, or credit at a local store proved too tempting to pass up. Many, of course, tried their luck at owning land, but frequent cases at the orphans' court and notices in local newspapers demonstrated that borrowing money to purchase land was a risky venture; those who failed lost their land and, if they died in debt, the courts bound out their children to serve as apprentices. This risk not only of failing but of breaking up the nuclear family was too high for many families who chose the safer road of tenancy. Even those who managed to obtain and keep a freehold were in all likelihood frequent customers at the landholders' stores and mills, thereby helping the wealthy to remain wealthy. Few of the settlers perhaps anticipated that many would not be able to acquire land, although tax lists reveal growing numbers of landless residents in the early nineteenth century.[34]

33. Jefferson to Madison, *Papers*, 8:682.
34. See, for example, Northumberland County Orphan's Court Docket 1, 18–20, NCCH. On growing numbers of landless see Tables 3 and 4 in the Appendix. Inequal-

The unequal distribution of wealth continued into the nineteenth century and beyond. In this respect the experiences of people in the upper Susquehanna Valley were far from unusual. Throughout the Midwest and West in the nineteenth century land that became available for settlement attracted speculators. Government policies often enhanced the purchasing power of speculators and led to land booms even in communities where, during the earliest years of settlement, there had been little stratification in wealth. In the rapidly expanding agricultural West, farm tenancy and wage labor emerged shortly after the initial settlement of the region. In much of the Midwest the difference in assets evident among those with their sights on newly available territory enhanced the wealth and power of those in control of capital and credit, whether they lived near their holdings or were nonresident speculators. Few pioneers were able to climb the economic ladder to become property holders. Early squatters became farm laborers or tenants or they moved on, like Natty Bumppo, seeking an independent life in a wilderness that proved ever elusive.[35]

The disparity between rich and poor in America, still one of our most pressing social problems, seemed evident everywhere by the end of the eighteenth century, if not earlier. The preconditions for this injustice developed in the early modern period; the Revolution reinforced the division between the wealthy and the less wealthy. No conspiracy was at work to make some prosper while others worked hard and never earned as much, although government action certainly could have changed the economic history of the rural backcountry. Enforcement of laws preventing the engrossing of vast tracts would have completely reoriented the economy of the region. But many in the valley, including tenants, would not necessarily have

---

ity of wealth was certainly not unique to the valley. Jeffrey Williamson and Peter Lindert described a significant increase in inequality in America from 1774 to 1860, and Lee Soltow, taking a different view of the long-term trend, noted the existence of "substantial" inequality in the United States in 1798. See Williamson and Lindert, *American Inequality: A Macroeconomic History* (New York, 1980), 36–38, and Soltow, *Distribution of Wealth and Income in the United States in 1798* (Pittsburgh, Pa., 1989), 190–191, 243, 252.

35. See John Mack Farragher, *Sugar Creek: Life on the Illinois Prairie* (New Haven, Conn., 1986), 183–187; and Paul Wallace Gates, *Landlords and Tenants on the Prairie Frontier: Studies in American Land Policy* (Ithaca, N.Y., 1973), 48–71, 238–325. On the relationship between landholding and migration for one township in the upper valley see Tables 5 and 6 in the Appendix.

wanted such action, especially if it limited their choices at local stores, meant more arduous travel between settlements, or exposed them to additional risks. Valley residents believed that they needed the wealthy landholders; without them there would have been fewer jobs, fewer opportunities to establish a secure farm in the hinterland, and less chance that state and local governments would improve the local transportation network.

In the wake of a war that devastated the upper Susquehanna Valley, residents had a chance that few ever have: to start over. But rather than employ the egalitarian rhetoric of the Revolution to create a society with minimal economic inequality, and thus put into practice what Joyce Appleby has referred to as a "vision of classlessness,"[36] these residents mostly tried to reestablish the prewar economy, which had been organized by a few wealthy landholders creating limited economic opportunity and security for cash-poor settlers. Public institutions, governments, and courts, all creations of the people, celebrated the rebirth of this economic system and provided funds to ensure its success and laws to prevent anyone from interfering with the landholders' commercial dreams.

Celebrating large-scale production for market, the heirs of the Revolution pursued profit wherever it lay, no matter what the consequences. Government officials, acting for the public good or, to use a more fitting eighteenth-century phrase, the "common wealth," supported these efforts. Few with economic power had demonstrated concern for the region's peltry stocks during the early part of the century, and the fur trade, as a result, led to depletion and the collapse of the trade. In the nineteenth century, when Americans sought yet different resources from the hinterland,[37] residents discovered that their rich supplies of lumber and coal could bring profit in the Atlantic market; few worried about squandering resources or polluting the environment when the profits were so enticing. In pursuing these industries the wealthy developers employed thousands of others who never became rich themselves. Like the

36. Appleby, *Capitalism and a New Social Order*, chap. 3.

37. The shift in the nineteenth century emphasizes that resources are cultural constructions. On this point see Cronon, *Changes in the Land*, 165–167. On the forces motivating the shift for at least part of the upper valley, see Diane Lindstrom, *Economic Development in the Philadelphia Region, 1810–1850* (New York, 1978), 93–151. For a superb study of changing perceptions of resources in a particular area see Richard White, *Land Use, Environment, and Social Change: The Shaping of Island County, Washington* (Seattle, Wash., 1980).

farmers who rented or purchased land from the prosperous land-holders before and after the Revolution, these nineteenth-century valley residents recognized that security came from working for the wealthy.

In some ways, the valley economy had changed little from the area William Penn had set his sights on in the seventeenth century. Entrepreneurial Americans in the age of William Cooper, like fur traders a century earlier, thought in terms of profits; they valued the hinterland for the commodities it could produce and established an economic system based on the procurement of those resources. The developers' economic sensibilities stressed profit and generally ignored any long-term environmental and social costs. In making this valley of opportunity part of the Atlantic commercial world, those who directed economic change in the eighteenth century ensured that most valley residents would become dependents in an age of independence.

Appendix

Table 1. Demographic profile of valley inhabitants, 1800, by age and county

	Under 16		16–45		Over 45		other free	slaves	total
	male	female	male	female	male	female			
New York									
Otsego	6,001	5,551	4,193	3,627	1,261	911	44	48	21,636
Tioga	1,911	1,763	1,349	1,188	342	276	33	17	6,879
Pennsylvania									
Luzerne	3,479	3,379	2,381	2,120	787	597	78	18	12,839
Lycoming	1,458	1,397	858	847	293	259	263	94	5,469
Northumberland	7,599	9,057	5,046	4,792	1,733	1,385	135	29	29,776
Total	20,448	21,147	13,827	12,574	4,416	3,428	553	206	76,599

Source: Return of the Whole Number of Persons within the Several Districts of the United States (Second Census) (Washington, D.C., 1808).

Table 2. Land distribution among taxable residents, by acres, in Muncy Township, Northumberland County, 1774–1790

Year	Acres						
	0	1–10	11–50	51–150	151–300	301–500	501 +
1774	52[1]	0	1	14	20	1	1
1790	42[2]	0	5	38	18	6	2

Source: Northumberland County Pennsylvania Board of County Commissioners Tax Records, LR 91.2 (1774) and LR 91.5 (1790), PHMC.
1. Including five listed as "poor."
2. Not including eleven single freemen listed without acreage.

Table 3. Land distribution among taxable residents, by acres, in Turbut Township, Northumberland County, 1792–1812

Year and status	Acres							
	0	town lot	1–10	11–50	51–150	151–300	301–500	501 +
1792								
Married men or widows	34	–	3	7	58	82	3	2
Single freemen	53	–	0	0	1	0	0	0
1802								
Married men or widows	121	61	11	26	84	89	13	2
Single freemen	47	0	0	0	0	0	0	0
1812								
Married men or widows	143	92	15	27	112	84	18	6
Single freemen	64	1	0	0	9	3	1	0

Source: Northumberland County Pennsylvania Board of County Commissioners Tax Records, LR 91.7 (1792, 1802) and LR 91.8 (1812), PHMC.

Table 4. Land distribution among taxable residents, by acres, in Shamokin
Township, Northumberland County, 1794–1802

Year and status	Acres						
	0	1–10	11–50	51–150	151–300	301–500	501+
1794[1]							
Married men or widows	15	1	10	48	49	8	4
1802							
Married men or widows	8	8	12	74	64	12	5
Tenants[2]	28	4	5	26	11	1	1
Single freemen	53	1	–	5	–	–	–

Source: Northumberland County Pennsylvania Board of County Commissioners Tax Records,
LR 91.6, PHMC.
1. Not including 12 single freemen listed without acreage.
2. Listed in record as "taxable occupant" with another person listed as "owner."

Table 5. Persons in 1792 who
remained or disappeared in 1802,
by acres held, Turbut Township,
Northumberland County

Acres	Remaining	Gone
0	17	70
1–10	1	2
11–50	5	2
51–150	18	41
151–300	36	46
301–500	2	1
501+	0	2

Source: Northumberland County Pennsylvania Board of County Commissioners
Tax Records, LR 91.7, PHMC.

Table 6. Persons in 1802 who
remained or disappeared in 1812,
by acres held, Turbut Township,
Northumberland County

Acres	Remaining	Gone
0	62	106
1–10	4	7
11–50	10	16
51–150	37	47
151–300	32	57
301–500	9	4
501+	2	0
Town lot	21	40

Source: Northumberland County Pennsylvania Board of County Commissioners
Tax Records, LR 91.7 (1802) and LR
91.8 (1812), PHMC.

Table 7. Prices of selected commodities and wages, Northumberland
and Lycoming counties, Pennsylvania, 1792–1795*

	Minimum			Maximum		
	£	s	d	£	s	d
Grain (per bushel)						
Wheat	–	4	6	–	6	0
Oats	–	2	6	–	3	6
Rye	–	3	0	–	5	0
Corn (maize)	–	3	0	–	4	6
Livestock						
Cow	3	1	0	7	10	0
Yoke of oxen	30	–	–	–	–	–
Horse	9	–	–	41	10	0
Land (per acre)						
Country (unimproved)	–	10	–	7	–	–
Wages (per day)						
In town	–	3	9	–	–	–
Surveying	–	2	6	–	5	0
Farm labor	–	2	6	–	6	0

Source: Day Book of Muncy Farm, Wallis Papers, Reel 6; Duke de la Rochefoucault Liancourt, *Travels through the United States of North America, the Country of the
Iroquois and Upper Canada, in the Years 1795, 1796, and 1797*, 4 vols. (London,
1800), 1:145–186, passim; Norman B. Wilkinson, ed., "Mr. Davy's Diary," *Pennsylvania History* 20 (1953), 260, 266, 268; Thomas Cooper, *Some Information Respecting
America* (London, 1794), letter IV.
*All figures in Pennsylvania currency.

Index

Library of Congress Cataloging-in-Publication Data

Mancall, Peter C.
   Valley of opportunity: economic culture along the Upper
Susquehanna, 1700–1800 / Peter C. Mancall.
      p. cm.
   Includes bibliographical references and index.
   ISBN 0-8014-2503-4 (cloth: alkaline paper)
   1. Susquehanna River Region—Economic conditions.   2. Susquehanna
River Region—Social conditions.   3. Entrepreneurship—Susquehanna
River Region—History—18th century.   I. Title.
HC107.A12M26   1991
330.974802—dc20
                                                              90-55719